Marilyn Narey

Editor

Making Meaning

Constructing Multimodal Perspectives
of Language, Literacy, and Learning through
Arts-based Early Childhood Education

Editor
Dr. Marilyn Narey
East Stroudsburg University of Pennsylvania
256 Baywood Ave.
Pittsburgh PA 15228-1310
USA
mjnarey@comcast.net

ISBN: 978-0-387-87537-8 (hardcover)   e-ISBN: 978-0-387-87539-2
ISBN: 978-0-387-87690-0 (softcover)
DOI: 10.1007/978-0-387-87539-2

Library of Congress Control Number: 2008938621

Printed on acid-free paper

springer.com

Making Meaning

EDUCATING THE YOUNG CHILD

VOLUME 2

This academic and scholarly book series will focus on the education and development of young children from infancy through eight years of age. The series will provide a synthesis of current theory and research on trends, issues, controversies, and challenges in the early childhood field and examine implications for practice. One hallmark of the series will be comprehensive reviews of research on a variety of topics with particular relevance for early childhood educators worldwide. The mission of the series is to enrich and enlarge early childhood educators' knowledge, enhance their professional development, and reassert the importance of early childhood education to the international community. The audience for the series includes college students, teachers of young children, college and university faculty, and professionals from fields other than education who are unified by their commitment to the care and education of young children. In many ways, the proposed series is an outgrowth of the success of *Early Childhood Education Journal* which has grown from a quarterly magazine to a respected and international professional journal that is published six times a year.

.For other titles published in this series, go to
www.springer.com/series/7205

Contents

Foreword

Mary Renck Jalongo

The bulletin board in the local hospital's pediatric playroom displays young patients' drawings of their doctors. Caitlin is a five-year-old with a chronic illness that requires frequent hospitalizations and her portrait of her doctor brings smiles of recognition to staff members and families alike. She has captured several of the pediatrician's dominant features--unruly gray eyebrows, sparse hair to match, and an intense facial expression. Today Caitlin is excited at the prospect of using a new box of 64 colored crayons "with the points still on" and, as she draws, she uses the self-guiding speech characteristic of her age. Anyone within earshot has access to Caitlin's thoughts as she draws an imaginary creature: "Now her floaty dress...her hair is gonna be golden...How to do wings? I have an idea! I'll swirl silver and white together!" After several minutes Caitlin seems satisfied with her drawing and announces, "Okay everybody, here's my pink fairy!" She then bends down close to the paper as if listening and reports back on what her creation has to say, much to the bemusement of everyone present. In this informal situation, a child's imagination is eagerly welcomed by the young woman who supervises the playroom, two college student volunteers, medical staff, and family members of the patients. The adults are entertained by Caitlin's imagination in the original sense of that word: to captivate for a time, engaging both heart and mind.

When Caitlin returns to school and kindergarten, however, expectations are very different. Her teacher feels considerable pressure to push, pull, or drag the kindergartners through scripted phonics lessons day after day in hopes of accelerating their reading achievement. Rather than appreciating five-year-olds' imagination, Caitlin's teacher approaches fantasy and imagination as frivolous, immature, and anathema to "real learning". The teacher is not alone in this point of view; both the field of education in general and early childhood education in particular are conflicted about children's imagination and the works that it produces (Imagine Nation, 2008). Such attitudes are rooted in the erroneous assumption that children's creative thought has no practical value and that even adults' imagination is worthwhile only if it saves money or labor, increases global competitiveness, or advances technology.

Indiana University of Pennsylvania, USA

M. J. Narey (ed.), *Making Meaning*.
© Springer 2009

Interestingly, two of the most influential educational theorists of our era—Piaget and Vygotsky—regard imagination as foundational to cognition. Piaget asserted that to understand is to invent while Vygotsky contended that imagination interacts with cultural tools and symbol systems to produce learning (Eckhoff & Urbach, 2008; Gajdamaschko, 2005). Although the areas of disagreement between Piaget and Vygotsky are more often the focus of discussion, on this they agree: imagination and cognition are inseparable. More recently, Brian Sutton-Smith (1988) posed the following series of questions that speak to this connection between imagination and cognition: "But what if the imagination is itself the very font of thought? What if the imagination is what permits thought to work by providing it with the images and metaphors that give it direction? What if the imagination is primarily not mere fancy or imitation, but is itself thought's direction? Presumably our educational foci would then be very different" (p. 7).

In this, the second volume in the series *Educating the Young Child: Advances in Theory and Research, Implications for Practice*, a group of educators with specialized expertise in the arts explore the important linkages among literacy, the arts, ways of knowing, and means of communicating. Frank Smith (2003), a prominent expert in literacy, also champions this cause. In stark contrast to many of his contemporaries in the field, he contends that human learning relies on the triumvirate of imagination, identification, and social interaction. Teaching/learning can never be successful in the absence of any one of the three. Children are motivated to become literate, not by dreary lessons, but by opportunities to make meaning and communicate with others. Engaging the child's imagination, far from being a distraction from full literacy, is the only enduring and effective route to it (Egan, 2006). To illustrate, even when the goal of a drawing is realism, as in science instruction, the accuracy of young children's drawings is influenced by their imaginations. Suppose that young children are faced with the task of drawing a pumpkin. They frequently portray not only what they observe at that moment (such as pumpkins being orange and round) but also their prior knowledge (what they know but may not see at that time, such as the stem and leaves, or seeds inside). Even more interesting is the way in which drawing is affected by their intentions and interpersonal relationships. Brenneman and Louro (2008), for example, asked preschoolers to represent apples and found that, when the goal was to make certain that their parent purchased their favorites at the grocery store, the children were deliberate about coloring realistically in order to suit their purpose (e.g., yellow delicious, red delicious, Granny Smith). This finding exemplifies the linkages among imagination, identification, and social interaction of which Smith (2003) speaks. Indeed, the pages of this volume—particularly the delightful art work produced by young children—give testimony to the fact that art is not merely the expression of feelings but also a language that conveys understanding and, as such, is a major cultural tool for social interaction.

When misguided early childhood educators approach the arts as mindless busywork and treat literacy with print as the only worthwhile pursuit in the curriculum, they seriously limit the range of communicative tools available to the young child. As Althouse, Johnson and Mitchell (2003) note,

A picture may be worth a thousand words, but these words can remain unsaid or misunderstood when adults do not attend to their development. Beyond fostering the artistic development of the young children we work with through media and processes, we must also guide children's aesthetic development—verbal and visual literacy in the aesthetic domain. Otherwise, their art may be misinterpreted or neglected and the young artists' meanings never communicated. (p. 79)

For the very young—even more so than human beings of other ages—visual images, spoken words, interpersonal interactions, and the printed word are all of a piece rather than neatly compartmentalized. The ultimate irony is that, after years of formal education have persuaded them to pigeonhole thought, they will need to reclaim that freewheeling, nonliteral type of thinking from childhood if ever they hope to excel in any field (Csikzentmihalyi, 1997; Shavinina & Ferrari, 2004). This book is a cogent reminder that everyone responsible for the care and education of young children has to acquire an abiding respect for "the hundred languages of children" of which Loris Malaguzzi, founder of the Reggio Emilia schools, speaks. There are many ways in which the very young can show what they know, acquire important skills, and develop the dispositions and attitudes that support life-wide/lifelong learning. Both as individual chapters and as volume, the message is clear: the arts contribute immeasurably to the quantity and quality of ways in which children can convey not just feelings but also thinking and attain not only creative expression but also academic achievement.

References

Althouse, R., Johnson, M. H., & Mitchell, S. T. (2003). *The colors of learning: Integrating the visual arts into the early childhood curriculum.* New York: Teachers College Press; Washington, DC: NAEYC

Bailin, S. (2007). Imagination and arts education in cultural contexts. In K. Egan, M. Stout, & K. Takaya (Eds.), *Teaching and learning outside the box: Inspiring imagination across the curriculum* (pp. 101–166). New York: Teachers College Press.

Brenneman, K., & Louro, I. F. (2008, in press). Science journals in the preschool classroom. *Early Childhood Education Journal,* 36

Csikszentmihalyi, M. (1997). Creativity: Flow and the psychology of discovery and invention. New York: Harper/Perennial.

Eckhoff, A., & Urbach, J. (2008, in press). Understanding imaginative thinking during childhood: Sociocultural conceptions of creativity and imaginative thought. *Early Childhood Education Journal.*

Egan, K. (2006). *Teaching literacy: Engaging the imagination of new readers and writers.* Thousand Oaks, CA: Corwin Press.

Gajdamaschko, N. (2005). Vygotsky on imagination: Why an understanding of the imagination is an important issue for schoolteachers. *Teaching Education, 16*(1), 13–22.

Imagine Nation. (2008). New poll reveals stifling imagination in schools underlies innovation and skills deficit. Retrieved May 25, 2008 from: http://www.theimaginenation.net

Jalongo, M. R. (2003). The child's right to creative thought and expression. *Childhood Education, 79*(4), 218-228. A Position Paper of the Association for Childhood Education International.

Shavinina, L. V., & Ferrari, M. (Eds.). (2004). *Beyond knowledge: Extracognitive aspects of developing high ability.* Mahwah, NJ: Lawrence Erlbaum.

Smith, F. (2003). *Unspeakable acts, unnatural practices: Flaws and fallacies in "scientific" reading instruction.* Portsmouth, NH: Heinemann.

Sutton-Smith, B. (1988). In search of the imagination. In K. Egan & D. Nadaner (Eds.), *Imagination and education* (pp. 3–29). New York: Teachers College Press.

Introduction

Marilyn J. Narey

> "I can read."
> The university visitor looked up from her papers and smiled at the confident countenance
> of the cherub-faced seven-year old child who stood before her.
> "That's wonderful!" the visitor exclaimed.
> "Reading is very important..." the child went on solemnly.
> The visitor began to nod enthusiastically in agreement. *Reading is very important.* Then,
> abruptly the visitor stopped nodding and her smile began to fade as the youngster
> continued, "... for the test!"

This brief exchange took place in an urban school classroom in the northeastern United States. To many early childhood educators across the globe, this story is all too familiar. The current push for educational accountability and reform has only reinforced what Eisner (2006) calls the "production vision of education" (p. 3), wherein schools are expected to work with assembly-line efficiency to achieve a prescribed set of outcomes. Although most education professionals would contest the view that our work with young children is only "important for the test," we have yet to articulate an alternative vision to guide our collaborative efforts. Secure in the assumption that it is important to promote young children's language, literacy, and learning, we do not typically step back to examine *why* this work is important; instead, we jump ahead to search for methods and techniques that align with the most recent mandate. As Eisner points out, "We often pursue aims and engage in practices that have become a deep part of our sub-consciousness without ever making them conscious" (p. 4). To make sense of the current state of our field and envision its future development, we must delve into the sea of meaning underlying our everyday work in classrooms, administrative offices, and universities. In other words, we must consider what we mean when we talk about "language," "literacy," and "learning." This requires that we reflect on the varieties and uses of language, interrogate what it means to be literate, and develop our own understanding of why learning is of value to the child and to the society as a whole.

East Stroudsburg University of Pennsylvania, USA

M. J. Narey (ed.), *Making Meaning*.
© Springer 2009

Out of the collective work of the authors of this volume, we put forward the following provisional definitions:

- A language is a system of communication structured by its rules of significa-tion, or "meaning-making." Languages can be constructed in a variety of sen-sory/representational modalities, not limited to human speech and writing.
- Literacy describes a person's ability to make/interpret meaningful signs in a particular representational modality (e.g., print, image, film, etc.)
- Learning is the process of making sense or creating meaning from experience.

Our perspective on language, literacy, and learning resonates with Malaguzzi's (1998) insight that "the child has a hundred languages...but [the school and the culture] steal the ninety-nine." (p. 3). Moreover, our expanded definition of liter-acy is supported by Millard and Marsh's (2001) critical assessment of the current British education system—that it "is foreclosing on children's culturally acquired resources for communicating meanings to others...by devaluing all but the prod-ucts of the writing process" (p. 55). In the chapters that follow, the authors provide evidence from research and practice to support the central arguments put forth in this volume: (1) that language, literacy, and learning are about making meaning, (2) that meaning-making is a multimodal process, and (3) that arts-based learning facilitates this multimodal process for children and the adults who work with them.

Children may draw, dance, sing, talk, and write their understandings of the world (Gallas, 1994), but most early childhood teachers enter the field with a "verbocentric" mindset, unprepared to effectively use the arts to develop these other modalities for making meaning. In early childhood education, the arts are frequently viewed as "directed production" manifested in holiday decorations (in the United States, orange construction paper Halloween jack-o-lanterns and cut-out Xerox totem poles for Native American units scheduled to coincide with Thanksgiving) or scripted performances primarily for parents' entertainment. Of-ten the arts are promoted as "self-expression," which many teachers mistakenly translate as allowing children free-time play in the art center or "dress-up" corner. Assuming (incorrectly) that the children's artistic or dramatic modalities will ad-vance on their own, these teachers take no responsibility for the learning that may or may not occur. Occasionally, the arts are taught in a limited manner: as a set of decontextualized skills or as "development of aesthetic impulses" (Millard and Marsh, 2001, p. 55) as teachers focus on mixing colors, or ask, "how does this painting make you feel?" Rarely are the arts perceived or taught as a meaning making process. Therefore, as pressures to achieve for "the test" filter further down to the youngest levels of early childhood education, some professionals dealing with the learning of young children may lament the diminishing ability to find time for the arts, but not have a substantive understanding of why the arts are important as a means of developing children's multiple modalities for language, literacy, and learning. It is this lack of understanding that we seek to address.

Purpose of this Book

The perspective on language, literacy, and learning we are advocating is supported by the work of respected theorists and researchers (see, for example, Dewey, 1934/1980; Dyson, 1993, 2003, 2004; Eisner, 1978, 1994, 2002, 2006; Harste, 2000; Heath & Wolf, 2005; Kress, 1997, 2003; Olson, 1992), by the National Council of Teachers of English (NCTE)(2005) guideline for multimodal literacies, and by recognized examples of practice, such as the schools of Reggio Emila (Edwards, Gandini, & Forman, 1998). In line with these models of research and practice, we developed *Making Meaning: Constructing Multimodal Perspectives of Language, Literacy, and Learning through Arts-based Early Childhood Education* by first asking, "What is it about language, literacy, and learning that we believe may have value for children, for the adults who work with them, for the society in which we all live, and for the future world we will shape?" We then began to consider, "How might we work to bring about the future we envision for early childhood education?" Inevitably, our experience with the arts has shaped our responses to these questions.

In this volume, we explicitly present art as a meaning-making process. While not all practitioners have backgrounds that would naturally lead them to a multimodal conceptualization of language, literacy, and learning, most educators acknowledge that the arts have a place in the early childhood curriculum, and many have expressed concerns that mandated prescriptive practices and high-stakes test preparation leave little time for arts experiences that were once central to the early childhood curriculum. We present a multimodal, child-centered understanding of art as a means of "coming to know" in order to underscore the early childhood education professional's responsibility to advance the arts in the various settings in which they work.

Thus, the purpose of this book is threefold: (1) to provoke readers to examine their current understandings of language, literacy, and learning through the lens of the various arts-based perspectives offered in this volume, (2) to provide them with a starting point for constructing broader, multimodal views of what it might mean to "make meaning," and (3) to underscore why understanding arts-based learning as a meaning-making process is especially critical to early childhood education in the face of narrowly-focused, test-driven curricular reforms. This text offers a provocative sampling of the work of distinguished authors whose fields of expertise include literacy, second language acquisition, semiotics, the arts and arts education, child development, and early childhood education. All of the authors who have contributed to this volume have years of professional experience as teachers, teacher educators, artists, administrators, and/or researchers in education. In this second volume of the series, *Educating the Young Child: Advances in Theory and Research, Implications for Practice*, our authors draw from their professional experience to integrate theory and research with stories of how children, teachers, teacher-educators, and pre-service teachers, along with parents, researchers, and other professionals engage the arts as meaning-making processes.

Overview of the Book

The concept of "meaning-making" presented in this book is not limited to arts processes and products of children, but also encompasses ways adults in the field of education work to make meaning: for example, constructing arts-based curricula, developing research methodologies for studying children's multimodal processes, investigating contextual influences, or designing arts-based pre-service teacher development. The chapters are organized into three sections: Beyond Words, Contexts and Layered Texts, and Visions.

Part One: Beyond Words provides the foundation for our discussions of making meaning through arts-based early childhood education. In the first chapter, Margaret Brooks explores the relationship between thought and drawing as a meaning-making process. Through five-year-old children's drawings of flashlights and light trap constructions, Dr. Brooks illustrates how drawing supports the movement from simple spontaneous concepts to the complex concepts that promote higher mental functions. She thoughtfully outlines how a specific Vygotskian socio-cultural framework can assist teachers in their understanding and support of young children's drawing as meaning making. In Chapter Two, university educators, Linda K. Crafton and Penny Silvers, and public school teacher, Mary Brennan, share a powerful example of a multimodal, arts-based approach to teaching critical literacy in a first grade classroom. Their research focuses upon a carefully constructed community of practice where art was "repositioned" to create a critical multiliteracies, multimodal early childhood curriculum built on social justice and identity development. In the third chapter, Maureen Kendrick and Roberta McKay underscore the need for teachers and educational researchers to recognize the social, cultural, and political understandings that students bring to the literacy experience. They suggest that children's drawings can offer a method of investigation that will bring a richer knowledge of what children perceive about reading and writing in their lives, both in and outside of school. In this intriguing description of their image-based literacy research methodology, Dr. Kendrick and Dr. McKay relate their own meaning-making process as they share the evolution of their analysis and interpretation of children's literacy drawings. In Chapter Four, Kim Sheridan presents the Studio Thinking Framework derived from research at Harvard University's Project Zero. Dr. Sheridan explains how eight studio habits of mind, typically developed in intensive high school art classes, can also be encouraged in the early childhood classroom. She describes how applying a Studio Thinking Framework to common activities, such as block building or drawing, contributes to young children's meaning-making as children become more observant, engaged, reflective on their work, and willing to explore and express ideas.

The chapters in Part Two: Contexts and Layered Texts are focused upon the authors' explorations into the diverse and often complex environments that influence children's multimodal, arts-based meaning-making. In Chapter Five, Eli Trimis and Andri Savva introduce the concept of *chorotopos* (space/place) as they explore young children's artistic learning in the context of museum environments and other cultural settings using their in-depth approach. They explain *chorotopos* as a critical component in this method of instruction and describe their research using the in-depth approach with children and teachers in northern Greece and Cyprus. In Chapter Six, Paula Purnell looks at how educational and societal contexts position children with diverse abilities, challenging early childhood teachers to question fundamental presumptions about learning that prevail regarding "differently-abled" children and the arts. Chapter Seven is centered on the home environment of English Language Learners, as Sharon Cecile Switzer discusses the influences of parents and family members on young Brazilian immigrant children. Dr. Switzer draws from her larger body of research to explore the multiple modes of communication, particularly music and visual art, that were prevalent in her findings and the implications that this has for early childhood educators working with English Language Learners. In Chapter Eight, Patricia Whitfield draws attention to the powerful influence of educational policy on children's abilities to make meaning through the arts and encourages early childhood teachers to ensure that all children have access to quality arts learning.

In Part Three: Visions, the authors look to the future as they investigate strategies to develop pre-service teachers' understandings of how children's many languages, literacies, and learning may be developed through the arts. In Chapter Nine, Kathy Danko-McGhee and Ruslan Slutsky draw attention to the importance of providing stimulating classroom environments that support and promote children's meaning making. Underscoring that teachers must go beyond merely making materials available, they describe two different sets of experiences designed to develop pre-service teachers' abilities to anticipate how children may interact with materials and to think critically about designing for this interaction. They examine both approaches to determine the greatest impact on the pre-service teachers' abilities to plan these environments and discuss the results. Next, in Chapter Ten, Lynn Hartle and Candace Jaruszewicz look at the integral relationships between arts and technology. They present examples of arts and technology in an early childhood classroom and discuss implications for pre-service teacher education. In Chapter Eleven, Kelli Jo Kerry-Moran and Matthew J. Meyer point out that not only do most pre-service teachers have very little knowledge in the dramatic arts, but that they also lack experiences in which they have been taught through dramatic techniques. Arguing that drama attends to numerous modes of human communication and is critically important to the meaning making process in pre-service teacher education, Dr. Kerry-Moran and Dr. Meyer provide a sample unit along with a thoughtful discussion of the theoretical connections supporting the unit's role in the development of children's and/or pre-service teachers' school literacies, community literacies, and personal literacies. In Chapter Twelve, I explore the process of making meaning through arts learning in the context of my elementary education methods course. Using Antoine de Saint Exupéry's (1943/1971) *The Little Prince* as a metaphor for the need to look beyond initial perceptions, I not only provide concrete examples of course learning experiences but also attempt to uncover the meaning making underlying our engagement with these experiences. Common theories-in-use are discussed alongside of current theory, research, and practice, and my observations and reflections of our meaning making are accompanied by two former students' personal stories of how they came to understand arts as language, literacy, and learning in the early childhood classroom.

Our early childhood education community understands the awesome promise and the enormous responsibility of our work with young children. The importance of this work should not be determined in terms of test scores, but rather viewed in light of the diversity, multiplicity, and complexity of ways our children are able to make meaning.

References

de Saint Exupéry, A. (1943/1971). *The little prince*. New York: Harcourt, Brace & World, Inc.

Dewey, J. (1934/1980). *Art as experience*. New York: Perigee.

Dyson, A. H. (1993). *Social worlds of children learning to write in an urban primary school*. New York: Teachers College Press.

Dyson, A. H. (2003). *The brothers and sisters learn to write: Popular literacies in childhood and school cultures*. New York: Teachers College Press.

Dyson, A. H. (2004). Diversity as a "handful": Toward retheorizing the basics. *Research in the Teaching of English, 39*(2), 210-214.

Edwards, C. P., Gandini, L. & Forman, G. E. (Eds.) (1998). *The Hundred Languages of Children: The Reggio Emilia Approach - Advanced Reflections* (2nd ed.). Greenwich, CT: Ablex.

Eisner, E. W. (1978). Reading and the creation of meaning. In E. W Eisner (Ed.), *Reading, the arts, and the creation of meaning* (pp. 13-31). Reston, VA: National Art Education Association.

Eisner, E. W. (1994). *Cognition and curriculum reconsidered* (2nd ed.). New York: Teachers College Press.

Eisner, E. W. (2002). *The arts and the creation of mind*. New Haven, CT: Yale University Press.

Eisner, E. W. (2006). *Two visions of education*. (The Arts Education Collaborative Monograph No. 2). Pittsburgh, PA: Arts Education Collaborative.

Gallas, K. (1994). *The languages of learning: How children talk, write, dance, and sing their understanding of the world*. New York: Teachers College Press.

Harste, J. C. (2000). Six points of departure. In B. Berghoff, K. A. Eawa, J. C. Harste, & B. T. Hoonan (Eds.), *Beyond reading and writing: Inquiry, curriculum, and multiple ways of knowing* (pp. 1-16). Urbana, IL: National Council of Teachers of English.

Heath, S. B., & Wolf, S. A. (2005). Focus in creative learning: Drawing on art for language development. *Literacy, 39*(1), 38-45.

Kress, G. R. (1997). *Before writing: Rethinking the paths to literacy*. London: Routledge.

Kress, G. R. (2003). *Literacy in the new media age*. London: Routledge.

Maluguzzi, L. (1998). No way. The hundred *is* there. In C. Edwards, L. Gandini, & G. Forman (Eds.), *The hundred languages of children: The Reggio Emilia approach—advanced reflections* (pp. 2-3). Greenwich, CT: Ablex.

Millard, E., & Marsh, J. (2001). Words with pictures: The role of visual literacy in writing and its implication for schooling, *Reading, 35*(2), 54-61.

National Council of Teachers of English. (2005). Multimodal literacies. Retrieved March 2, 2008 from http://www.ncte.org/about/over/positions/category/literacy/123213.htm

Olson, J. L. (1992). *Envisioning writing: Toward an integration of drawing and writing*. Portsmouth, NH: Heinemann.

Part One
Beyond Words

Chapter 1
Drawing to Learn

Margaret Brooks

Abstract This chapter will demonstrate how a specific Vygotskian socio-cultural framework can assist teachers in their understanding and support of young children's drawing processes. Using examples of children drawing in a kindergarten and year one classroom, I will explore the notion that in drawing there is evidence of a relationship between thought and drawing that becomes visible through the study of meaning-making processes. Drawing supports the movement from simple spontaneous concepts to more complex concepts and plays an important role in promoting higher mental functions. When drawing is used in a collaborative and communicative manner it becomes a powerful meaning-making tool. When drawing is recognized as a meaning making process, supporting drawing then becomes central to the teaching and learning of young children.

Keywords drawing, Vygotsky, meaning making, early childhood, higher mental functions, socio-cultural

Drawing provides children with their first means of making a permanent, tangible, concrete, and communicable record of their ideas so that most young children have a strong desire to draw. Drawing, and mark making, are also among the child's first efforts at abstraction and the use of a symbol system (Athey, 1990; Cox, 1991; Eisner, 1972; Matthews, 1999). Facility with abstractions and symbol systems are essential for school-based literacy like mathematics, information technology, reading and writing (Athey, 1990; Barratt-Pugh & Rohl, 2000; Gifford, 1997).

In this chapter we will see how young children, in an early childhood classroom in Canada, productively used drawing in a range of contexts to make sense of the world in which they live. The children were encouraged to talk about, share, revise and revisit their drawings. Drawing slowed responses to stimulus by engaging the child with the subject in meaningful ways for longer periods. Drawing mediated between thought and action to support progressively complex ideas. These

University of New England, Australia

M. J. Narey (ed.), *Making Meaning*.
© Springer 2009

drawing processes extended the children's thinking as well as their awareness of different possibilities for representation and their drawing repertoire. In everyday life the arts often explore 'big ideas'. The arts give form to some very complex concepts. This distillation (and often crystallization) of concepts allows us to make connections between ideas and concepts that we might not normally easily make.

The writings of Lev Vygotsky (1962, 1978, 1987, 1998) offer us a rich and productive way of examining young children's drawing processes that acknowledges both the children's context and their intentions. Socio-cultural theory, as proposed by Vygotsky (1987), offers a way of understanding mental processes through disclosure of their emergence and subsequent growth. He viewed learning and development as dialectical in nature, working together as a dynamic process in a socio-cultural context. The learner brings prior knowledge and combines it with new knowledge through his or her interaction with others. Expertise is shared in order to negotiate and construct meaning (Duran & Syzmanski, 1995; Rogoff, 1990). Development of the individual is 'a process in which children grow into the intellectual life of those around them' (Vygotsky, 1978).

Drawing is also dialectical in nature and this chapter describes how drawing can be a powerful tool for mediating learning within a community of learners. Drawing in a social context mediates new knowledge and understanding. Focusing on children's drawing processes and applying an explicitly Vygotskian analysis is a departure from the way we have traditionally analyzed drawing, where individual drawings have typically been viewed in a de-contextualized and developmental manner (Brooks, 2002). By examining drawing events over time, threads of children's thinking can be followed, illuminating the consequential progression of increasingly complex ideas.

Thought and Drawing

Vygotsky was interested in the connections between thought and speech. He suggested that "the rational, intentional conveying of experience and thought to others requires a mediating system, the prototype of which is human speech born of the need of intercourse during work" (Vygotsky, 1962, p.6). However, he also considered other forms of communication such as symbols, algebraic systems, art, drawing, writing, and diagrams (Vygotsky, 1962). These signs and symbols might also be considered forms of language and a way of communicating. Vygtosky was not able to pursue his exploration of these other symbol systems in his short lifetime. My work builds upon Vygotsky's initial ideas and explores them further in relation to drawing. I chose drawing because it is something most children do and is considered to be foundational to the visual arts. If we also consider drawing to be a language of sorts, then we can begin to see how drawing might contribute to the formulation of thinking and meaning. The diagram (Fig.1.1) illustrates Vygotsky's theory of the connection between thought and speech and the development

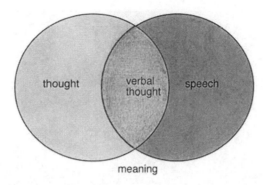

Fig. 1.1 Verbal thought. (adapted from Wink and Putney, 2002, p. xxv)

of verbal thought. Verbal thought is "the linkage of multiple layers of language and thought as they transform themselves into greater mental abilities, the joining of thought and language to make meaning" (Wink & Putney, 2002, p.152). Speech informs thought and thought is given life through speech. Meaning is created at the intersection of, and through a dynamic relationship between, thought and speech. Vygotsky proposed that it is in "word meaning" that thought and speech join to become verbal thought and that through the study of meaning-making we might find ways to understand children's thinking. He proposes that it is, "in meaning (that the) answers to our questions about the relationship between thought and speech can be found" (Vygotsky, 1962, p. 5).

Vygotsky wrote about two forms of meaning: meaning as reference and abstraction; and meaning as contextualized personal sense (Wertsch, 2000). There are also two basic assumptions about meaning as reference and abstractions. One is that "language meaning is a matter of referential relationships between signs and objects," and the other is that "the development of meaning is a matter of increasing generalization and abstraction" (Wertsch, 2000, p. 20). Vygotsky believed that an understanding of the difference between what he termed a child's spontaneous concept and a child's scientific concept depended on one's understanding of these two assumptions. It is in the spontaneous concept, which occurs in a child's first encounter with an experience that the referential use of language plays an important role. However, for meaning to develop further into abstraction the child has to move beyond this direct linking of referent to object to a more generalized meaning. Objects are grouped into categories rather than remaining single objects.

I suggest that drawing assists this movement and later in the chapter I present several examples of what this looks like for young children in the context of the early childhood classroom. The diagram (Fig. 1.2) borrows from Vygotsky's theory and illustrates a possible connection between thought, drawing and the development of visual thought (Brooks, 2002, 2003). When drawing informs thought and thought is given life through drawing we can begin to see the connection between thought and drawing and the value of drawing in the creation of meaning.

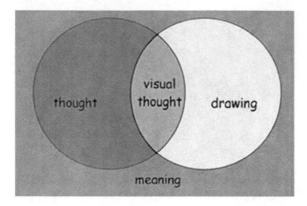

Fig. 1.2 Visual thought.

If we consider drawing to be a communication system that supports meaning and that might operate in similar ways to language, and if we replace the word 'language' with the word 'drawing' in the above hypothesis, then we can begin to understand how drawing might function at the referential level as well as be a mediator between a child's spontaneous concept and a child's more complex and scientific concept. Vygotsky (1962) describes a thought as being both whole and simultaneous. It does not consist of individual words like speech nor is it always connected to speech. What is contained simultaneously in thought unfolds sequentially in speech (Vygotsky, 1987). There is simultaneity of ideas and concepts in a completed drawing that parallels Vygotsky's description of thought. A drawing is seen as whole and simultaneous, whereas speech has a more linear and temporal order. Perhaps the power of drawing for children (and adults) is that it more closely represents thought.

The materiality of a drawing offers opportunities for ideas to be shared with others as well as revisited, re-evaluated and reworked. The relative permanency of drawing over speech offers children possibilities for an extended dialogic engagement with and around the drawing and the ideas it represents; this might not be as possible to achieve with speech. When young children do not yet have fluency with text, or perhaps even oral language, then drawing offers a means of communication and a viable mediating role for collaboration, meaning making and problem solving. Drawing provides a bridge to thinking that could have some advantages over speech or writing.

The rest of this chapter will illustrate, and expand on, four important concepts in relation to drawing and a Vygoskian theoretical framework. These are: drawing in the social context of the classroom; interpersonal and intrapersonal drawing dialogues; how drawing supports higher mental functions and the consequential progression of ideas through drawing. Each concept relates to the other while also building upon each other.

Drawing in the Social Context of the Classroom

In the context of a dark Canadian winter, 'light' was a meaningful and relevant topic for the children in this year one classroom to investigate. The children brought a variety of light sources from home so that everyone in the class could examine them more closely (Fig. 1.3). They also brought their own understanding of light that was acquired from their experiences and interactions with their families and friends outside of the classroom. In the classroom a new social context for sharing the collective understanding about light was created. These children were now exposed to a range of ideas that might be very different, and sometimes conflicting, from their own.

Vygotsky suggests that cognitive construction is influenced by past experiences as well the immediate social contexts and that both affect not just what is learned, but also how it is learned (Moll, 2002; Vygotsky, 1962, 1978; Wink & Putney, 2002). The differing ideas helped to raise the questions that provided the impetus for further investigation by individuals and small groups. Drawing was crucial element of the investigations. Compiling and comparing observational drawings gave the children a reference upon which to build and elaborate their ideas. Through shared reviewing, as well as discussions, the drawings prompted a deeper understanding of the concepts in question. For example, the differences amongst flashlights became evident through drawing and through comparison of the different drawings.

Fig. 1.3 Observational drawing of flashlights by three 5 year olds

Blair has made an inventory of different flashlights (Fig. 1.4). He uses this drawing to investigate the very different purposes of these flashlights. He notices that each has a different level of light that suits its purpose. His drawing provides the impetus for an exploration of the concept of candlepower and how we much light we need to see to read.

Comparing flashlights against different criteria helped the children to group and categorize in more complex ways, ways that acknowledged the scope of the technology of the culture in which they live. The children in this class were encouraged to formulate good questions and to investigate these questions either in small groups or independently. Drawing was supported and encouraged as an investigative and meaning making tool. Vygotsky (1978) suggests that new knowledge exists first in a shared, or interpersonal level before it is internalized. He recognized the school as an important site for promoting the shift from personal experiences and interpersonal dialogues to more complex thinking. Drawing helped to make the children's thinking visible. When their ideas were given some form of tangible, external permanency through their drawings then the children were able to use the drawings to discuss, compare and elaborate on their own and each others ideas. When children are exposed to different ideas through these interactions with others in their community they are able to grow into the intellectual life of those around them. In this model the cultural, historical and social elements of a child's life that are so crucial to a Vygotskian framework are acknowledged so that teaching and learning become truly dialogic in nature (Vygotsky 1978).

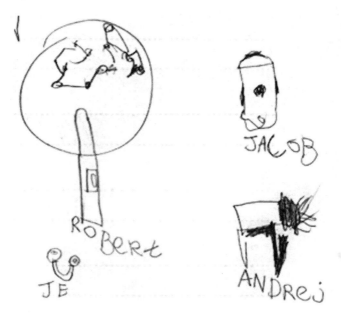

Fig. 1.4 Blair's drawings of four different flashlights.

Interpersonal Drawing Dialogues

In the social context of the classroom children are able to borrow the ideas of others and try them out for themselves and so they become part of their own mental processes. The notion of socially shared cognition is one of the unique contributions Vygotsky has made to our understanding of how children learn (Vygotsky 1978). The following example explores how one child develops an idea he has and how he considers, and sometimes incorporates, the ideas of others through his drawings.

A flashlight that had a four-way switch (see larger flashlight in Fig. 1.3) to produce three levels of light particularly fascinated Ed and challenged his notion of the concept of 'on' and 'off'. He told me that he thought the light changes had something to do with the switches. However, his friend Blair suggested instead that the changes had more to do with some mechanism around the bulb. Ed began his investigation of this flashlight by doing a detailed observation drawing of it. His initial drawing was a fairly detailed representational drawing that brought the flashlight into the realm of symbolic. This drawing represents his immediate encounter with the flashlight where he is working from the object and using his drawing to help him clarify the concept he is working with.

At an interpersonal level, one of the functions of drawing is to provide a referent to the object, thus drawing the experienced object into the symbolic realm. When Ed was drawing the flashlight he was taking his accumulated experiences of flashlights along with his observations and compiling the information into an immediate and holistic representation of the salient features of this flashlight. His drawing became a symbolic representation of some of the ideas he had about the flashlight. While he was drawing the flashlight, he was also talking with his peers about it. He was looking at other drawings children had done of the flashlight as well as receiving responses from his peers about his drawing. The drawings provided a common point of reference that was shared amongst the children. The drawings and discussions are examples of new knowledge existing in a shared context.

Intrapersonal Drawing Dialogues

Ed drew the flashlight with the light on and brought his recent experience of observing the flashlight in a dark space into his drawing by coloring the background to the flashlight black to represent darkness. In order to represent his initial idea of 'on and off' he took a black colored square of paper and made a cover for his drawing of the light bulb on the flashlight. When the black paper square covered the drawn light this represented the 'off', or 'no light', and when the black square was removed to reveal the drawn light this represented 'on' (Fig. 1.5).

Fig. 1.5   Ed demonstrates how the "on/off" flap works. The flashlight is 'off' when he covers the light part of the drawing with a black paper square and 'on' when he removes it.

This was Ed's way of representing the contrast between light and dark and the corresponding notion of on and off. Linking these two concepts through his drawing process moved him beyond a more immediate referent/object response to an intrapersonal level of interaction with his drawing. In this action drawing Ed is giving symbolic form to his initial idea. When he is able to give a physical and symbolic form to his thinking through his drawing, he is then able to play with his ideas. One of the powerful features of drawing is the way it helps to focus attention, aid in planning, develop deliberate memory and logical thinking, and mediate perception. Ed wanted a way to connect his dark colored piece of paper to his drawing so that it created a flap that opened and closed and would not get lost. To solve this problem he drew a plan (Fig. 1.6), as he drew he thought aloud of the various possibilities.

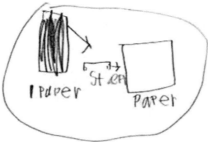

Fig. 1.6 Ed's plan for how to make a flap

   Drawing his plan helped him to select from a range of options and to organize the materials he needed to assemble to make the flap (i.e. the flap, a staple and the drawing). In a busy classroom, his plan reminded him what he needed to do. It focused his attention and provided a logical series of steps.

   Ed then attached two pipe cleaners to his drawing and tucked another black colored piece of paper under them to represent the switch on the flashlight. The two pipe cleaners held the switch in place while also allowing it to move back and forth like the switch on the flashlight did. Now he could synchronize the moving of the switch with the opening of the flap over the light bulb (Fig. 1.7).

   This drawing is a good example of drawing functioning as a learning activity that was leading Ed's development. He extended his notion of on and off to include the notion of four levels of "on/off". His drawing was more than a replica of what he saw. The process of drawing out his ideas and observations and playing with them has moved him to higher levels of thinking. Ed has been able to build upon his initial observations of the flashlight and develop an increasingly complex set of ideas. The focus in these drawings has consistently been upon the meaning the drawing holds in the construction of new knowledge. Any attempts Ed made at likeness or verisimilitude seem to have been to better understand the functioning of the flashlight, rather than to create a more realistic drawing. When drawing dialogues like this support meaning making in the social context of the classroom then children will be able to function at much higher levels of thinking.

Fig. 1.7 Ed's final drawing of the flashlight

Drawing in this context is a metacognitive tool. The progression from an inter-personal dialogue to an intrapersonal dialogue with drawing might be considered as part of the law of the development of higher mental functions (Vygotsky, 1978). However, when adults are reluctant to engage meaningfully with children's drawing, the shift from interpersonal to intrapersonal is compromised. The teacher has a very important role in assisting children's competencies with a cultural tool like drawing. It is important that teachers recognize that drawing is part of the de-velopment of higher mental functions and a powerful way of making meaning for young children.

Higher Mental Functions

In order to know how we can better help children move to higher levels of think-ing it is important to understand what Vygotsky means by the terms, 'spontaneous concepts' and 'scientific concepts' (Vygotsky, 1987). Vygotsky believed that a child's spontaneous concept differs from a child's scientific concept; particularly in the path the child takes in his or her thinking.

> The birth of the spontaneous concept is usually associated with the child's immediate encounter with things . . . In contrast, the birth of the scientific concept begins not with an immediate encounter with things, but with a mediated relation to the object. With the spontaneous concept the child moves from the thing to the concept. With the scientific concept, he is forced to follow the opposite path - from the concept to the thing. (Vygotsky, 1987, p. 219)

It is the referential nature of the relationship between the sign and the object that is the key to understanding the differences between everyday spontaneous concepts and more abstract, scientific concepts.

> The key difference . . . is a function of the presence or absence of a system. Concepts stand in a different relationship to the object when they exist outside a system than when they enter one. The relationship of the word 'flower' to the object is completely different for the child who does not yet know the words rose, violet or lily than it is for the child who does. Outside a system, the only possible connections between concepts are those that exist between the objects themselves, that is, empirical connections . . . These relationships mediate the concept's relationship to the object through its relationship to other concepts. A different relationship between the concept and the object develops. Supraempirical connections between concepts become possible. (Vygotsky, 1987, p. 234)

Table 1.1 summarizes the shift of thinking as the child moves from a spontaneous concept to a scientific concept. So for example, when a child is working at a spon-taneous conceptual level they tend to have "a referential relationship between signs and objects" (Wertsch, 2000, p. 20) and when they move to a scientific con-ceptual level this referential relationship changes to show "increasing generaliza-tion and abstraction" (Wertsch, 2000, p. 20).

Table 1.1 The Relationship between Spontaneous and Scientific Concepts

Spontaneous concept	Scientific concept
Referential relationship between signs and objects.	Increasing generalization and abstraction.
First, or immediate encounter with an experience or object.	Mediated relation to the object.
Referential use of language.	Objects grouped into categories.
The child moves from the thing to the concept.	Child moves from the concept to the thing.
Absence of a system.	System in place.
Empirical connections between objects.	Supra empirical connections between concepts become possible.

Vygotsky (1962) states that it is not enough to have labels for objects in order to think and solve problems. What is also needed is the ability to manipulate these labels across contexts that will allow for connections that promote thinking at a more abstract and conceptual level and so develop higher levels of thinking. However, the ability to manipulate labels across contexts is dependent upon the child's adequate understanding of the concept. The acquisition of word labels does not necessarily presume a clear understanding. Vygotsky (1962) suggests that a working, or experiential understanding is needed.

Drawing helps with the definition of words, that initially often only otherwise exist at the level of recitation, by providing the child with a working experience. Drawing plays an important role in focusing children's attention on the spontaneous concept as well as allowing them to make connections between concepts. Drawing will often contain and make visible the essence of an idea or concept. When these thoughts or concepts exist outside of the child, the child can then work with the idea in relation to other ideas. Drawing, when used as a medium of exchange, can form a dynamic function that allows an elaboration of an initial idea and the definition of a concept as well as assisting with building supra-empirical connections between concepts and systems.

The next series of drawings done by Ed demonstrates the shift from spontaneous concepts to scientific concepts and the important role drawing plays in the development of higher mental functions. When the children were exploring flashlights they discovered that flashlights often cast a shadow. This observation led most children in the class into a wider exploration of shadows. We began by going outside with our drawing clipboards to observe shadows in natural settings

Ed's exploration of shadows

The shadow of the bike rack (Fig. 1.8) was the subject of Ed's next investigation. He said, "I drew the bike rack because the shadow looked so different from the rack." He wondered why that would happen. He was surprised that shadows were not necessarily replicas of the objects that created them. Referring to both his drawing (Fig. 1.9) and the bike rack, Ed was able to point out to me how the hoops of the bike rack were separate circles that were attached to the bar at the top while the shadows appeared to be a continuous loop. Ed's motivation for drawing the bike rack and its shadow was to discover more about the nature of shadows. In this context, drawing was a meaning-making tool. Ed began with the spontaneous encounter and concept and through his drawing moved to a higher level of thinking. Ed discovered that shadows were not necessarily replicas of the objects that created them. Drawing acted as the mediation tool that allowed this new understanding to occur.

When I encountered Ed drawing the bike rack, our discussion focused upon what he had chosen to draw, why he had chosen to draw it, as well as what he was discovering in the process. Back in the classroom, when sharing his drawing with his peers, he talked about how he had discovered something new about shadows and how this discovery became clearer to him while he was drawing.

Fig. 1.8 The bike rack and shadow

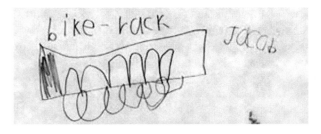

Fig. 1.9 Ed's drawing of the bike rack and shadow

In the classroom the children set up some mannequins and a light to reflect their shadows (Fig. 1.10). Ed launched into an ambitious drawing of the whole setting (Fig. 1.11). He singled out one figure to pay particular attention to and began to draw its shadow. He said, "Look, the shadow is bigger than the head." He had noticed that there was a difference between the size of the figure's head and the size of the shadow cast by the head. The shadow of the head was much bigger than the head.

There is a connection between this drawing and Ed's drawing of the bike rack and its shadow. Ed is interested in the size and shape of the shadows in relation to the objects that cast them. He is intrigued that there should be a difference in size and shape between the two. This latest drawing allowed Ed to try out a similar idea in a different context. The drawings allow Ed to move between concepts, operate at a supra empirical level and develop higher mental functions. Ed continued with his exploration of the size and shape of shadows by making a plasticine figure, directing light onto it from different angles and tracing and comparing the shadows.

Vygotsky (1978) considered the shift from everyday concepts to scientific concepts important in the formation of higher mental functions. A scientific concept allows empirical connections between concepts. A system is in place and increasing generalizations and abstractions are possible. Spontaneous concepts reach up into scientific concepts while scientific concepts reach down and pull the spontaneous concept up. In both cases the abstraction of drawing requires a level of interpretation and engagement that works to raise the level of thinking so that the children engage in more complex thinking. When children are encouraged to make observational drawings, or to draw out their initial ideas or experiences, they can then revisit, revise and recontextualize their drawing as well as compile a series of related drawings. Drawing processes such as this can play a critical role in the movement between spontaneous concepts and scientific concepts and the development of higher mental functions.

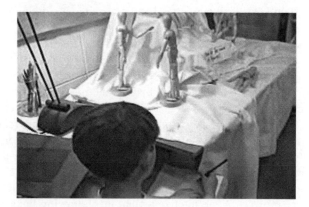

Fig. 1.10 Lamp, mannequins and shadows

Fig. 1.11 Ed's drawing of the head's shadow.

Drawing and the Consequential Progression of Ideas

Mapping the consequential progression of ideas is one way of linking the notions of a social context for drawing and learning, with interpersonal and intrapersonal dialogues as well as with higher mental thinking. Consequential progression for the children in this classroom is a process whereby the interactions amongst children and the interactions through and with their drawings, build cyclically over extended periods of time so that the understanding of the group becomes increasingly complex. The understanding that builds through this increasingly complex dialogic engagement also becomes a cultural resource that allows the group to progress as a strong learning community. Drawing becomes part of the cultural resources of the group. When drawings are shared between and amongst the children on an ongoing basis they play a vital and accessible mediating role in knowledge building.

Central to an understanding of consequential progression is the notion of intersubjectivity (Wink & Putney, 2002). Intersubjectivity in this context is the collective history and mutual meanings shared by a group of people, in particular the children in my classroom. This collective history and mutual meanings are negotiated and accumulated through drawing. Drawing creates intersubjective spaces in the classroom. Intersubjectivity comes about through the dynamic relationship between intertextuality and intercontextuality. Drawing acts as an intertextual event so that the cultural significance of artifacts and ideas is brought forward within the classroom community. Drawing allows the children to recognize each other's thoughts and ideas, link them to their own and to carry these thoughts and ideas forward to future projects. At an intercontextual level drawing links cultural practices and concepts with ways of being or actions taken. Drawing allows children to explicitly link previous experience with new learning. Drawing helps children to trust their own knowledge and provides a vehicle to work together to jointly construct a mutual understanding. These understandings become increasingly complex as the knowledge base expands.

Another idea, or topic, that grew out of the children's initial study of flashlights was how to trap light. During class time small groups and individual children drew plans and worked on the floor with flashlights and at the light table to enclose light with unit blocks. They seemed to have formed a common agreement that all of the traps should be made from unit blocks. Each day before leaving the classroom we gathered as a class and tested the traps by putting out the main lights, plunging the classroom into darkness. This way we could better see if light was escaping from any trap.

To help us better understand the notion of a consequential progression of ideas I will describe how a small group of five and six year old boys used drawing to explore ideas in relation to building the light traps. I will demonstrate how drawing in a social context mediated new knowledge and understanding for these children. I will examine drawing events over time and follow threads of children's thinking and the consequential progression of increasingly complex ideas.

Ed's light trap

Ed was one of the first children to build a light trap. While he chose to work by himself on the light table it is important to remember that he was working within the context of the classroom where there had already been many discussions about, and shared drawings of, light traps. Ed began by drawing a plan for his trap. His drawing contained elements of ideas from his peers as well as his own emerging ideas (Fig. 1.12). The drawing brought the accumulated knowledge of light traps forward into Ed's particular project.

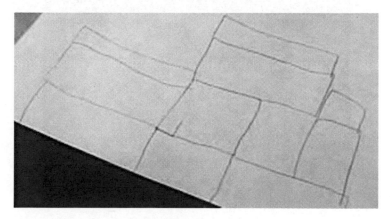

Fig. 1.12 Ed's drawing of his light trap

After drawing his plan, Ed collected the blocks he thought he needed and took them to the light table. His drawing helped him make decisions about which blocks to choose and how many (Fig. 1.13). His drawing mediated between thought and action to make his actions more deliberate. Ed's drawing fulfilled a significant role in his knowledge construction and understanding. Ed's drawing was functioning as an intertextual event so that the cultural significance of ideas was brought forward within the classroom community through drawing. Ed's aim seemed to be to build a structure that absolutely contained the light without any of it escaping. His focus was on the 'light tightness' of a basic box, block structure (Fig. 1.14) however he could not solve the problem of light escaping from around his structure.

Fig. 1.13 Ed uses his plan to help build the light trap

Fig. 1.14 Ed's finished light trap (Stuart and Anton's light trap is behind it)

Stuart and Anton's light trap

Stuart and Anton decided to build a light trap next to Ed. The two boys sat together to plan their light trap. Each made a drawing of how they thought the light trap would look. As they drew they talked with each other about their plans and looked at each other's drawing. The drawings allowed each child to see what the other was thinking. This facilitated a common understanding. Stuart and Anton were also aware of Ed's drawing and construction and were keen to try to address the problem Ed had with light escaping. Stuart and Anton also gained access to Ed's idea through the sharing of his drawing at a large group meeting.

Mirrors featured in Stuart and Anton's conversation from the very beginning. When previously studying flashlights the boys had noticed the reflecting mirror around the bulb in the flashlight and seemed convinced that mirrors and light had to go together. Stuart said the mirror gave the light "more power". Here drawing is functioning at an intercontextual level that works to link cultural practices and concepts with current ways of being or actions taken. Stuart and Anton's drawings allowed them to explicitly link previous experiences with new learning. In the first drawing Stuart placed the mirror under the drawbridge (Fig. 1.15). His rationale was that any light that escaped from around the castle walls would be trapped in the mirror and bounced back down to where it came from. Anton, however, drew the light going up inside the towers. He wanted to trap the light within the hollow towers. Anton's drawing showed two hollow towers connected by a drawbridge (Fig. 1.16).

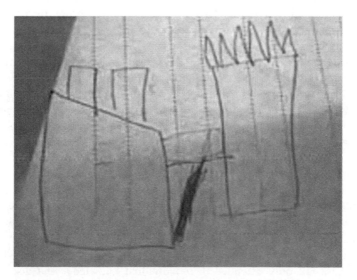

Fig. 1.15 Stuart's first drawing of a light trap with the mirror placed below the drawbridge to catch the light from the table

Fig. 1.16 Anton's first drawing of a light trap. Two towers and a drawbridge. The light goes up one tower and across the drawbridge.

However, Stuart pointed out that the light could only travel successfully up one tower because the other had windows in it where the light could escape. Stuart suggested a mirror be placed in the tower with the windows. Anton ignored that suggestion and pointed out that the drawbridge was hollow. He reasoned that the light would only be able to go up the tower, through the drawbridge and down the other tower. There would then only be one path for the light to travel and it would not be able to go anywhere else. This plan seemed to make the mirror redundant. Stuart suggested trying to incorporate the mirror at the end of the drawbridge. The two boys discussed the necessity of the mirror. Stuart insisted that it was the mirror that made the light "bounce off" and "keep moving". When Stuart mentioned, "keep moving" Anton paused and suddenly seemed to understand the purpose of the mirror. If they placed a mirror strategically at both ends of the drawbridge then the light would be forced to travel back and forwards across the drawbridge indefinitely thus creating the perfect trap. Anton revised his drawing to show how the light would bounce between the mirrors at either end of the drawbridge. Stuart also revised his drawing to incorporate Anton's ideas with his own.

Drawing helped the two boys take some initial and tentative ideas about how to trap light and elaborate and extend them through their drawing, talking, and building. In this series of drawings we can again also see the movement between spontaneous concepts and scientific concepts to higher mental thinking as well as the consequential progression of ideas.

In this case the two boys worked together to share their existing knowledge and in the process not only extended their individual knowledge but also extended their collective knowledge. Revising their drawings after they had built their structure helped to transform new knowledge from an interpersonal state to a more intrapersonal state as each was able to recall and retell, through the drawing, the new knowledge they had acquired. Sharing their new knowledge with the class through their drawings added to collective knowledge of this group of children.

Conclusion and Recommendations

In this chapter I have focused on what children bring to drawing, their interactions with their environment and how they work to solve the problems or questions they encounter through their drawing. The focus has not been on the performance level the children achieved in drawing but rather on the methods or the process by which performance was achieved. I would suggest that it is important to pay close attention to the kinds of activities, opportunities, and discussions that can support drawing in the social context of the classroom. I have shown that drawing can help children make their ideas visible and that it is often through drawing that children's ideas, questions, and misconceptions can be effectively processed. When drawing is one of the modes of exchange in a classroom then drawings can be preserved as a record of children's thinking that can be reviewed and revisited by both teacher and child while also serving as a vehicle of exchange within the wider learning community.

"A child does not just become a thinker or a problem solver: she becomes a special kind of thinker, rememberer, listener, and communicator that is a reflection of the social context" (Bodrova & Leong, 1996, p.10). In the context of the school setting, ideas and ways of processing information are shared amongst the teachers and children. When we value collaborative work and structure our classroom space, time and materials in ways that supported this value position, then much of the burden for learning is shifted from the teacher and shared among the whole class group. This provides a richer and more dialogic learning environment. When the nature of the interactions between teacher and child, and child and child, are ones that encourage a dialogue about ideas, meaning, and learning then children hear that this is something their learning community values. Strategies for learning, thinking, and using drawing as a meaning-making tool need to be modeled and talked about individually, in small groups, as well as in large group discussions. This approach to learning recognizes the particular skills and experiences each child brings to the learning situation and works to involve the child in a continuous dialogic spiral where the collective understanding and discussions work to support individual constructions. Drawing functions well as part of this dialogic model.

One of the great strengths of drawing lies in its ability to immediately reflect back to the person drawing the ideas that are revealed. This is perhaps why young children find drawing such an attractive and powerful tool. It is immediately holistic and interactive in ways that writing is not. The examples used in this chapter have demonstrated that children are able to represent complex ideas in their drawings. It has also demonstrated that children are able to absorb information from the contexts in which they work and to assimilate and transform new ideas through their drawings. However, the support, time, and opportunity for children to pursue complexity in their drawing also have to be part of the teaching and learning environment.

The focus of the discussion around the drawing has to be on the meaning and information it contains rather than on drawing skills and aesthetic qualities. This shifts the focus from a performance based criteria to one that is concerned with the meaning that the children are trying to make of certain phenomena through their drawing. This approach opens a dialogue that actively involves children at a cognitive level. I would suggest that when our focus is primarily on the meanings represented through drawing we could begin to see drawing as an invaluable teaching and learning tool.

Drawings like those I have just described provide valuable insights into children's thinking and provide records of children's cognitive growth and development. If we think of drawing involving many steps and perhaps many drawings in the pursuit of an idea, this opens possibilities for children using drawing over again in many different ways and contexts. The generative and divergent possibilities offered by drawing are among its most important qualities. When young children take their drawings home each day we lose important records. It is important that drawings are easily accessible and carefully stored in the classroom.

When drawing is viewed as a tool that is part of a meaning-making repertoire this helps teachers to see drawing as part of a learning process rather than as a product that is indicative of a more rigid stage of development. When the drawing skills involved become part of the child's struggle to articulate meaning then teachers can work with the child to clarify the meaning with the assumption that it may take several drawings to reach a desired level of understanding. These examples show that while it is important to draw at the interpersonal level it is worthwhile pursuing the cognitive complexity and abstraction that drawing seems to support at an intrapersonal level. This often means asking more from children through drawing.

A Vygotskian theoretical framework has helped us to look at drawing as much more than recreation and decoration. It has helped us understand how meaning and understanding can be facilitated through drawing and that drawing can play a significant role in the growth and development of young children's thinking and education.

References

Athey, C. (1990). *Extending thought in young children*. London: Paul Chapman Publishing.
Barratt-Pugh, C. , & Rohl, M. (2000). *Literacy learning in the early years*. Australia: Allen & Unwin.
Brooks, M. (2002). *Drawing to Learn*. Unpublished PhD thesis. University of Alberta, Canada.

Brooks, M. (2003). Drawing, thinking, meaning. TRACEY,
    http://www.lboro.ac.uk/departments/ac/traccy/thin/Brooks.html

Bodrova, E., & Leong, D. J. (1996). *Tools of the mind - The Vygotskian approach to early child-hood education.* Columbus, OH: Merrill/Prentice Hall.

Cox, M. V. (1991). *The child's point of view* (2nd ed.). London: Harvester Wheatsheaf

Duran, R. P., & Syzmanski, M. H. (1995). Co-operative learning interaction and construction of activity. *Discourse Processes, 10*(1), 149-164.

Eisner, E. W. (1972). *Educating artistic vision.* New York: Macmillan.

Gifford, S. (1997). When should they start doing sums? A critical consideration of the emergent mathematics approach. In I. Thompson (Ed.), *Teaching and learning early number* (pp. 178-183). Buckingham, UK: Open University Press.

Matthews, J. (1999). *The art of childhood and adolescence: The construction of meaning.* London: Falmer Press.

Moll, L. (2002). Inspired by Vygotsky: Ethnographic experiments in education. In C. D. Lee & P. Smagorinsky (Eds.), *Vygotskian perspectives on literacy research: Constructing meaning through collaborative inquiry* (pp. 256-268). New York: Cambridge University Press.

Rogoff, B. (1990). *Apprenticeship in thinking: Cognitive development in social context.* New York: Oxford University Press.

Vygotsky, L. S. (1962). *Thought and language.* Cambridge, MA: M.I.T. Press

Vygotsky, L. S. (1978). *Mind in society.* Cambridge, MA: Harvard University Press.

Vygotsky, L. S. (1987). Thinking and Speech. In L. S. Vygotsky, *The collected works of L. S. Vygotsky, Vol. 1, Problems of general psychology* (pp. 39-285) (R. W. Rieber & A. S. Carton, Eds.; N. Minick, Trans.). New York: Plenum Press.

Vygotsky, L. S. (1998). The history of the development of higher mental functions. In L.S. Vygotsky, *The collected works of L.S. Vygotsky, Vol. 4, Problems of general psychology* (pp.39-285) (R.W. Rieber& A. S. Carton, Eds.; N. Minick, Trans.). New York: Plenum Press.

Wertsch, J. (2000). Vygotsky's two minds on the nature of meaning. In C. D. Lee & P. Smagorinsky (Eds.), *Vygotskian Perspectives on Literary Research: Constructing Meaning through Collaborative Inquiry* (pp. 19-30). New York: Cambridge University Press.

Wink, J., & Putney, L. (2002). *A vision of Vygotsky.* Boston: Allyn and Bacon.

Margaret Brooks
University of New England
Armidale, NSW   Australia

Dr Margaret Brooks' passion is drawing. Not only is she a practicing artist in her own right, with drawing being her particular medium, but she is also interested in the drawing processes of young children. As a senior lecturer at the University of New England, Australia, she is responsible for teaching, Young Children and the Creative Arts, Play, and Young Children and Mathematics. As a researcher of young children drawing she uses visual ethnography because this visual method honours the visual processes of the children she is researching.

Chapter 2
Creating a Critical Multiliteracies Curriculum:

Repositioning Art in the Early Childhood Classroom

Linda K. Crafton, Penny Silvers, and Mary Brennan

Abstract Traditional early childhood curricula tend to separate the arts and literacy as different meaning-making systems. However, current multiliteracies theory and practice suggests that a broader view of literacy and learning is necessary for 21st century living. The notion of multiliteracies allows us to expand not only our definition of literacy from traditional print views to digital ones but also promotes broader understandings of the arts as semiotic systems integral to meaning making. More importantly, multiliteracies theory moves educators from a curriculum-as-neutral stance to a critical pedagogy stance that encourages young learners to take on a social justice identity from the start. This chapter features the critical multiliteracies research and practice of one teacher and two university educators researching in a first grade classroom over several years. An extended curricular example illustrates how art can be repositioned in early childhood instruction and curriculum to become an integral component of critical multimodal learning. The chapter shows how young children move seamlessly in and out of curricular engagements based on their interests and multimodal needs necessary for functioning in their classroom and the world beyond.

Keywords multiliteracies, emergent literacy, early literacy, critical literacy, critical visual literacy, multimodal learning, semiotics, arts and literacy, arts and identity, transmediation

University of Wisconsin-Parkside, USA
DePaul University, USA
Pritchett Elementary School, USA

M. J. Narey (ed.), *Making Meaning*.
© Springer 2009

Introduction

Classrooms rich in writing, literature, and read-alouds, often create a strong bond between children and books. Following Ray (1999), many teachers have learned to use touchstone, mentor texts that they go back to again and again to highlight features to support students in particular writing techniques. But just as often, it is the children who decide which books will take on a significance beyond the read-aloud or the reader response; which story and experiences with it will be their constant companion to help them grow beyond themselves (Harste, Short, & Burke, 1988). And so it was with Tori and Karen during their first grade year in Mary Brennan's classroom. From its introduction in the fall and well into their second grade year, *Ruby's Wish* (Bridges, 2001), the story about a young girl growing up in China long ago who is determined to attend university when she grows up, just like the boys in her family, became a tool to think with, a text to transform, and one resource used to shape a new identity. Their story, however, like all others, is situational; it unfolds within a particular sociocultural context in which the teacher and her researcher colleagues were intentional about the ways and means of learning, literacy and change. This chapter analyzes and describes the path taken by Tori and Karen as they lived one year with a teacher and class-mates exploring a multiliteracies, multimodal curriculum with social justice and identity development as the core. Mary worked within a community of practice alongside two teacher educators, Linda and Penny. As a collaborative team, they came together on a weekly basis to explore the theory and practice of a pedagogy steeped in 21st century understandings of what it takes to become a successful citizen in a pluralistic society.

As early childhood educators, we are interested in creating learners "who are agents of text rather than victims of text" (Albers, 2007, p. ix). Critical mul-tiliteracies/multimodal actions not only promote increased abilities in particular sign systems, they encourage the investigation of possible selves. The powerful visual and written texts created by Tori and Karen around a specific focus, al-lowed them to unpack various systems of meaning and to enact developing identi-ties. They helped us understand that visual literacy and the critical interpretation of visual texts is indispensable in the achievement of a fully realized critical liter-acy.

An Expanded Theoretical Base Informs Our Inquiries

We approach our research and curriculum work drawing from a rich network of theoretical views, chief among them are: semiotics, sociocultural theories, and multimodal/multiliteracies.

Semiotics

As small children, we lived in a multimodal world. We discovered that art was a language with as much communication power as speech. Later we learned, like oral language, the arts could act as a bridge to reading and writing and that music and movement had the same potential for contributing to our expression of meaning and self. There were so many languages and literacies when we were young, so much playful, joyful movement among them as we began to learn the stunning communication potential within us all as human beings. As we entered the formal structures of school, our languages and literacies were systematically downsized and we were left with fewer semiotic resources from which to draw, just at a time when our meaning-making should have been at its richest, undifferentiated peak.

We live in a society in which language is privileged as the dominant communication system – in and out of the classroom. We value the orator over the dancer and we warn children of dismal futures should they not become proficient readers and writers. Semiotic theory expands our understanding of literacy and communication by gently sliding language from its central position to work alongside other semiotic modes, particularly the arts, with greater parity. Semiotics is the study of signs, how acts and objects function as signs in relation to other signs in the production and interpretation of meaning. Working together, multiple sign systems produce "texts" that communicate ideas. Texts can take a number of different forms (written, spoken, painted, performed, etc) but within each text, it is the complex meaning-relations that exist between one sign and another that breathe life into the communication event.

Semiotics teaches us that every text can be viewed as a multiplicity of signs (e.g., writing is both a linguistic sign and a visual one, an image can be interpreted both visually and linguistically); texts, then, are inherently intertextual. Intertextuality is a semiotic notion introduced by Kristeva (1980). The term suggests that individual texts are not discrete, closed-off entities; rather, every text and every reading depends on prior texts. Kress (2003) points out that individuals are "not mere users of a system, who produce no change, we need to see that changes take place always, incessantly, and that they arise as a result of the interested actions of individuals" (p. 155).

In our research and curriculum explorations, we use semiotic theory to remind us that, when reading a picture book, for example, there are many sign systems operating in one text entity (print, visual display of print, illustrations, photographs); together, these elements come together to create a meaning gestalt. Albers (2007) notes that "Representation occurs across and within forms, and expression of meaning is semiotic" (p. 6). Read aloud time, then, becomes a rich opportunity to not only read and discuss print meanings in relation to the linguistic and visual aspects of print but to read images in terms of how the illustrator uses line, color, light and placement on the page to communicate and their relationship to the print elements. Collectively these systems support particular interpretations.

However, communication very often occurs through combinations of sign systems, juxtaposed to create a more powerful effect. Albers, for example, describes how in the movie, *Jaws*, Spielberg (1975, as cited in Albers, 2007) uses music and visual elements – the shark, underwater scenes, and actors' faces – to strike fear in the hearts of viewers. This combination is so memorable that many adults who experienced it now only have to hear the music to be thrown into some level of anxiety.

Sociocultural Theory

We know from sociocultural theorists (Gee, 1992; Vygotsky, 1986; Wells, 1999) that learning is an active process involving social participation. Dewey (1938) helps us understand that individuals develop by interacting meaningfully with their environment. Children bring prior knowledge and their personal social worlds to the classroom and, as they are involved in the work of the classroom community, they learn through their interpersonal engagements and interactions with multimodal tools. "We have learned that when primary classrooms open up social learning space and encourage collective use of the available multimodal tools of the classroom culture, children and teachers transform and, in the process, transform the very culture of the classroom itself" (Crafton, Brennan, & Silvers, 2007, p. 517).

Wenger (1998) also helps us see the importance of the work of the community and the need for children to engage in inquiry using a variety of learning tools. He presents a theory of learning as participation, situated in our lived experiences in the world. As we all belong to multiple communities and construct identities in relation to these communities, our participation shapes not only our own experience and competence, but shapes our community as well. This reinforces the notion that learning is about identity construction – for the individual as well as the group.

Multiliteracies

A developing body of research about multiliteracies, also called "new literacies" (Kress, 2003), has helped us understand that literacy is multimodal (print, art, drama, language) and multimedial (combining various means of communication such as Internet, music, video) (Vasquez, Egawa, Harste, & Thompson, 2004). Children in the 21st century have to learn to negotiate multiple literacies to achieve work and overall life success (Kress, 2003). They have to learn to consider different perspectives, to analyze and problem-solve complex issues, and to think critically about social issues.

Traditional views of early literacy focus mainly on print. From this perspective, literacy is primarily thought of as decoding and making meaning. However, a different dimension of literacy emerges when it is considered as social practice (Vasquez, Egawa, Harste, & Thompson, 2004). Luke and Freebody (1997) elaborate on this through their four resources model that presents practices necessary for full literacy development. These include:

- Code Breaking (decoding written texts; understanding basic features of language including the alphabetic principles; and understanding broader cultural codes or ways of talking and acting within various communities).
- Meaning Making (constructing meaning through writing, visual representation, digital technology, movement, music, and oral language).
- Using texts (ways that texts are used for cultural and social purposes).
- Critical analysis (texts of all kinds are socially constructed and can be changed or deconstructed. Similarly, readers need to understand that texts position them in particular ways that can be accepted or rejected. Readers have the power to question, consider different perspectives, and resist being positioned to think or believe in a particular way).

As noted by Janks (2000), we need to understand the relationship between language and power and that language is a cultural resource that can be used to challenge or maintain systems of dominance. When this critical perspective becomes a part of literacy practices, literacy must be defined more broadly to reflect, "all literacy events are multimodal, involving the orchestration of a wide variety of sign systems" (Short, Harste, & Burke, 1996, p. 14). A multiliteracies classroom includes a focus on community and social practices, on multimodal means of representing and constructing meaning, and taking a critical social justice stance leading to change and identity transformation. It supports teaching for social action, cultural critique, and for democracy, inside and outside of school (Bomer and Bomer, 2001).

It is important that teachers learn to use multiliteracies as tools to help even young children acquire the literacy resources for appreciation, understanding, analysis and action – and to take on the New London Group's (2000) challenge to nurture the critical engagements that are necessary for students to design their social futures and provide them with access to the language of work, power, and community. Children can understand social issues and should learn from the beginning of school that they can make a difference in the lives of others. Through play, art, music, technology, and language, children can address complex issues that concern them and their world (Dyson, 1993).

Social Practices in Mary's Classroom

Tori and Karen were members of a first grade classroom in a northern suburb of Chicago where changing demographics have shifted from rural to a more urban, multiethnic, multicultural community.   With a variety of languages and cultures represented, Mary worked hard to develop a community of practice in her class-room, to provide space for inquiry, support engaged learning, scaffold emerging literacy practices, and help her students learn to care about each other and about the world beyond the classroom.   Critical literacy (Anstey & Bull, 2006; Comber, 2003; Vasquez, 2003; Wink, 2005) is part of our research study of multiliteracies as an expanded view of literacy practices.   A particular emphasis in Mary's teach-ing was helping the students learn to take a critical stance and to understand that agency is an important outcome of critical work – that they can take action, make a difference, and change what they feel isn't working within their classroom, the school, or their community and beyond.

As researchers in Mary's classroom, Linda and Penny became participant ob-servers, often working alongside Mary, talking to students, facilitating group work, preparing read-alouds, joining inquiry groups, and participating in the life of the classroom.   On occasion, Linda and Penny joined Mary in assessing individual students whose literacy/learning growth concerned us.   Other times, they distanced themselves from the learning community, taking fieldnotes, observing and docu-menting the complex interactions through video recordings, and collecting student artifacts to broaden their understandings of student learning and change.

Mary was intentional about establishing particular social practices in her class-room.   She slowly transformed her classroom into a community of practice (Wen-ger, 1998) taking the time to reflect on learning experiences together with the stu-dents, verbalizing her own learning processes and "noticing" out loud what she saw the students doing as a way of validating their talk, collaboration, and inquir-ies.   She intentionally highlighted student strengths and made sure everyone knew who the experts were – experts at using technology, drawing pictures, telling sto-ries, dramatizing stories, reading, writing, illustrating, and organizing routines. Inquiry groups were another way students were able to collaborate, problem-solve, and take responsibility for making learning decisions based on their interests, needs, and teacher expectations.   Transmediation (Suhor, 1992; Harste, 2000) be-came a central strategy in Mary's curriculum.   Transmediation is a process of re-thinking something that is known in one sign system (like print) through another sign system (like art or music). For example, students can use *Sketch to Stretch* (Harste, Short, & Burke, 1988) as a strategy to symbolize what a story or concept means to them.   As their unique visual representations are discussed together in the classroom, students gain new insight and come to understand something in a new way. Each sign system generates a particular perspective, and contributes something unique to the meaning-making process.   Students learn to think diver-gently, metaphorically, and collaboratively as they negotiate meaning and add the language of each sign system to their interpretive tool box. Rather than a literal representation of a story, a drawing can reflect a way of expanding meaning to other aspects of life.

From the beginning, Mary made a variety of learning tools available for the students to use as they explored topics of interest and importance. For example, Mary had a rotating daily schedule of who would use the 4 computers in the room. She had a box of stories and books the children could select from to engage in Reader's Theater. Students were encouraged to dramatize stories they read or wrote; illustrate and make posters or banners, or use the computer to make pictures for their writing; music was available through a variety of CD's stored in the classroom to set the mood for various subjects; and materials for writing, drawing, reading, and investigating were always available. Reading and writing, drawing, dramatizing, and interacting together were the primary ways in which authentic learning experiences were developed and problems were solved.

Mary also used talk as a powerful learning tool. For example, Mary commented that Gaby's illustrations were filled with color, showing everyone what colors could do to help the viewer feel the warmth and happiness in her picture. From students' positive reaction to her statements, Gaby began to take on the identity of an artist who flooded her canvas with beautiful primary colors – colors that reminded her of Mexico and her family visits. When Mary told Jay that she liked "reading" his picture-story about computer characters, he began to place his characters in various activities in his drawings and revise his story as he authored his visual text. Soon after, he told the class that he might want to be a writer and make a book about all of his computer games at home. Reading pictures took its place alongside reading words as part of the literacy practices in Mary's room. Pictures were a text and words were a text – children were learning to read everything and move seamlessly between the two.

Read-aloud time became an important instructional strategy and Mary used think-alouds during oral reading to help the children learn the language of visual interpretation. Using phrases like "I wonder why the artist used contrasting colors; or placed the pictures this way on the page; or showed the characters taking these actions" helped the students learn to ask critical questions of visual as well as print texts. She found ways to make learners understand that all visible texts have invisible meanings that underpin them and it is their job to discover what those are. Through Mary's guidance, the discourse surrounding visual images gradually became the language of artists and illustrators: What do you notice? What do you feel? What do you think the artist/illustrator wants you to feel? What tools does s/he use to achieve that (e.g., color, line, placement, light source, top frame, vertical and horizontal orientation, multiple perspectives, positioning of people)?

As we all learned more about critical literacy, issues of power, equity, and justice became a more visible part of the classroom dialogue. Inquiry groups provided a way for students to choose areas of inquiry, pursue their own interests, and have multiple opportunities to work together. Early in the year, Linda brought up

the issue of gender and provided a small text set of books and materials that supported an inquiry into gender roles, gender equity, and gender in the media. *The
Piggy Book* (Browne, 1986) led to heated discussions about what moms and dads
do and the questions that we asked the children became the core questions that
were asked when interpreting and interrogating all texts – print, visual, digital,
musical, or dramatic.

Bringing Social Justice Close to Home

As the students were learning to critique texts and interpret them from multiple
perspectives, Mary helped them connect their emerging social justice awareness to
life in their own community. One day she brought in an article from the local
community newspaper with the intention of sharing a real life example of citizenship and community activism. Little did she know that this article about an elderly
woman about to lose her home would become so important and meaningful for her
students and for herself (see also Crafton, Brennan, & Silvers, 2007).

> This experience [Grandma Ruth] is representative of so many opportunities this year for
> 1st graders to become empowered learners. Opening up space in the curriculum for
> students to think critically, to care, and to use the tools of 21st century learners was
> transformational for me. The support of our community of practice, the theory that I
> revisited, relearned, and was introduced to this year became the support I needed as I
> returned to teaching the multimodal world of 1st grade (Mary, personal journal, 6/05)

While Mary historically had reserved an honored place in her early childhood
curriculum for the arts, particularly drama and the visual arts and connecting them
to subject matter learning, the difference now was to recognize their force in identity development, and to deeply engage in the "arts essentials like personal voice,
brainstorming, making creative choices and reflecting on their impact" (Booth,
2008). A more fluid movement between text and image and back again became
characteristic of Mary's teaching...and when you ask Mary, she is quick to respond that it began with Grandma Ruth.

In mid-December, a local newspaper ran a cover story about an elderly woman
who was being evicted from her house and placed in a nursing home apparently
against her will. Later articles revealed how a real estate developer wanted to
build more expensive homes on this woman's neglected property. Mary felt this
article would support the first grade social studies curriculum and its focus on
learning about the traits of responsible citizenship as well as her growing interest
in critical literacy.

At first Mary was a little hesitant about sharing this article, as the subject matter seemed to be rather adult. But she felt that the work with critical literacy and
care supported the use of this compelling story, and she forged ahead. The picture
on the front page grabbed the students' attention and the headline caused them to

gasp in horror. Staring straight out of the black and white photo, front and center, Grandma Ruth was declaring, "They can kill me first!"

The first reading and sharing of this story began with a discussion of the headline and the front-page photo. Mary simultaneously discussed how the reporter purposefully used the headline, carefully crafting the words, to grab the reader's attention; and that the photographer used a "demand image" to do the same. She helped her students relate to the headline by sharing ways that they use this same expression, e.g. "Oh, no, I lost my jacket. My mom is going to kill me." Mary also asked her students to tell what they noticed about the woman:

"She looks sad," responded Jordyn.

"She is looking at us," added Kevin.

"What do you think she is saying to us?" asked Mary.

"Help me!" was Brittany's response.

Mary re-read this article several times over the next few days. Her students were engaged—this was a real story about a real person. Together they examined the photo of this woman's home (a smaller photo in the same article). Again they simultaneously discussed word choice and images and wondered aloud why that photo was chosen and what did it tell them about her?

"I don't think it looks so bad," said Ricardo.

"Yes, it does," replied Lizzie, "look at all that garbage!"

"Why don't the neighbors help her clean it up?" asked Daniel.

"Hey look at those old tires," said Jackie.

"It's an 'eyesore'," shouted Kyle, borrowing words from the article. Students liked the expression, "eyesore," the word the reporter used to describe her home. They also noticed that in the article the woman was referred to as "Grandma Ruth". "She looks sort of like my grandma," said Pearl and, from this point on, the students referred to her as Grandma Ruth.

A follow up article elaborated her plight. This article offered a possible solution. A developer would purchase her land and build several homes on it, including one for Grandma Ruth. By this time Mary's students were beginning to understand Grandma Ruth's perspective and Kevin said, "She doesn't want a new home! She wants this one!" This led to discussions about possible solutions, kinds of action that could be taken, and a heated dialogue about fairness, rights, economics, and power. The children drew pictures of possible solutions, and some went right to the computers to create their stories about why this was wrong. Solutions included having an "extreme makeover" for the house, collecting money to help save the house, getting community members to clean the house, and sending Grandma Ruth letters from the class to be courageous and not move out if she didn't want to (Fig. 2.1).

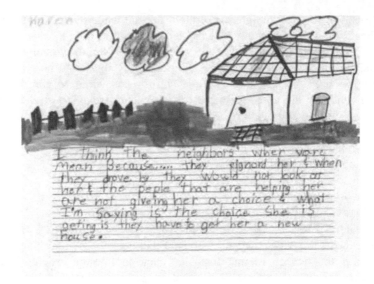

Fig. 2.1 Karen's letter to Grandma Ruth

Under Mary's guidance, the children continued to write stories, prepared a digital slide show, wrote and illustrated letters to the newspaper, and used process drama as a way to explore possible solutions. They danced, acted, drew, wrote, and talked their way to understanding the complexity of the situation and the need for taking social action. One concrete action came when the children wrote a letter to Grandma Ruth and sent it to the newspaper. It was forwarded to Grandma Ruth.

On the very last day of school, the children received a letter back from her, thanking them for caring, for helping her, and encouraging them to be good students and value their education.

May 25

Dear Mrs. Brennan:

    I thank you very much for being such a wonderful teacher, teaching your young Kings and Queens to love and care for others. It was a wonderful letter I received from you and your Kings and Queens from Kara S. at the newspaper. She is also so wonderful.

    To the Kings and Queens you are teaching, let them know that I appreciate their caring about Grandma Ruth and that I am fine and still fighting the people that want to take my home away from me. You see, I had wonderful teachers, like you, and it has carried me through life's journeys, so keep learning and always be honest to yourself and others and you will get to age 83 with much love and caring. May blessings be with you always.

With all my love.
Thank you so much.,
Grandma Ruth

P.S. I have kept all the papers and pictures you sent close to my heart.

Four years later, Mary's students, now in 4th grade, continue to ask about Grandma Ruth. The reporter is no longer at the paper and repeated e-mails have not answered questions about her saga…but it made an impact on these young citizens. Recently, Mary asked one of her former students to share the story of Grandma Ruth and his response began… "Well, Grandma Ruth lived in a house that was an 'eyesore' and the government wanted to take it from her, but it was hers …"

Tori & Karen Embark on a Path: Using Text and Image as Tools to Reposition Self

Our work together this first year was purposeful and exploratory. Linda, Mary, and Penny were together in Mary's classroom on a regular basis observing and capturing the dynamic learning in this setting. Conversations and learning outside of the classroom seamlessly transferred back into the classroom setting. Early in the fall, we began to identify and share picture books that highlighted social issues, useful for the critical conversations that would be threaded throughout the school year in relation to a broad range of texts, including art, drama and music.

One purpose of this chapter is to focus on findings revealed in the analysis of multiple, multimodal data sources that point to identity shifts in two students in Mary's classroom. The transcribed dialogues, fieldnotes, pieces of student art, and videotaping of role playing all provided evidence of change.

Daily read alouds were an integral part of Mary's practice. Using literature selected to encourage critical conversations and reflections was a time when Penny and Linda sat outside of the learning circle and observed the dialogue that Mary facilitated. When engaged in critical literacy, the author/reader pays particular attention to how texts represent meanings about the self and others, that is, texts make available certain social roles. She believed, as Harste (2008) noted, that the ability to sound out words and make meaning from texts makes children good consumers rather than good citizens and to be truly literate, children have to understand how texts work.

During reading, Mary invited responses and interpretations of stories using basic questions of engagement like:

Why do think the author wrote this book?

Why do you think the illustrator …?

Who has the most power in the story?

What words/images make you think that?

Who doesn't have much or any power?

Whose voice is silenced?

Why do you think s/he, they don't have a voice?

The sustained critical inquiry about Grandma Ruth had a significant impact on the students. Children recognized, from the start, that the work they did was important. They listened to the books Mary read to them and had thoughtful discussions. They added new words to their vocabulary and began to use words like empathy, connecting, and caring. Mary developed an expanded text set of picture books and read-alouds pertaining to social issues (see Fig. 2.2). Her read-alouds included books about homelessness, different cultures, coming to a new country, learning new languages, gender, and race.

Favorite Books: Gender & Identity
Amazing Grace by Mary Hoffman
Chrysanthemum by Kevin Henkes
Hooway for Wodney Wat by Helen Lester
Koala Lou by Mem Fox
My Great Aunt Arizona by Gloria Houston
Oliver Button is a Sissy by Tomie DePaola
The Piggybook by Anthony Browne
The Rainbow Fish by Marcus Pfister
Ruby's Wish by Shirim Yim Bridges
William's Doll by Charlotte Zolotow

Fig. 2.2. Mary's text set of picture books.

Ruby's Wish

In February Mary's students were learning about China and celebrating the Chinese New Year. They were fascinated with Chinese traditions. By this time, her students had engaged in critical discussions around a dozen or more books, and had extended from them into art or drama or personal inquiry. Mary decided to read aloud *Ruby's Wish* (2001) by Shirin Yim Bridges to her class. Ruby is a young girl in Ancient China who defies the traditional female role and achieves her dream of attending the university in a male dominated society. This book had a different focus than the books about Chinese celebrations, but its focus was one with which her students were familiar. It supported the kinds of critical questions and thinking Mary had been encouraging. In one section of the book, the author says:

"... most girls were never taught to read or write." Mary paused to open up space for reader response:

Kevin: (gestures his response with a thumbs down, waving motion, frowning.)

Karen says: "That's really unfair. That the boys get to learn but the girls don't get to read and write."

Tori: (turning to Logan and whispering) "Some times you do that – on the playground, you don't let us play and that's not fair."

Mary: "Let's stop and think about that. What's really happening?"

Zack: "Well... I don't know... the boys have to go to school but the girls get to stop, so... the girls get to do what they want, so that's not so bad."

Karen: "Well... no... maybe... but... What if we have an assignment to write and the girls don't have to write then we wouldn't learn how to do it." (pause) Why can't they be together doing the same things?"

Mary: "We've thought about this before with other books – girls having the same choices or opportunities as boys..."

Tori: "Well... like Piggybook and Magic Fish where it wasn't fair but in this book it's more unfair because only one girl got to go."

Logan: "Yeh... maybe Ruby would feel sad that some girls didn't get to go and she might not want to go."

Karen: "Well, she has to go or she wouldn't get to learn."

Eric: "It was unfair at the beginning but fair at the end."

Carmen Luke (2000) states that meanings that readers make of various texts are negotiated in relation to one's different situations and positioning (e.g. adult, child, teenager, male, female, race, ethnicity, socioeconomic class) and cultural contexts. In this exchange, Mary gently pushed her young readers to consider what covert messages might be lurking under the words she was reading. Tori quickly made a connection from the text to the playground and her own experience with unfairness. Certainly, first graders of both genders are not novices when it comes to unequal treatment, but Mary raised the bar with this and other books suggesting that boys often have more power than girls in social settings. Karen focused on the injustice of not being able to learn and not having opportunities to read and write while Logan suggested that Ruby may not want to go unless everyone has the chance. Albers (2007) notes that "critical discussions can lead to students' awareness of what they have learned, and with dialogue, they can unlearn beliefs that tend to stabilize culture, gender, race and ideology" (p. 168). The social construction of meaning in this situation laid a tentative conceptual foundation that was revisited again and again by Tori and Karen.

A short time after the reading of *Ruby's Wish*, students were asked to choose their favorite book from a set of read-alouds so they could discuss its meaning with others and then represent their ideas through art. Tori and Karen joined Linda and one boy who lost interest in the activity and wandered to another group. Initially, Tori retold the story of Ruby, her wish, and how the wish was granted. As in the previous dialogue, the comments about it being unfair and how girls should get to do the same things as boys surfaced. Together, Linda, Tori and

Karen decided to draw a picture of Ruby that showed her important traits, like being brave and courageous by standing up to her grandfather and saying over and over again that her life was unfair.

Tori and Karen gathered the art supplies and continued talking about how their drawing could show something so abstract as bravery. They immediately pulled out their red markers, remembering that the color red is an important color in China. Tori recalled the line from the story that said that Ruby still wears a little red each day. Karen added that red is the color of bravery and power. Linda suggested that sometimes size in a picture can communicate ideas like that too and so the young artists used simple lines and color to fill the page with their first image of Ruby (Fig. 2.3). The vertical orientation of their drawing forces the viewer to read top to bottom, first encountering Ruby's sad face with undifferentiated eyes and red cheeks; she is saying "it is unfair". The children's earlier dialogue, Tori's retelling and the first piece of art produced in relation to the literature all provided connected opportunities to make and consolidate meaning in relation to the narrative.

The second image of Ruby came months later as a gift from Tori and Karen to Linda who was now visiting the classroom less and less. During the intervening weeks of image 1 and image 2, Mary had continued to highlight gender issues through an extended unit on China where the students learned that girls were not as valued as boys in that culture. Tori and Karen had also been involved in an extended inquiry group focused on gender issues.

Fig. 2.3 First drawing of Ruby by Tori and Karen (Translation: It isn't fair. It is a true story.)

In this second drawing (Fig. 2.4), Ruby changed from a tearful, frowning girl depicted by simple lines to an older, smiling more sophisticated girl/woman wearing makeup and earrings. This time Ruby is a smaller figure but the whole of the work itself is richer, more textured with Ruby shown in a setting that reveals Chinese culture – Chinese symbols are shown on a wall hanging and close by is a hanging ball with tassels, also an Asian artifact. However, this isn't a pure Chinese setting as a close look at the right of the drawing shows -- two rugs are seen drawn in pink with hearts and stars decorating them – décor more representative of an American girl's home than a Chinese one. Albers (2007) notes that in art with a horizontal orientation, the meaning should be read left to right and the left side often presents information that is already known or given, while information on the right is new information (p. 141). In this image, Tori and Karen seem to be transitioning their understandings of gender from one culture to another; with one foot still in the narrative of Ruby, they have begun to create their own social narrative.

While Ruby is still declaring, "It's not fair" in this picture, the artists have included more writing to express their growing knowledge of gender inequality:

> her Grandfather doesn't understanet
> it's still happening in China.
> All the boy's get's the atteunton.
> She's not being treated right.

Fig. 2.4 Second drawing of Ruby by Karen and Tori

   This text not only includes a cross-cultural message, it is an intertextual, multimodal creation reflective of the increasing salience of multiple modes of meaning available in all contemporary text displays (Fairclough 2000). It is worth noting that Ruby's face is dramatically different from the first drawing, particularly the eyes and mouth, which are almost, stylized versions of other images of girls and women found in many popular American magazines. These young learners show that many prior texts influence current ones and that visual literacy as well as print literacy is not only intertextual but intervisual as well. Tori and Karen use a range of semiotic resources at their disposal to create one text; their understandings of what it means to be female in America comes from many places. This is the most powerful reason to engage in critical literacy from an early age, arming all students with the tools necessary to uncover and resist the ways others may seek to position them.

   Tori and Karen's final artistic rendering of Ruby came at the beginning of second grade when they produced the text (Fig. 2.5) and brought it to Mary. The critical experiences with text and image they had had in first grade stayed with them throughout the summer and resurfaced one more time in another visual exploration of Ruby. Here, Tori and Karen themselves have entered the text as Ruby was transformed into a Western girl with ponytails not unlike Karen's and a t-shirt with jeans, similar to the clothes both girls wore to school. Gone is the provocative, sexual look and heavy make-up of the last drawing and, in its place, Tori and Karen show an image of a contemporary girl, smiling, once again full-face forward looking out at her viewing audience.

Fig. 2.5 Final drawing of Ruby

The only remnants of the previous texts are their use of the color red and the chopsticks protruding from the girl's hair. The eyes, however, are reminiscent of the second drawing, almost doll-like in their expression, they predictably reveal the continued influence of contemporary texts in their lives. Their label in the bottom left of the picture shows that, indeed, this is still a representation of the meanings they constructed from the book, *Ruby's Wish*, but those critical perspectives have now been internalized. The words to the immediate right of Ruby say: "P.S. on that scroll Tori wrote in Hebrew." This is a strong intertextual, intervisual move by Tori, who is Jewish, to identify herself as integral to the communication.

Bakhtin (1981) tells us that when an author composes a text, he or she also composes a social self. While he was referring to written texts, we interpret this image as both a social and cultural statement about an identity that Tori and Karen have been exploring over time and have finally realized. Revealed in the details and visual codes of this image, we see how reading, writing, talk, and art mediate new understandings of self and the world.

Importantly, Tori and Karen have divided this work into two parts: one primarily visual and the other entirely written. The right side of the text shows a letter written to Mary:

> Dear Ms. Brennan,
> You are a great
> teacher we miss
> you so much.
> We want to
> know how
> grandma Ruth
> is doing. does
> grandma Ruth
> still have
> her house.
> From: Tori Bar-Shalom & Karen Skyla

Considering Tori and Karen's final representation as a whole, it is easy to see that the girls are seeking to reestablish a treasured relationship with their teacher, but a closer look reveals much more. Their work is unified by their concern for social issues. Their semiotic texts are both culturally and personally situated (Albers, 2007), and demonstrate that the experiences these girls have had, the critical conversations, the explorations that revolved around images and purpose was truly transformational. Without Tori and Karen's first image, it would be more difficult to interpret their last; reading images across representations, like the process of assessing growth in writers, gives teachers and researchers access to a learner's history as well as cues to the topics that would be most productive to discuss. Knowing that many meaningful, multimodal topic-related opportunities happened in the spaces between each of the drawings underscores the value of ongoing opportunities to move among sign systems. While each picture positioned Tori and Karen as writers and artists, each also provided a reflective opportunity to consider who they are becoming and who they want to be in the future.

Conclusion

Mary's classroom and, specifically, Tori and Karen's work, reveal the parallel processes of the arts and literacy, their reciprocity in the evolution of learning and their impact on identity construction. What is essential to reading and writing is also essential to art and other semiotic systems: bringing life experiences to bear, focusing on big ideas, drafting, revising, presenting and reflecting. Each sign system brings with it a different potential, its own rhythms of learning, and each alternative construction of meaning a new opportunity to transform the self. Transmediation and the intertextual moves visible in Tori and Karen's art and writing reveal how multiple semiotic systems support personal inquiries. When substantive talk, the creation of images and the reading and writing of literature brush up against one another in a continuous cycle, teachers are provided with prime opportunities to raise current social and cultural assumptions to consciousness and help students relearn oppressive views. Students, then, can enter into an active examination and control of socialized beliefs, challenging them rather than passively accepting them.

Maxine Greene (1995) repeatedly turns our attention to the notion of "wide-awakeness," the awareness of what it means to be fully present in the world. "Meanings spring up all around as soon as we are conscious, and it is the obligation of teachers to heighten the consciousness of who ever they teach by urging them to read and look and make their own interpretations of what they see" (p. 35). Our work raises questions about exactly what constitutes effective teaching and learning in the early childhood classroom.

We know that students today live in an increasingly visual culture. We recognize that the adult world of Mary's students is one that we can only imagine. In Mary's school, first graders attend an art class once a week at the end of the day. Even the time slot allotted for art gives the message that it is not as important as the academic subjects. Our work in language, literacy and the arts is different than the "arts experiences that are inserted into the school day without deep connections to the core curriculum of the classroom (Eisner, 1982, 2002; Grumet, 2004). Primary teachers have traditionally embraced the arts (i.e. music, drama, visual expression) and, yet, at a time when their importance should be increasing, it is waning. Our role as early childhood educators is to provide the resources of all semiotic systems to our young learners. Our research is helping us to see that in today's world this is not only a responsibility, it must be a priority.

Our experiences with Mary's class demonstrate that young children are capable of challenging (or helping to perpetuate) social injustices related to gender, race, and class differences. Issues of equity and social justice are part of young children's lives and are appropriate dimensions of a semiotic curriculum.

When texts that deal with critical social issues are read, discussed, and represented through multiple modes in primary classrooms, they can open up space for children to consider alternative perspectives, make intertextual connections, critique and analyze author assumptions and develop a sense of self and agency. Tori's and Karen's renditions of Ruby speak to shifts in their identities that may hold promise for their futures as strong, independent, socially aware women.

The children in Mary's class engaged in important work. The curriculum expanded to embrace authentic experiences and multiple ways of knowing and expressing. Linda, Mary, and Penny looked for meaningful ways to integrate the arts with a range of other sign systems— and the students were willing participants. "Every instance of making and sharing meaning is a multimodal event involving many sign systems in addition to language...When we limit ourselves to language, we cut ourselves off from other ways of knowing... Children whose strength is not language are denied access. Children whose strength is language are not given opportunities to extend their knowing and thereby develop new ways to communicate with themselves and others" (Harste, 2000, p. 4).

As teachers and learners we must ourselves be visionary and provide ways for our students to "move gracefully and fluently between text and images, between literal and figurative worlds" (Burmark, 2002, p. 1). Future research opportunities include looking for ways to expand curriculum to embrace the arts. Visual literacy, especially connected with digital literacy, is an area that warrants exploration. As early childhood educators, we have an obligation to look for new social practices, practices that will help to fulfill a dream of a fully functioning participatory democracy. Along with the other authors in this book and colleagues in our own arts and literacy communities, we must continuously challenge ourselves and those who would contain our students within the point of a number 2 pencil.

This research is supported by a grant from the Spencer Foundation.

References

Albers, P. (2007). *Finding the artist within*. Newark, DE: The International Reading Association.

Anstey, M., & Bull, G. (2006). *Teaching and learning multiliteracies: Changing times, changing literacies*. Newark, DE: The International Reading Association.

Bakhtin, M. (1981). *The dialogic imagination: Four essays*. Austin, TX: University of Texas Press.

Bomer, R., & Bomer, K. (2001). *Reading and writing for social action*. Portsmouth, NH: Heinemann.

Booth, E. (2008). Taking AIM, Reaching the mark. In C. Weiss & A.L. Lichtenstein, (Eds.), *AIMprint: New relationships in the arts and learning* (pp. i-ii). Chicago: Columbia College Chicago.

Bridges, S. (2001). *Ruby's wish*. San Francisco, CA: Chronicle Books.

Browne, A. (1986). *The piggybook*. New York: Alfred Knopf, Inc.

Burmark, L. (2002). *Visual literacy: Learn to see, see to learn*. Alexandria, VA: ASCD.

Comber, B. (2003). Critical literacy: What does it look like in the early years? In N. Hall, J. Larson, & J. Marsh, (Eds.), *Handbook of early childhood literacy* (pp. 355-369). Thousand Oaks, CA: Sage.

Crafton, L., Brennan, M., & Silvers, P. (2007). Critical inquiry and multiliteracies in a first-grade classroom. *Language Arts, 84*(6), 510-518.

DePaola, T. (1969). *Oliver Button is a Sissy.* New York: Harcourt Brace.

Dewey, J. (1938*). Experience and education.* New York: Collier.

Dyson, A. H. (1993). *Social worlds of children learning to write in an urban primary school.* New York: Teachers College Press.

Eisner, E. (1982). *Cognition and Curriculum.* New York: Longman.

Eisner, E. (2002). *The Educational Imagination.* Columbus, OH: Merrill Prentice Hall.

Fairclough, N. (2000). Multiliteracies and language: Orders of discourse and intertextuality. In M. Kalantzis & B. Cope (Eds.), *Multiliteracies: Literacy learning and the design of social futures* (pp. 162-181). London: Routledge.

Fox, M. (1988). *Koala Lou.* Melbourne, Australia: Drakeford.

Gee, J. (1992). *The social mind: Language, ideology and social practice.* New York: Bergin & Garvey.

Greene, M. (1995). *Releasing the imagination: Essays on education, the arts, and social change.* San Francisco, CA: Jossey-Bass.

Grumet, M. (2004). No one learns alone. In N. Rabkin & R. Redmond (Eds.), *Putting the arts in the picture: Reframing education in the 21st century* (pp. 49-80). Chicago: Columbia College.

Harste, J. (2000). Six points of departure. In B. Berghoff, K. Egawa, J. Harste, & B. Hoonan (Eds.), *Beyond reading and writing: Inquiry, curriculum, and multiple ways of knowing* (pp. 1-16). Urbana, IL: National Council of Teachers of English.

Harste, J. (2008). Visual literacy thought piece. In M. Lewison, C. Leland, & J. Harste (Eds.), *Creating critical classrooms: K-8 reading and writing with an edge* (pp. 52-58). New York: Lawrence Erlbaum.

Harste, J., Short, K., & Burke, C. (1988). *Creating classrooms for authors.* Portsmouth, NH: Heinemann.

Henkes, K. (1991). *Chrysanthemum.* New York: Mulberry Books.

Hoffman, M. (1991). *Amazing Grace.* New York: Dial Books

Houston, G. (1992). *My Great Aunt Arizona.* New York: HarperCollins.

Janks, H. (2000). Domination, access, diversity, and design: A synthesis for critical literacy education. *Educational Review, 52*(2), 15-30.

Kress, G. (2003). *Literacy in the new media age.* London: Routledge.

Kristeva, J. (1980). *Desire in language: A semiotic approach to literature and art.* New York: Columbia University Press.

Lester, H. (1999). *Hooway for Wodney Wat.* New York: Houghton-Mifflin.

Luke, A. & Freebody, P. (1997). Shaping the social practices of reading. In S. Muspratt, A. Luke, & P. Freebody (Eds.), *Constructing critical literacies* (pp. 185-225). Cresskill, NJ: Hampton.

Luke, C. (2000). Cyberschooling and technological change: Multiliteracies for new times. In M. Kalantzis & B. Cope (Eds.), *Multiliteracies: Literacy learning and the design of social futures* (pp. 69-91). London: Routledge.

New London Group. (2000). A pedagogy of multiliteracies: Designing social futures. *Harvard Educational Review, 66,* 60-92.

Pfister, M. (1992). *The Rainbow Fish.* New York: North-South Books.

Ray, K.W. (1999). *Wondrous words: Writers and writing in the elementary classroom.* Champaign Urbana, IL: National Council for Teachers of English.

Short, K., Harste, J., & Burke, C. (1996). *Creating classrooms for authors and inquirers.* Portsmouth, NH: Heinemann.

Suhor, C. (1992). Semiotics and the English language arts. *Language arts, 69*(3), 228-230.

Vasquez, V. (2003). *Getting beyond "I like the book": Creating space for critical literacy in K-6 classrooms.* Newark, DE: International Reading Association.

Vazquez, V., Egawa, K., Harste, J., & Thompson, R. (Eds.). (2004). *Literacy as social practice.* Urbana, IL: National Council of Teachers of English.

Vygotsky, L. (1986). *Thought and language*. Cambridge, MA: The MIT Press.

Wells, G. (1999). Dialogic inquiry: Toward a sociocultural practice and theory of education. Cambridge, UK: Cambridge University Press.

Wenger, E. (1998). *Communities of practice: Learning, meaning, and identity*. Cambridge, UK: Cambridge University Press.

Zolotow, C. (1972). *William's Doll*. New York: Harper & Row.

Linda Crafton
University of Wisconsin, Parkside
Kenosha, WI   USA

Dr. Linda Crafton is Professor of teacher education and literacy at the University of Wisconsin, Parkside. Formerly Director of Teacher Education Assessment at Northwestern University, she is currently a member of the Elementary Section Steering Committee for the National Council of Teachers of English. Dr. Crafton has written several books on the holistic teaching and learning of reading and writing and published in many journals including *Language Arts, Journal of Reading and Reading Teacher*. For the past six years, her collaborative research interests have focused on critical literacy, multiliteracies, multimodal learning and intertextuality.

Penny Silvers
DePaul University
Chicago, IL   USA

Dr. Penny Silvers is an Assistant Professor in teacher education and literacy at DePaul University in Chicago, Illinois. She is a former elementary teacher and reading specialist and has written numerous articles and book chapters relating to language arts and reading practices. Penny is active in the National Council of Teachers of English and is a former member of the Commission on Reading. Her collaborative research interests include 21st Century literacy practices, multimodal learning, critical literacy, and professional study groups as communities of practice.

Mary Brennan
Pritchett Elementary School
Buffalo Grove, IL   USA

Ms. Mary Brennan is a National Board Certified first grade teacher in Buffalo Grove, Illinois and a doctoral student at Northern Illinois University. She is teaching National Board certification courses at Roosevelt University and mentoring teachers through the NBCT process. Mary's research interests include multiliteracies, multimodal learning, critical communities of practice, cultures of care, and critical literacy. She is involved in curriculum development and literacy practices in her district and has given many state and national presentations about multiliteracies in early elementary classrooms.

Chapter 3
Researching Literacy with Young Children's Drawings

Maureen E. Kendrick and Roberta A. McKay

Abstract Our research indicates that young children's drawings of reading and writing are a compelling source of information about literacy in their lives both inside and outside of school. This chapter will focus on the research methodology we have developed to elicit young children's drawings of reading and writing and on the various ways that we have analyzed and interpreted the drawings. We outline our argument, including theoretical stance, for drawings as a powerful but often ignored symbol system in which young children create and express meanings about literacy. Educators of young children will be challenged to see the potential of drawings to inform their understanding of young children's literacy.

Keywords multiliteracies, images of literacy, multimodal representations, early literacy, image-based research

Art educators such as Wilson and Wilson (1982) have long recognized that children draw to know, that is, drawing is one way that children create and express complex meanings about their worlds. They suggest that children's drawings may convey a number of realities including that of everyday common experience, the reality of self, of right and wrong, and the reality of anticipation and control of the future. Further, Wilson and Wilson (1982) argue that "unlike the structure of language, the structure of drawing does not demand a precise placement of elements in order to convey meaning" (p. 36) and is a more flexible way for children to develop ideas.

Children's drawings have been utilized by researchers in various fields including psychology and anthropology to learn more about children's constructions of their worlds (Adler, 1982; Dennis, 1966, 1970; Diem-Wille, 2001; Koppitz, 1984). Only a very limited number of educational researchers, however, have used drawing as an alternative mode of investigating children's knowledge and understand-

University of British Columbia, Canada
University of Alberta, Canada

M. J. Narey (ed.), *Making Meaning.*

ing of particular topics. Examples include Weber and Mitchell's (1995) study of children's conceptualizations of teachers, Peterson's (1997) research on children's knowledge of science, Piscitelli and Anderson's (2001) explorations of children's perceptions of museums, and Wetton and McWhirter's (1998) work on children's perceptions of health and safety concepts. Such research clearly demonstrates that children are able to express powerful and imaginative ideas and problems through visual modes.

Although children's drawing have been included by literacy researchers in their studies of the development of reading and writing (i.e., Clyde, 1994; Dyson, 1992; Nixon, 2001; Rowe & Harste, 1986; Voss, 1996), few literacy researchers, if any, have as a research tool asked children to draw their images of reading and writing. The development of teaching and research methods that utilize a variety of forms of representation as a means of examining what children know and understand remains largely unexplored in the field of literacy despite the fact that a growing number of literacy researchers recognize that children make use of the multiple sign systems available to them in the culture to construct and express meaning (Anning, 2003; Berghoff, 1998; Siegel, 2006). We have been researching children's images of literacy, utilizing children's drawings since 1997 (Kendrick, Anderson, Smythe, & McKay, 2003; Kendrick & McKay 2002/2003, 2004; McKay & Kendrick, 2001a, 2001b). The research has been conducted in multicultural urban classrooms, with a range of socioeconomic conditions, in Canada and in New Zealand. This chapter offers an articulation of the research methodology used to elicit drawings of reading and writing, with specific attention given to the evolution of how we have analyzed and interpreted the drawings. It is our contention that calls from literacy educators and theorists for a multiple literacies perspective (e.g., New London Group, 1996) remain largely unheeded and that much literacy research remains grounded in verbocentric perspectives. When visual modalities are used, little attention is paid to their analysis. Researching literacy with young children's drawing provides one avenue for addressing a multiliteracies agenda.

A Multimodal Stance

An increasing number of language arts educators and researchers are calling for a multiple literacies perspective that recognizes art, music, dance, drama and film as vital modes of representation and communication that play an important role in the development of children's lives. This broader definition of literacy goes beyond language symbols to that of multiple symbols. Critical to this perspective is the understanding that symbol systems other than language are not 'tack-ons' but rather relevant options for creating and expressing meaning. Kress and Jewitt (2003) emphasize that a multimodal approach to learning begins from a theoretical position that treats all modes of meaning making as equally significant.

The sociocultural theory of Vygotsky (1978) provides the basis for the conceptual framework we adopt in our literacy research using children's drawings. Two of Vygotsky's premises are particularly significant to our research, the first being that the transmission and acquisition of cultural knowledge such as literacy takes place on an interpersonal level between individuals as a precursor to internalization of such knowledge on an intrapersonal level within the individual. An understanding of this relationship between the individual and the culture enables us to view the children's individual meaning construction as embedded in their social and cultural milieu. Vygotsky's (1978) second formulation that informs our research is that of spontaneous concept development. Spontaneous concepts develop from the child's experiences. The images of literacy constructed by the children in their drawings provide us with insights into their personal experiences of literacy, that is, what sense they have constructed of the complex world of literacy in which they are situated. In other words, the drawings provide a window on the children's spontaneous concept development in relation to literacy.

Art educators, Kindler and Darras (1997), also draw upon the conceptual work of Vygotsky in their formulation of an alternative model of the artistic development of children. They reject stage theories of artistic development that are rooted in Piagetian views of cognitive development and instead propose a model grounded in semiotic and sociocultural foundations. Their model considers pictorial production as a semiotic activity, therefore having communication potential. Kindler and Darras suggest that this communication may consist of "thoughts, ideas, emotions, values, states, understandings, or realities" (1997, p. 19). This model of artistic development of children argues that pictorial production occurs in an interactive social environment and is an integral part of a pluri-media process in a context that includes words, sounds, and gestures.

Taking a multimodal/social semiotic theoretical stance (Kress, 1997, 2000; Pahl, 2003; Stein, 2003) calls for a much broader view of literacy than portrayed by traditional language-based approaches. This stance also necessitates a research strategy that goes beyond traditional language-based research approaches. In our literacy research, we adopt a qualitative, interpretative research approach, specifically, that of image-based research (Prosser, 1998; Rose, 2001; van Leeuwen & Jewitt, 2001). Image-based research includes moving forms such as films and videos, as well as still images such as photographs, drawings, graffiti and cartoons (Prosser, 1998). Image-based research is relatively new in qualitative research and Prosser suggests that it has only been within the last 30 years that qualitative researchers have given serious consideration to the use of images with words to enhance understanding of the human condition. Images such as the drawings of literacy produced by young children provide us, as researchers, with data that are ordered differently and allow us to perceive that data in different ways. The production of the drawings also provides the children with a different mode to create and express what they know and thereby offer portrayals of themselves that may be quite different from those they may offer in words. From a social constructivist stance, image-based research enables us to investigate the potential of drawing as an alternative way for children to create and represent their knowledge of literacy.

Visual anthropology also broadly informs our understanding of multiple modes of representation within specific social and cultural settings. Visual anthropologists contend, "much that is observable, much that can be learned about a culture can be recorded most effectively and comprehensively through film, photography or by drawing" (Morphy & Banks, 1997, p. 14). They also argue that neglecting visual data may be a reflection of Western bias (the privileging of the intellectual over the experiential or phenomenological) or a disregard for the importance of visual phenomena across cultures. We would add that neglecting visual data may also be a reflection of an adult communication bias, which typically privileges written modes over visual. In visual anthropology, traditionally researchers rather than research participants have used visual modes for recording culture. We view our participants as co-researchers and put the visual tools of pencils, crayons, and felts in their hands to enhance our understanding of their every day literacy practices.

Collecting Drawings Of Literacy

Collecting drawings of literacy from young children is relatively straightforward and is a practical technique for both researchers and teachers. Researchers in other fields (i.e., Koppitz, 1984; Wetton & McWhirter, 1998) who have elicited drawings from young children as a data source also confirm the ease with which drawings can be obtained by teachers and researchers. The procedure we have followed in soliciting drawings of reading and writing has remained consistent and has included group discussions followed by a drawing task. In all instances, standard academic research ethics approvals were obtained and anonymity and confidentiality guaranteed. The participating students in each of the classrooms where we have conducted the research met in groups with one or both of the researchers for approximately 60 minutes to discuss and draw pictures of their ideas about literacy in their lives in school, outside of school, and in the future. The groups ranged in size from 4 to 21 children, with the average group size being 17 children. The participating children and the researchers met outside of the classroom, usually in an art room or other vacant room of the school. The classroom teacher was not present in almost all instances. Because our goal was to explore children's images and ideas as evident in their drawings, the questions outlined below were used to guide the discussions rather than rigidly format them. The directions for the drawing task, as outlined in the last question of the following list, were deliberately left open-ended and did not specify who or what should be in the drawing or where it might take place.

1. What kind of reading/writing do you do in school/outside of school?
2. Why do you read/write in school/outside of school?
3. Where do you read/write in school/outside of school?
4. How is reading/writing in school both similar and different from reading/writing outside of school?

5. How do you think you will use reading/writing in the future, as you grow older?
6. Draw a picture of reading or writing. It can be a picture of reading or writing that you do now or that you think you might do when you're older.

The discussion provided the impetus for drawing and we were aware that hearing the ideas of their peers could influence what the children might draw. Group discussions of approximately 15 minutes proved to be sufficient time for children to respond to the questions and maintain a focus on the discussion. The children were provided with a standard sized piece of white paper, pencils, and colored crayons or markers. Following the discussion and drawing session, the children were asked to provide an explanation of their drawings. Older children wrote explanations on the back of their drawings, whereas younger children dictated to one of the researchers. The explanations we requested in the earlier research were to include who and what was in the drawings and when and where the literacy event or activity took place. In the more recent studies, we have also asked children to explain why they chose to draw what they did. Each drawing was color photocopied and the accompanying explanation provided by the children was either photocopied or transcribed on the back of the color photocopy. In every case, the original drawings were returned to the children.

Analyzing Drawings of Literacy

While children's drawings of literacy practices may be collected with relative ease, they are more difficult to analyze due to the very qualities that make them so compelling and revealing, that is, their complexity, richness, simultaneity and multilayered nature. Rose (2001) points out that although there is a substantial amount of academic work being published in the social sciences on "things visual, there are remarkably few guides to possible methods of interpretation and even fewer explanations of how to do those methods" (p. 2). Interpreters of visual images broadly agree that there are three sites at which the meanings of an image are made: the site of production, the site of the image itself, and the site where the image is viewed by various audiences (Rose, 2001). Many of the theoretical disagreements about visual interpretation relate to disputes over which of these sites is most important and why. It is our position that the three sites at which meanings are made are inextricably connected and relational to each other, and this is reflected in our discussions of each site, which follows.

As researchers, we have seen an evolution in our analysis and interpretation of young children's drawings of literacy, which has primarily been provoked by the children's drawings themselves. Particular drawings challenged us to think more deeply about the unique texts children produce, and the ways in which they weave their personal and social histories. We view these drawings as "pivotal" lessons learned in our ability to understand more fully what the children are able to communicate about the diverse ways they see themselves and others as literate beings.

Lesson 1: The Site of Production

In our early research (McKay & Kendrick, 2001a), we relied predominantly on content analysis to interpret the children's drawings. Our interpretation focused on the image as the site of meaning-making. Specifically, we counted occurrences of what we thought we saw in the images and developed corresponding categories (e.g., Bell, 2001; Rose, 2001). These categories included the presence of human figures, the setting or context, (e.g., home, school, work), the depiction of self or others in direct engagement in reading or writing, the presence of any written text, the depiction of literacy tools, (e.g., pencils, paper, books, computers) and literacy artifacts (e.g., letters, stories, environmental print), and the depiction of other elements such as pets or symbols (e.g., the corporate symbol of Nike).

We learned, however, that any mode of analysis that restricts itself to the elements in the image alone may not by itself "demonstrate how viewers understand and value what they see or hear (Bell, 2001, p. 26). Art educators Wilson and Wilson (1982) emphasize how crucial it is to ask children about their drawings in order to "be allowed to enter all of the realities of the child's drawing world" (p. 37). Thus, our methods for analyzing the children's drawings departed from strict content analysis in that we utilized what the children told us about the drawings as a central part of our analysis and interpretation. Creating opportunities for the children to offer interpretive explanations *during* rather than after the drawing process was a critical component of learning to understand the specificity of the children's visual language (Kress & van Leeuwen, 1996).

For example, in an early study where we found that one of the most predominant images apparent in young children's drawings was family as the focal point of literacy, the children's explicit talk about reading with their mothers, sending messages and letters to absent parents, and listening to stories read by older brothers and sisters provided a living context for the images. Two drawings, which were designed as books, serve to illustrate how the children's interpretive explanations shaped our understanding of their intended meaning. One child made a book to give to her mother and the other made a book about topics she wanted to read about in the future. In the first example, Vicki (Age 6) wrote a poem to her mom. In talking about her drawing she made reference to the hearts she had drawn on the front of the book (Fig. 3.1) and then, after opening the cover, said:

> *"Now we're going into the middle. Let me read this to you: 'I like hearts. Hearts like me. I like me.' There's my momma and here's me. And I drew these hearts for my momma, and now at the back, here's a star, and here's my mommy, and here's tiger heart (a striped heart)."*

Fig. 3.1 Drawings from Vicki's book

Vicki appeared to have a clear sense of audience and this was demonstrated in the importance she placed on giving the book to her mother, who at the time lived in a separate residence. Unlike the other children who agreed to let us borrow their pictures until a later date, Vicki was insistent upon having the original book that day to give to her mother.

Although Ashley (Age 6) also made a book, she had a different intent than that communicated by Vicki. Ashley's book contained images of books about which she said, "When I grow up, I'm going to read a book about scary dinosaurs and tornadoes and about Valentines and dogs" (Fig. 3.2). The book cover includes a dinosaur, a book with the message: "I Love You Mom and DaD," a dog, two hearts, and a tornado. Inside the book, Ashley has drawn herself with a book in her hands, her name, and again included a dog, a tornado, and a Valentine heart (Fig. 3.3). Interestingly, both Vicki and Ashley also demonstrated an awareness of the physical format of a book (e.g., front, middle, back). Rose (2001) argues that content analysis alone does not adequately deal with the cultural meanings of an image and, in particular, how meanings are made by the producer (and viewer) of the image. Including the children's own interpretations in our analysis of an image's meaning was crucial for understanding how and why the image was produced and the particularities of how a specific audience might view the image (Rose, 2001).

Fig. 3.2 Ashley's book cover

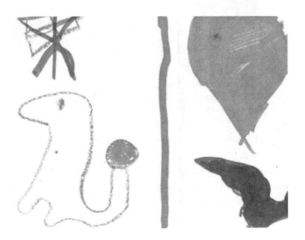

Fig. 3.3 Inside Ashley's book

Drawings similar to those by Vicki and Ashley provoked us to regard the images of literacy as more than a collection or series of elements such as figures, locations, and literacy tools and artifacts. The drawings in fact have "voice" in much the same way that Graves (1994) described "voice" in children's writing process. He argues that "voice is the imprint of ourselves on our writing" (p. 81) and is the driving force of the writing process. The children's drawings are an imprint of each child's self. As Graves suggests, "teachers who attend to voice listen to the person in the piece and observe how that person uses the process components" (1994, p. 81). We learned that, as researchers, we needed to do the same "listening" to each child's drawing and explanation and that indeed, the child's voice was the driving force of the images of literacy created.

Lesson 2: The Image Itself

Building on our initial use of content analysis and the children's interpretive explanations, we developed a more holistic categorization scheme that included primary, secondary, and 'unknown' images of literacy. Primary images included drawings in which literacy was the central topic of the drawing (e.g., a picture of someone reading books, writing stories and letters, or teaching the alphabet); secondary images included drawings where literacy artifacts or events were "add-on" components of the drawing (e.g., a drawing that is predominantly about dinosaurs that includes a small sketch of a book in the corner of the page), and unknown images which included drawings that did not appear to relate to reading and writing, in particular, or language learning, in general (e.g., drawings of sports equipment or animals). In each of our previous studies, a small number of students (1 to 2 in each grade) produced drawings that had no apparent relationship to reading or writing. Our tendency had been to dismiss these images as anomalies and attribute them to the possibility that children had difficulty understanding the directions for the task or difficulties understanding the nature of reading and writing. Indeed, in reporting results, we focused mainly on children's primary and secondary images of literacy, discarding to a large extent those that we had identified as "unknown." Our interpretation of these "unknown" images established both the site of production, which included the children's explanations, and the image itself as equally important to the interpretive process.

We use as an example one boy's image of literacy, categorized initially as "unknown," to illustrate how a closer examination of the drawing from the child's perspective illuminated a more expansive and inclusive view of literacy than our initial categorization scheme revealed. We believe that the process we underwent as researchers reveals the importance of adopting multiple perspectives in understanding the complexity of children's constructions of literacy and identity. In Ramo's drawing, he has drawn himself suspended in the air above his bed (see Fig. 3.4). His written description of his drawing was "I jumped on the bed". When asked about his drawing, Ramo (age 6) told one of the researchers quite emphatically, "I am jumping on the bed. I am NOT reading and writing".

As we began to consider our role as 'audience' for the drawings, we were able to build alternative interpretations of Ramo's drawing that enabled us to see that his drawing was indeed providing us with information about his views of literacy. Rather than dismissing the drawing, we could speculate that perhaps what Ramo was telling us with his drawing as a response to our request was that reading and writing did not play a significant role in his life right now and that he would rather be active. His emphatic oral explanation of his drawing supports this interpretation and also underscores the importance of having the children describe and explain their drawings.

Fig. 3.4 "I am jumping on the bed. I am NOT reading and writing"

Dustin's drawing provides another powerful example of how focusing on the 'unknown' in children's drawings can provide a window on their literacy narratives which comprise children's perceptions and interpretations of their social interactions about the cultural materials and experiences to which they are exposed both inside and outside school (see Kendrick & McKay, 2002/2003). Dustin (age 10) wrote the following on the front of his drawing: *I shot my first buck with a doble barel shotgut. It is at my grapernts farm. My dad Helped me.* As the text indicates, his drawing was of a freshly killed buck, hanging upside down, blood dripping from its neck (see Fig. 3.5). Dustin, rifle in hand, is drawn beside the buck. It would have been easy for us as researchers to overlook Dustin's drawing or attribute its content to low achievement or disinterest in reading and writing. By revisiting Dustin's drawing, as he interpreted it for us within the context of his life both inside and outside the classroom, we were able to tap into his own perception of the multiple layers of meaning embedded in his drawing. Dustin engaged in the drawing activity with considerable secrecy, asking questions such as: "Can we draw anything we want about reading and writing?" and "Does our teacher get to see it?" Once reassured that he was free to draw what he chose, and that his teacher would not see the drawing without his permission, he set to work with quiet determination.

We suspected from his secrecy that guns and hunting were not topics that he thought would meet with his language arts teacher's approval; they were topics that, according to him, constituted "violence," something he said he was "not allowed to write about." An interview with Dustin's teacher confirmed that guns, blood, and dismemberment were banned from classroom drawing, writing, and reading as part of the school's "zero tolerance" policy on violence. Dustin's drawing represents what he was not allowed to write about at school. Dustin's interpretation of this policy was evident in his blank journal; when he was told on the Monday mornings following his weekend hunting trips with his father and grandfather to write about his weekend, he sat in silent residence.

Both Ramo's and Dustin's drawings, as well as other drawings we categorized as initially having an "unknown" relationship to literacy, have unrealized potential for helping uncover the scripts or literacy narratives students bring to school and use to make sense of reading and writing (Gallas & Smagorinsky, 2002, p. 58). These literacy narratives can be situated within Vygotsky's (1978) Zone of Proximal Development (ZPD) framework. Cummins (1994) described the ZPD as an interpersonal space where new understandings arise through collaborative interaction and inquiry. Similarly, Newman, Griffin, and Cole (1989) labeled this space as the "construction zone." They pointed out, however, that the construction zone could become a constriction zone if the context limits rather than extends children's identities and learning. The drawings we have collected serve as an important and alternative construction zone for young children to communicate their understanding of themselves and the world.

Fig. 3.5 Dustin's drawing of himself standing next to his first buck

Lesson 3: The Site of Viewing

Adopting a social semiotic perspective (e.g., Iedema, 2001; Jewitt & Oyama, 2001) enabled us to shift our analytic focus more specifically to understanding our own meaning making at the site of viewing (e.g., Kendrick & McKay, 2003). Jewitt and Oyama argue that social semiotics is concerned with the study of images in their social context and must be interpreted by researchers using "whatever resources of interpretation and intertextual connection they can lay their hands on to create their own new interpretations and interconnections" (2001, p. 134). Rose (2001) asserts that a critical approach to interpreting visual images requires that as researchers, we take images seriously, think about the social conditions and effects of visual objects, and consider our own way of looking at images. She further argues that, "the ways in which images become culturally meaningful are illuminated by raising questions of how the image is made, what it looks like, and how it is seen" (2001, p. 188).

Brandy's drawing in particular engaged us in more critical examination of how we as researchers view literacy practices, including their associated identities and relationships. Her drawing, which depicts letter writing with her father, highlights the role of literacy in maintaining emotional ties with absent family members. During the drawing activity, she talked about writing a letter to her father, who did not live in the same household and worked for long periods outside of the city. The drawing includes a pencil and a letter that reads, 'Dear Dad How are you doing Love Brandy' (see Fig. 3.6). On the reverse side (see Fig. 3.7), she drew her father and his written response to her letter: 'Dear Brandy. I love you very much.'

Fig. 3.6 Brandy's drawing about writing a letter to her Dad

Fig. 3.7 Brandy's drawing of her dad answering her letter

For Melody, a young New Zealand girl, reading and writing at home are strongly associated with her family's religious practices. In her drawing, she is sitting on her bed surrounded by multiple copies of prayer books (see Fig. 3.8). She writes: "I am getting a book of prayers at home. I am reading the book of prayers at home. It is cool reading the book of prayers. it was fun. I love reading at home. I am 7 yrs old. I love reading and writing. I love reading prayers."

Both Brandy's and Melody's depictions of literacy focus not on reading and writing as activities in and of themselves, but rather, what motivates their individual desires to read and write. Brandy associated writing with communicating with her father when he was away. For Melody, reading was associated with practicing her prayers. Drawing provides a space for young learners like Brandy and Melody to negotiate their own identities and relationships with others in relation to literacy. In this way, the producers of the images also constitute a kind of private audience. As researchers, however, we have learned that we serve as a public audience for these images. As Collier (2001) explains, "Analysis of visual records of human experience is a search for pattern and meaning, complicated by our inescapable role as participants in that experience" (p. 35). How we understand the patterns and meanings evident in the drawings must be contextualized in relation to our own associations, experiences, and ways of valuing literacy, which have in turn influenced the very nature of how we solicited the children's drawings. In essence, we have come to view the drawings as co-constructions that involve both the researchers' and children's understandings of literacy.

Fig. 3.8 Melody's depiction of literacy

We are reminded of Rosenblatt's (1978) idea of transaction, a coming-together as it were, of a reader and a text. We have begun to understand our viewing of the children's drawings as a coming-together of researcher (reader) and drawing (text). Just as Rosenblatt argues that creating the meaning of the text involves both the author's text and what the reader brings to it, we recognize that analysis and interpretation of the "meanings" of the drawings involves both the drawing and what the viewer brings to it.

In addition to recognizing and considering how we as researchers viewed the children's drawings as a form of 'audience' (reader), we also began to consider how the teachers viewed the drawings as another form of 'audience'. This was particularly salient in one of the research schools, where teachers had described their students (Grades 1-3) to us at the onset of the research project as having very limited knowledge about literacy. When the children's drawings and our interpretations were presented to the classroom teachers, they were extremely surprised that their students were able to construct such rich images of literacy. The teachers had not considered that the children may be able to create and express meaning about literacy in a symbol system other than language and were not familiar with viewing children's drawings of literacy as a powerful source of information.

The Potential of Researching the Literacy of Young Children through Their Drawings

Our image-based literacy research uses young children's drawings as a new way of investigating the educational, social and cultural context of what primary school children know about literacy in their lives both inside and outside of school. We believe that the inclusion of multimodal opportunities for young children to create and express what they know about literacy is essential for expanding our understandings of children's knowledge of literacy in their lives. Such opportunities may be particularly significant for those students who are better able to represent their meanings and understandings through alternative and preferred modes of communication, which may include symbol systems other than verbal language. In her study of Douglas, Clyde (1994) found that the more global nature of art enabled a young boy to make and share meaning in ways that the linear demands of oral and written language did not. "To view Douglas through verbocentric eyes would miss the brilliance of this young mind, the deliberateness and sophistication of not only his inquiries but also his strategies for exploring them" (Clyde, 1994, p. 32). Words are important but are only one way of creating and expressing meaning. A verbocentric focus excludes many young children. The inclusion of multimodal representations in understanding more fully children's knowledge of literacy is both critical and timely if we are to provide alternatives for children who may appear to be failing when only verbal or written measures are utilized as evidence of what they know about literacy.

Our use of drawings as a means of increasing our understanding of what young children know about literacy has proven to be a valuable and easily facilitated method for us as teachers and researchers to collect information and for children to provide information. As Peterson (1997) pointed out in her science research using drawings, children in different language groups and in different age groups all provided significantly more information from visual memory than from verbal memory. As a research method, she speculates that utilizing drawing and oral and written language, in relation to each other, as ways of accessing what children of various cultures and ages know has "the potential to modify the dominant view of verbal knowledge as the primary representation of what average people know, and ultimately to advance knowledge of the role visual memory plays in human understandings of the world in which we live" (p. 7).

Ultimately, the development of broader and more inclusive methods of representing knowledge will provide teachers and researchers with insights into children's strengths, difficulties, and preferred modes of representation, and may also lead to more effective and meaningful literacy curriculum development. By using drawings as another method to access the literacy knowledge of children, teachers will be better able to build curriculum that incorporates and maps in innovative ways children's perceptions about what literacy is and its significance in their lives. Knowing how to teach children more effectively centers on developing a richer and more refined method of investigating what they know and understand about literacy in their lives both inside and outside of school. As teachers and educational researchers, we need to pay careful attention to what students bring to the reading and writing experience, and at how literacy is a social, cultural, and political experience.

In this chapter, we have argued that although children's drawings are relatively easy to collect in research and classroom contexts, they are far more difficult to analyze. The lessons we have learned in researching literacy with young children's drawings have taught us that each of the three sites of meaning making must be equally weighed in the interpretive process. At the site of production, it is critical to understand the children's intent and to include their interpretations in the analysis of the image. At the site of the image itself, investigating both what is *not* readily evident in the image (i.e., the 'unknown') along with what is evident provide key information about the literacy narratives children bring to school and use to make sense of their experiences. At the viewing site, we need to be aware of our own interpretive lenses as researchers and teachers, and to understand how our definitions of literacy, including how we value literacy and what we associate with it, shape our own meaning making process. As Rose (2001) suggests, however, in the end, successful interpretation of images is not about discovering their 'truth' but rather, is dependent upon a passionate engagement with what you see.

References

Adler, L. L. (1982). Children's drawings as an indicator of individual preferences reflecting group values: A programmatic study. In L. L. Adler (Ed.), *Cross-cultural research at issue* (pp. 71-98). New York: Academic Press.

Anning, A. (2003). Pathways to the graphicacy club: The crossroad of home and pre-school. *Journal of Early Childhood Literacy, 3*(1), 5-35.

Bell, P. (2001). Content analysis of visual images. In T. van Leeuwen & C. Jewitt (Eds.), *Handbook of Visual Analysis* (pp. 10-34). London: Sage.

Bergohoff, B. (1998). Multiple sign systems and reading. *The Reading Teacher, 5*(6), 520-523.

Collier, M. (2001). Approaches to analysis in visual anthropology. In T. van Leeuwen & C. Jewitt (Eds.), *Handbook of Visual Analysis* (pp. 35-60). London: Sage.

Cummins, J. (1994). From coercive to collaborative relations of power in the teaching of literacy. In B. Ferdman, R. Weber, & A. Ramírez (Eds.), *Literacy across languages and cultures* (pp. 295-331). Albany, NY: State University of New York Press.

Clyde, J. A. (1994). Lessons from Douglas: Expanding our visions of what it means to "know". *Language Arts, 7*(1), 22-23.

Dennis, W. (1966). *Group values through children's drawings.* New York: John Wiley & Sons.

Dennis, W. (1970). Goodenough scores, art experience and modernization. In I. Al-Issas & W. Dennis (Eds.), *Cross-cultural studies of behavior* (pp. 134-152). New York: Holt, Rinehart & Winston.

Diem-Wille, G. (2001). A therapeutic perspective: the use of drawings in child psychoanalysis and social science. In T. van Leeuwen & C. Jewitt (Eds.), *Handbook of visual analysis* (pp. 119-133). London: Sage.

Dyson, A. H. (1992). The emergence of visible language: Interrelationships between drawing and early writing. *Visible Language, 16*, 360-381.

Gallas, K., & Smagorinsky, P. (2002). Approaching texts in school. *The Reading Teacher, 56*(1), 54-61.

Graves, D. (1994). *A fresh look at writing.* Portsmouth, NH: Heinemann.

Iedema, R. (2001). Analysing film and television: A social semiotic account of Hospital: An Unhealthy Business. In T. van Leeuwen & C. Jewitt (Eds.), *Handbook of visual analysis* (pp. 183-204). London: Sage.

Jewitt, C., & Oyama, R. (2001). Visual meaning: A social semiotic approach. In T. van Leeuwen & C. Jewitt (Eds.), *Handbook of Visual Analysis* (pp. 134-156). London: Sage.

Kendrick, M., Anderson, J., Smythe, S., & McKay, R. (2003). What images of family literacy reveal about family literacy practices and family literacy programs. In C. Fairbanks, J. Worthy, B. Maloch, J. Hoffman, & D. Schallert (Eds.), *52nd Yearbook of the National Reading Conference* (pp. 245-271). Oak Creek, WI: National Reading Conference, Inc.

Kendrick, M., & McKay, R. (2002/2003). Uncovering literacy narratives through children's drawings: An illustrative example. *Canadian Journal of Education, 27*(1), 45-60.

Kendrick, M., & McKay, R. (2004). Drawing as an alternative way of understanding young children's constructions of literacy. *Journal of Early Childhood Literacy, 4*(1), 109-128.

Kindler, A., & Darras, B. (1997). Map of artistic development. In A.M. Kindler (Ed.), *Child development in art* (pp. 17-42). Reston, VA: National Art Education Association.

Koppitz, E. M. (1984). *Psychological evaluation of human figure drawings by middle school pupils.* Orlando, FL: Grune & Stratton, Inc.

Kress, G. (1997). *Before writing: Rethinking the paths to literacy.* New York, NY: Routledge.

Kress, G. (2000). Multimodality. In B. Cope & M. Kalantzis (Eds.), *Multiliteracies: Literacy learning and the design of social futures* (pp. 182-202). London: Routledge.

Kress, G., & Jewitt, C. (2003). Introduction. In C. Jewitt & G. Kress (Eds.), *Multimodal literacy* (pp. 1-18). New York: Peter Lang.

Kress, G., & van Leeuwen, T. (1996). *Reading images: The grammar of visual design.* London: Routledge.

McKay, R., & Kendrick, M. (2001a). Children draw their images of reading and writing. *Language Arts, 78*(6), 529-533.

McKay, R., & Kendrick, M. (2001b). Images of Literacy: Young Children's drawings about reading and writing. *Canadian Journal of Research in Early Childhood Education, 8*(4), 7-22.

Morphy, H., & Banks, M. (1997). Introduction. In M. Banks & H. Morphy, *Rethinking Visual Anthropology* (pp. 1-35). New Haven, CT: Yale University Press.

New London Group. (1996). A pedagogy of multiliteracies: Designing social futures. *Harvard Educational Review, 66*, 60-92.

Newman, D., Griffin, P., & Cole, M. (1989). *The construction zone: Working for cognitive change in school.* Cambridge, MA: Cambridge University Press.

Nixon, H. (2001). "Slow and steady – not enough pace!": The absence of the visual in valued middle primary literate competencies. Paper presented to the Australian Association for Research in Education National Conference, Fremantle, December 2-6, 2001.

Pahl, K. (2003). Children's text-making at home: Transforming meaning across modes. In C. Jewitt & G. Kress (Eds.), *Multimodal literacy* (pp. 139-154). New York: Peter Lang.

Peterson, R. W. (1997). *Visual memory and language: A study of children's use of art and language to communicate their knowledge of science.* Paper presented at the annual meeting of the National Association for Research in Science Teaching, Oak Brooks, IL.

Piscitelli, B., & Anderson, D. (2001). Young children's perspectives of museums settings and experiences. *Museum Management and Curatorship, 19*, 269-282.

Prosser, J. (1998). *Image-based research.* London: Falmer Press.

Rose, G. (2001). *Visual methodologies.* London: Sage.

Rosenblatt, L. (1978). *The reader, the text, the poem: The transactional theory of the literary work.* Carbondale, IL: Southern Illinois University Press.

Rowe, D., & Harste, J. (1986). Metalinguistic awareness in writing and reading: The young child as curricular informant. In D. Yaden & S. Templeton (Eds.), *Metalinguistic awareness and beginning literacy: Conceptualizing what it means to read and write* (pp. 235-256). Portsmouth, NH: Heinemann.

Siegel, M. (2006). Rereading the signs: Multimodal transformations in the field of literacy education. *Language Arts, 84*(1), 65-77.

Stein, P. (2003). The Olifantsvlei Fresh Stories Project: Multimodality, creativity, and fixing in the semiotic chain. In C. Jewitt & G. Kress (Eds.), *Multimodal literacy* (pp. 123-138). New York: Peter Lang.

van Leeuwen, T., & Jewitt, C. (Eds.) (2001). *Handbook of visual analysis.* London: Sage.

Voss, M. (1996). *Hidden literacies: Children learning at home and at school.* Portsmouth, NH: Heinemann.

Vygotsky, L. (1978). *Mind in society: The development of higher psychological processes*. Cambridge, MA: Harvard University Press.

Weber, S., & Mitchell C. (1995). *That's funny, you don't look like a teacher*. London: Falmer Press.

Wetton, N., & McWhirter, J. (1998). Images and curriculum development in health education. In J. Prosser (Ed.), *Image-based research* (pp. 263-283). London: Falmer Press.

Wilson, M., & Wilson, B. (1982). *Teaching children to draw: A guide for teachers and parents*. Engelwood Cliffs, NJ: Prentice-Hall.

Maureen E. Kendrick
University of British Columbia
Vancouver, BC   Canada

Dr. Maureen Kendrick is an Associate Professor in Literacy Education in the Department of Language and Literacy Education at the University of British Columbia. Her research interests include literacy and multimodality, and literacy and international development.

Roberta A. McKay
University of Alberta
Edmonton, AB   Canada

Dr. Roberta McKay is a Professor in Language Arts/Literacy in the Department of Elementary Education at the University of Alberta. Her research interests include children's images of literacy, language and learning, and constructivist teacher professional development.

Chapter 4
Studio Thinking in Early Childhood

Kimberly Sheridan

Abstract The visual arts provide important and unique learning opportunities for young children. In this chapter, I use the Studio Thinking Framework, developed from research at Harvard University's Project Zero that involved close observation of studio art classrooms to see what teachers intend to teach and how they teach it, to inform how we can think about learning in the early childhood classroom. I describe strategies teachers can use to create a "studio classroom" that fosters children's development of broad "habits of mind," such as becoming more observant, more engaged and persistent, reflective on their work, and willing to explore and express ideas. I discuss how teachers can use this focus on developing students' habits of mind in the arts to build connections to other learning areas.

Keywords art education, early childhood education, visual arts, thinking, dispositions, art appreciation, young children, teaching methods

Ask someone what young children learn in the visual arts and they might say something like they learn to draw, paint or shape with clay. Some might question the word "learn" and instead consider young children's work in the arts more in terms of opportunities for self-expression than learning. Thinking back to their own elementary school days, they might conjure up images of making of holiday-oriented crafts and view the arts as a special, fun activity, a break from the real work of school. In all these views, the arts seem separate from other academic learning, and perhaps to some, less important.

But in Harvard Project Zero's Studio Thinking project's investigation into what students really learn in the visual arts instruction, our answers were quite different. Students learn to observe and become more attentive to their world and their work; they learn to engage in problems of interest and persist through difficulties. Students express themselves in their art, but they learn a lot about expression: how to communicate ideas and feelings, and how to interpret ideas in other visual forms such as paintings, films, and advertisements. They learn to reflect on

George Mason University, USA

M. J. Narey (ed.), *Making Meaning.*
© Springer 2009

their work and working process; they learn to try out new ideas, challenge themselves and embrace learning from mistakes. They learn to imagine and plan in more complex and effective ways. Students learn "habits of mind" or ways of thinking in the studio, that extend beyond the making of a specific drawing, sculpture or digital video (Hetland, Winner, Veenema, & Sheridan, 2007). In this view, the connections between arts and other areas of learning become more apparent and profound. Studio arts classrooms can foster ways of thinking that characterize the types of learning we want to happen throughout, in all areas of learning.

The visual arts often have a strong presence in early childhood education. For instance, the connections between literacy and visual arts learning in the early childhood classroom are particularly robust. Literacy learning is frequently saturated with visual forms in early childhood classrooms. Books are richly illustrated and children are encouraged to look at the pictures for contextual clues to the text. Students' create narrative drawings to accompany their own oral and written stories. These links between visual and language arts are developmentally appropriate for young learners; researchers identify rich connections between students' interrelated development of writing, reading and drawing (e.g., Atkinson, 1991; Baghban, 2007; Kendrick & McKay, 2004; McKay & Kendrick, 2001). These links also make for richly engaging and memorable learning experiences, as they engage multiple modalities and senses. Finally, linking visual arts and language arts reflects current conceptions of literacy, which include a wide range of visual forms. Increasingly in contemporary society, visual and textual forms are intertwined and students need to learn how to create and interpret them in relation to one another.

The presence of visual arts activities in a classroom, however, does not mean that students are developing the complex habits of mind we describe in the Studio Thinking project. Students need to be supported so that art experiences develop complex thinking and build connections to other areas of learning. And, despite the fact that visual arts have a strong presence in early childhood classrooms and are increasingly a part of a broader view of literacy, there is often little guidance for early childhood educators for how to use the visual arts to promote children's learning. Many early childhood educators feel ill-equipped to support visual arts learning. Unlike the other domains they teach, their own experiences may be somewhat limited, and their teacher preparation background often does not adequately fill that gap. While elementary arts specialists are tasked with providing students' ongoing, sequential instruction in the arts, general educators need tools to make sure that the arts experiences in their classrooms are meaningful and promote understanding, rather than just activity. In this chapter, I discuss how early childhood educators may use the Studio Thinking Framework to help support complex thinking in and through the arts.

Introducing the Studio Thinking Framework

The Studio Thinking Framework is comprised of two main parts. The first part identifies what is being taught in studio classrooms. We describe eight Studio Habits of Mind that studio arts classes seek to develop: Develop Craft, Engage & Persist, Envision, Express, Observe, Reflect, Stretch & Explore, and Understand the Art World (Table 4.1). These habits are not a set of isolated skills; they are better described as dispositions, broad ways of thinking that studio art teachers try to develop in their students. These habits are not independent of one another; most art learning integrates them in complex ways. Teachers may highlight a particular habit in a given lesson, but most studio lessons draw on all eight habits. This focus on habits of mind reflects a view that the aim of education is not primarily a body of work, rather a student who takes an engaged, attentive, creative, thoughtful, and skilled approach to work and working. While we developed the framework through observation of arts classes, we think these habits of mind can and should be developed in all realms of learning. As Eliot Eisner (2002) describes, "Work in the arts is not only a way of creating performances and products; it is a way of creating our lives by expanding our consciousness, shaping our dispositions, satisfying our quest for thinking, establishing contact with others, and sharing a culture" (Eisner, 2002, p. 3).

Table 4.1 The Studio Thinking Framework: Eight Studio Habits of Mind Developed through Studio Arts Instruction (adapted from Hetland, Winner, Veenema & Sheridan (2007). Studio Thinking: The real benefits of visual arts instruction. Teachers College Press: New York.).

1	Develop Craft	Technique: Learning to use tools (e.g., viewfinders, brushes), materials (e.g., charcoal, paint). Learning artistic conventions (e.g., perspective, color mixing). Studio Practice: Learning to care for tools, materials, and space.
2	Engage & Persist	Learning to embrace problems of relevance within the art world and/or of personal importance, to develop focus and other mental states conducive to working and persevering at art tasks.
3	Envision	Learning to picture mentally what cannot be directly observed and imagine possible next steps in making a piece.
4	Express	Learning to create works that convey an idea, a feeling, or a personal meaning.
5	Observe	Learning to attend to visual contexts more closely than ordinary "looking" requires, and thereby to see things that otherwise might not be seen.
6	Reflect	Question & Explain: Learning to think and talk with others about an aspect of one's work or working process. Evaluate: Learning to judge one's own work and working process and the work of others in relation to standards of the field.
7	Stretch & Explore	Learning to reach beyond one's capacities, to explore playfully without a preconceived plan, and to embrace the opportunity to learn from mistakes and accidents.
8	Understand Art World	Domain: Learning about art history and current practice. Communities: Learning to interact as an artist with other artists (i.e., in classrooms, in local arts organizations, and across the art field) and within the broader society.

The second part of the framework is how these habits of mind are taught; the three Studio Structures that make up a studio class. These are: Demonstration-Lectures, Students-at-Work, and Critiques (Table 4.2). These studio structures are flexible components of a studio class; teachers use them in a variety of ways. They may do mini-demonstrations and critiques punctuating student work time. For instance, we observed critiques of students' work that lasted 2 minutes and others that lasted two hours. Each of these studio structures involves strategies, techniques and approaches that help develop students' habits of mind. I will discuss these in detail later as I describe ways of using them in early childhood classrooms. The Studio Thinking Framework was initially developed from close observation and analysis of intensive, high school level visual arts classes, looking at what habits of mind teachers intend to teach, how they go about teaching them, and how we know students have learned them. Developed through repeated observations of classes (including close analysis of videotaped teacher-student interaction in studio classes), interviews with teachers and students, and documentation of students' learning over the course of years of instruction, the Studio Thinking Framework identifies the types of thinking students develop through serious engagement in visual art.

Table 4.2 The three classroom structures described in the Studio Thinking Framework (adapted from Hetland, Winner, Veenema & Sheridan (2007). *Studio Thinking: The real benefits of visual arts instruction.* Teachers College Press: New York.).

The Studio Thinking Framework: Three Studio Structures

Studio Structure 1: Students-at-Work

Students make artworks based on teachers' assignments

Assignments specify materials, tools, and/or challenges

Teachers observe and consult with individuals or small groups

Teachers sometimes talk briefly to the whole class

Studio Structure 2: Demonstration-Lectures

Teachers (and others) deliver information about processes and products and set assignments

Information is immediately useful to students for class work or homework

Information is conveyed quickly and efficiently to reserve time for work and reflection

Visual examples are frequent and sometimes extended

Interaction occurs to varying degrees.

Studio Structure 3: Critiques

Central structure for discussion and reflection

A pause to focus on observation, conversation, and reflection

Focus on student works

Works are completed or in progress

Display is temporary and informal

On the surface, a framework developed from intensive high school art classes may seem to have limited connection with the general educational environment of early childhood. However the studio habits of mind are capacities that are fundamental to work in the arts, whether at the preschool or professional level. Non-art specialists and arts specialists, working with students at a wide range of levels and diverse contexts, have found the framework useful in designing and guiding instruction that develops studio thinking.

Studio Thinking in Early Childhood Education

In some ways the early childhood classroom may be particularly suited to using the Studio Thinking Framework to guide instruction. Many have remarked on the creativity and expressivity of young children's artistic work and thinking. Howard Gardner calls age five, the "golden age of creativity" (Gardner, 1982, p. 86). Whether they are formally working on something traditionally thought of as "art" or are expressing themselves aesthetically through different forms of play, the ages roughly between three and seven years old are a time of metaphors and playful thinking (Gardner, 1990; Piaget, 1962). Given these developmental proclivities, it makes sense to make the arts a central part of learning in early childhood. The arts can serve as an inviting entry point into many realms of learning.

There are a range of ways early childhood educators can use the Studio Thinking Framework to transform the everyday arts experiences in their classrooms into opportunities for setting the foundation for developing students' creative, disciplined, and reflective habits of mind. In what follows, I will discuss how early childhood educators can use the Studio Thinking Framework to target the development of students' habits of mind through the common arts activities of young children such as block building or drawing. I will then move on to consider how to lead thoughtful, developmentally appropriate discussions on the art and visual culture that surrounds children in their daily lives. Then I will discuss how the arts may be explicitly integrated into activities in other areas of the early childhood curriculum to promote engaged work and reflective and creative thinking.

Using "Studio Structures" to Support Arts Learning in the Early Education Classroom

Our observation of high school studio classes showed them to have characteristics that set them apart from most other high school classes, and that we argue are important for developing "Studio Habits of Mind." First, the bulk of student in-class time was spent working individually or collaboratively on open-ended projects under the observation of a teacher, who would have brief consultations with students about their work. Lectures were limited, and generally involved demonstrations to give information and insight into the techniques and concepts guiding the day's work. Frequent, and sometimes extended, visual examples were used. Finally, students' work was looked at and discussed as a group at various stages of completion through formal and informal critiques.

Early childhood classrooms share some commonalties with these high school studio classes. Students spend much of the class time engaged in work under the guidance of the teacher, who may circle around, keeping kids engaged in working and assisting them as needed. Lectures are rare in early childhood classes, and when they occur they often combine telling with showing in some fashion and are immediately relevant to students' work at hand. This studio-like structure is an advantage for easily applying the Studio Thinking Framework to early childhood education.

Early childhood educators can use the Studio Thinking Framework to help them envision new ways to support children's visual art making. There are typically art-making experiences in early childhood general classrooms, whether it's a preschooler painting at an easel, a kindergartener building a city scene with blocks, a first grader illustrating a story, or a second grader creating a geometric pattern with tangrams. These activities offer potential for developing the types of habits of mind described in Table 4.2, but they are often done with little instruction to scaffold more complex thinking.

Let's take the example of block building. Unit blocks are a mainstay in early childhood education. Blocks are argued to support important learning and cognitive development in a variety of domains—social, logical-mathematical, aesthetic, spatial. While important learning happens through open-ended free play with blocks, educators can use the Studio Thinking Framework to scaffold and target more complex thinking and building, while still providing opportunities for free exploration and experimentation with blocks. In particular, the three Studio Structures can be used in flexible ways to target learning in the different habits of mind.

Using Demonstration-Lectures to Develop Habits of Mind

For instance, prior to (or midway through) a children's building session with blocks, teachers can use a demonstration-lecture to target the types of habits of mind they wish to encourage in block use in a particular session. If a teacher was targeting *Observe* and *Develop Craft*, she may demonstrate a particular skill such as building of arches, asking children to watch very carefully her different methods of arch-building, and try them out in their own buildings. She may ask students to look closely at images of buildings with arches and try to find ways to recreate them with blocks. She might describe some of the challenges you might run into in building an arch and demonstrate strategies for handling those challenges.

However, if a teacher was targeting *Envision* and *Stretch & Explore*, he might lead a discussion that involves getting students to imagine and plan what they are going to build, and encouraging them to stretch beyond their initial conceptions.

For instance, if students were planning on building a city scene he might ask them questions to generate memories of things they have seen or read about in cities, probing questions like "what are some different ways people travel around in cities?" or "what are some types of buildings?" As a group, they might explore how to represent their ideas with their blocks. The goal in this case would be to assist students in developing more detailed and elaborate mental images for what they were going to build, to encourage them to explore more possibilities than just what initially came to mind, to get excited about their ideas, and to provide some initial examples of building techniques that might help them make progress on their envisioned plan.

Targeting Habits of Mind during Students-at-Work

During "Students-at-Work" in studio classes, students work independently or collaboratively and the teacher circles around consulting with them on their work. In our analysis of studio classes, we found this to be a particularly important time for targeting students' development of the habits of mind. While from the outside perspective it looks as if the teacher's role is fairly minor—monitoring students' activities—we found that good studio teachers used this time to really gain insight into what students' could understand and could do. Teachers observe students' work and working process and give them "just in time" advice to advance or deepen their thinking. This advice may be aimed at helping students develop any of the eight habits of mind, but often a teacher may particularly target one or two in a given session or assignment.

An early childhood educator working to develop habits of mind through block building can take a similar approach while the students are working. For instance, if she is targeting Observe and Develop Craft through highlighting the use of arches, she may point out features of the arches in students' buildings, ask them questions about what they notice about theirs' and others' arches, and as she talks to individual students, ask them questions about their strategies and techniques for building, what they have learned. To a student who has mastered a simple arch construction, she may pose a more difficult technical challenge, or ask them to assist a student who is struggling. When she praises students' work, she might reinforce the focus on *Observe* with comments such as "nice, careful looking" and *Develop Craft* by pointing out parts that are built particularly well.

If he is instead targeting *Envision* and *Stretch & Explore* his comments and questions may focus more on what they are imagining or planning to do next and how they might elaborate or expand on that idea. He may encourage two students who have very different building styles or ideas to work together to form a collaborative building. His praise may focus on noting good ideas, or noting when students try something new.

Regardless of the particular habit(s) targeted in a session, a teacher nearly always works on *Engage & Persist* during the Students-at-Work time, encouraging

students to find ways to become interested and stay interested and persist through
the difficulties they encounter (e.g., their arch collapsing, not having the "right"
blocks to complete a structure). This is often important for young children, as
they may not have yet developed strategies for maintaining their attention on a
project, or for working through frustration.

Reflecting on Learning through Critiques

Critiques are a central part of studio art classes. They are a chance for students to
pause and reflect on what they have done and where they are going in a particular
project. At various points during a project, the teacher may stop the working process and have students look at and discuss their own and each others' works.
Sometimes the works are looked at as a whole group, sometimes students are
asked to look at what one student has done if it illustrates a key idea. In a studio
class, critiques provide important time for students to Reflect on the formal and interpretive properties of the work, and learn from one another. But critiques are not
just a tool for reflection, they are also important to do midway through a project to
help students collaboratively Envision new ideas for their work. For instance, a
student may want to try to build an arch that another student has done, or be challenged to do one taller or wider.

Critiques are a powerful learning tool that is underutilized in education outside
of upper level studio art. Students are often excited by the opportunity to look at
and talk about each other's works. Critiques can be used to support learning in a
range of ways in the early childhood classroom. For instance, in the block example, time can be taken for students to look at each other's buildings, and discuss
them in different ways. The teacher can scaffold the discussion to target particular
habits of mind. For instance, for the goal of *Develop Craft*, the teacher could ask
students to point out the different approaches they see to the arch building task.
As they try to describe the differences, they may need to use numbers, relative size
and positional words. They can be taught to notice and describe elements such as
symmetry and patterns. They can discuss important design features such as func-
tionality (e.g., is the arch the right size for what they want to go through it? is it
built sturdy enough not to collapse?).

If the targeted goal was developing the habit of mind of *Envision*, much of the
critique may instead focus on having children discuss how they might elaborate on
structures. This kind of discussion can get quite animated and complex as the
children picture what something would look like with another layer, a balcony, a
turret, and try to describe to one another what they envision. Or the envisioning
might focus on how the block structure could be used in pretend play. The important learning here is that students are using an object that they see in front of them
and mentally picturing different possibilities for it. They are both devising strategies on how to create those possibilities and how to communicate to one another
their ideas for doing this. Other researchers have found this type of thinking process to be particularly fostered by the arts. Shirley Brice Heath, in her analysis of

after-school groups, found that in the arts, language that focused on imagining possibilities and creating plans to put them into action were much more common in arts focused groups than those in sports or computers (Heath, 1999, 2001).

The aim in this discussion of studio structures is not to suggest that early childhood education classrooms should be run exactly like art studios. Rather, the types of pedagogical structures we see in studios can be a useful tool for early childhood educators as they create open-ended learning experiences for their students that develop students' habits of mind.

Developing Studio Thinking through Talking about Art

Arts in early childhood education need not be limited to art making experiences. Talking about art and visual culture provides a way to both develop students "studio thinking," and a complex and engaging forum for building young children's oral language and analytic skills. In addition to providing guidance for open-ended arts activities in the early childhood classroom, the Studio Thinking Framework can be used to guide discussions about art and visual culture so that they support the development of habits of mind.

There are many ways to highlight studio habits of mind in children's every day encounters with visual objects in the classroom. For instance, reading picture books is a mainstay of early childhood education. As children look at the book illustrations, questions can be framed to target the particular studio habits of mind a teacher wants to encourage:

1. Develop Craft--What do you think the artist used to make this picture? Have you ever used that material? If you were illustrating this book what materials would you use? Why?
2. Engage and Persist—Do you think the artist got tired doing all these drawings? How do you   think she kept herself interested?
3. Envision—What did you imagine this [specific character/scene] looked like? How is this the same or different from how the illustrator drew it? (Or, while reading the text, you might ask them to imagine how an author might illustrate it before showing them the illustration).
4. Express—How does this picture make you feel? What do you see in it that you think gives you that feeling? How does it fit with the mood in the story?
5. Observe—What stands out to you most in this picture? What do you have to look closely to notice? What are some of the colors (shapes, types of lines, objects, patterns) you can find?
6. Reflect—Question and Explain: What do you wonder about when you look at this picture? Evaluate—What do you think is good about the illustration? Anything you don't like about it?
7. Stretch & Explore—What are some other ways you can think of to show this same scene in the book?

8. Understand Art World—What is the job of a book illustrator? What is the difference between a book illustrator and other kinds of artists? Would you be interested in doing that kind of work?

These represent just a few of the many questions that could be used to target different Studio Habits of Mind while looking at children's book illustrations. It is not essential (nor advisable) that each "Studio Habit of Mind" be addressed in a given discussion. Rather, the eight habits of mind give insight to educators of the range of ways over the course of their interactions with children over time, on broad areas they can support children's learning.

The Studio Thinking framework can be extended to foster discussion, analysis, and interpretation of not only artworks and illustrations, but the many forms that are important elements of children's visual culture: toys, food packaging, computer and video games, television shows and movies, and advertisements. Discussing these every day objects helps children become more observant of and reflective about the world around them (e.g., Freedman, 2003; Wilson, 2004). For instance, art educator and theorist, Terry Barrett describes leading kindergarteners through an analysis and interpretation of the design and aesthetic properties of their teddy bears. Students discuss why a designer wouldn't make a teddy bear with sharp teeth, and why the property of softness is more important than color in making a good teddy bear (Barrett, 2003).

Framing questions about artworks and visual culture around the Studio Habits of Mind yields important learning in a number of ways. For young children, talking about the properties of art works and other elements of visual culture, provides a concrete reference for learning a new and rich vocabulary. Students learn a vocabulary of adjectives describing color, shapes, patterns, lines, and moods. They gain experience using a vocabulary of relational words as they describe what is above, next to, beneath, behind, or in the corner of a picture, (and see the ways others might not understand if they are not clear or accurate in their terms). They learn words to describe the often wide and varied subject matter of the art works. And, particularly highlighted in the Studio Thinking Framework, they learn a vocabulary to describe thought processes, using words such as notice, wonder, look, feel, imagine, and plan as they think about the meanings of the work and the decisions that went into making it.

As students learn to adopt a vocabulary that highlights different thought processes (e.g., seeing, feeling, imagining, looking, noticing, wondering, planning) involved in the creation of artworks, they become more aware of their own thinking. Educational psychologists focus on the importance of this awareness, or metacognition, in learning and transferring learning to new situations (e.g., Bransford, Brown & Cocking, 1999; Bransford & Schwartz, 1999). While students usually develop metacognitive strategies later in elementary and middle school, at even the earliest ages, students can begin to think about the thoughts, decisions and meanings that underlie the visual culture in their worlds and their own art making processes. To be sure, a kindergartner's description and analysis of the design of his teddy bear or of John Burningham's (1970) pen and ink drawings in *Mr.Gumpy's Outing* or of his marker drawing of his family are going to be quite different than an adolescent's analysis of her art and visual culture. However, they both can be encouraged to develop the studio thinking described above in developmentally appropriate ways.

Discussions about art and visual culture that focus on thought processes can be an important part of creating a classroom culture of thinking. A language of thought in the classroom can help children become more aware of their own thinking and can learn to adopt more complex and effective thought processes both inside and outside the classroom (Perkins, 1992; Ritchhart, 2002; Ritchhart & Perkins, 2000, 2005). As children engage in discussions with their teacher and one another, they gradually internalize the dialogue process into their own thinking (Vygotsky, 1962). They develop thinking dispositions that they can carry with them outside the classroom (Perkins, Jay, & Tishman, 1993; Perkins, Tishman, Ritchhart, Donis, & Andrade, 2000). Again, these metacognitive strategies are more developed and explicit in older grades, but an engaging studio approach that highlights thought processes seems like a good foundation for later development of metacognitive strategies.

Art and Other Subjects

The habits of mind developed through studio arts instruction are broad habits that have correlates in many areas. Learning to *Observe* is important whether you are doing science, art, social studies, gym, or just walking down the road. Being able to *Envision* things not seen is central in math, science, creative writing, literature and history. Most areas of learning require you to *Engage & Persist, Express* ideas and *Reflect* on what you have learned. And to innovate in any field or endeavor requires the ability to *Stretch & Explore*.

However, that the arts share habits of mind with other areas of learning does not mean that developing these habits of mind through studio art will then automatically transfer those abilities to other areas of life and learning. For instance, we do not know whether learning to envision possibilities for a drawing makes you any more likely to envision possibilities for outcomes of a scientific experiment. Most psychological research has found that much of our learning is domain-specific. Documenting transfer of learning from one subject to another has proved to be particularly difficult. In a meta-analysis of claims that learning in the arts transfers to other skills, Winner & Hetland (2000) found limited empirical evidence for the claim that studying the arts causes gains in other academic areas.

In my view, transfer between the arts and other domains may be an interesting psychological question (e.g., what does it mean about cognitive processing that there is a relationship between listening to classical music and performance on some spatial cognition tasks?) but not one that is enough well-developed to influence educational policies. Rather than thinking of learning in the arts as transferring abilities to other domains, it is more useful to consider the value of building thoughtful connections between the arts and other disciplines through arts-integrated curricula or projects. Integrating arts into other forms of learning can be an inviting pedagogical approach for young children and over the years of schooling it is important to learn the overlap and distinctions between fields, such as the different sciences and arts, which have been an important part of human inquiry and activity throughout history.

Art Integration

Compared to secondary schools, the boundaries between academic disciplines are fluid in early childhood and elementary schools. The arts are a frequent part of "units" that transverse multiple boundaries. Arts integration into other academic units often focuses on content (e.g., when studying Ancient Egypt, students create their own hieroglyphs, when studying the family students draw portraits of their family members). These arts activities can provide an engaging and memorable connection to the content.

The Studio Thinking Framework provides an additional route to think about arts integration, one oriented around shared habits of mind. For instance, the habits of mind can be used to explore connections between drawing and writing. Both are important forms for communicating ideas, with drawing as a form of written communication preceding writing for many children. As discussed earlier, researchers have commented on the important connections between drawing and writing. The same can be said for habits of mind. In drawing, Observe, that is, looking closely and noticing details and nuances, is importantly connected to Envision, creating and manipulating mental images of things not currently seen. As students become more close observers, they also develop their visual memory and ability to create mental images to draw upon when they make their works. For instance, when my first grade son recently drew a picture of someone shooting an arrow he was able to envision, based on prior observation, that people close one eye when they aim. His drawing, though drawn from his imagination, creates a much more convincing feeling of the action of aiming an arrow because of his developing abilities to Observe and Envision and build connections between them. This same quality of being observant is important in story telling, whether oral or written. Students who notice nuances and details, and then can draw on their memories of them when writing, can create richer more descriptive and engaging stories.

Projects that integrate writing and drawing can be specifically targeted on this shared value of Observe and Envision. For instance, students could be asked to imagine and draw and describe in words a place in the school that they had been before. Then they could go to the room and Reflect on how well they had envisioned what they had previously seen, and how they could further elaborate or change their drawings or descriptions based on close observation. Listening to stories is another way to build connections between Envision with words and images. Instead of looking at the illustrations in a story, students could be asked to close their eyes and imagine in detail what is going on in the story (a kindergarten student whose class tried this approach described it as "making movies of the book in our minds"). This active envisioning may make students more engaged and attentive to the story and thus, improve their comprehension. It also helps them in the artistic process of translating words and ideas into visual forms. Furthermore, supporting this connection between words and mental images gives students who may be predisposed to either learn more visually or verbally a route into both reading comprehension and visual art that builds on their strengths.

Teachers' Learning

To this point I have focused on what research has found about the types of complex thinking that are involved in the working in the arts and how teachers can support that type of thinking in their students. However, in my interactions with teachers, I often find this work is just as important in transforming their own understanding of learning in the arts. All too often, while a teacher may recognize the importance of learning, she may exclaim, something along the lines of, "I have no talent in art; I can't draw at all!" or "I don't really know much about art" when talking about her own abilities, interest and experience in the arts. While it is true that many people do not develop their drawing skills beyond the skills of an average 10-12 year old, the formal vocabulary of discussing artworks can seem esoteric; the arts are much broader than these conceptions. The Studio Thinking Framework highlights the many components of learning in the arts that do not require extensive technical skills or content knowledge in the arts.

The Studio Thinking Framework provides a broader and a more accurate account for both teachers and students of what it means to be talented in art. Typically, as children move through elementary school they regard the students who can draw most accurately representational or copy professional forms (e.g., cartoon characters) most precisely as the talented "artists," and students who do not perceive themselves as skilled are self-critical and drop out of working in arts (e.g., Davis, 1997; Soep, 2004). However, this conception of art often is just related to developmental differences in fine motor control, and it represents skills in a very narrow area (in Studio Thinking terms it could be represented by a narrow slice of *Develop Craft* and a narrow aspect of *Observe*). By broadening students' and teachers' conceptions to consider many elements of artistic thinking, there are more routes for success and the arts become more accessible.

One of the first responses teachers often have to using the Studio Thinking Framework is a sense of validation. They realize that they are implicitly already teaching students in ways that develop at least some of these habits of mind. The framework is a tool to become more mindful about what they are already doing, make it more explicit to students and their parents, and to find new opportunities to develop students' habits of minds.

A Shared Language for Learning

Thinking in terms of these studio habits of mind and the activities that develop them, can be a powerful way to clarify learning from complex, open-ended activities. An important aspect of the Studio Thinking Framework is that it can help educators see, label and communicate to others the learning they observe in their classroom. Often early childhood educators sense the value of the playful, open-ended projects in their classrooms but lack a way to communicate more specifically what students learn to those who do not interact with the children in the classroom each day. The eight habits of mind identify broad categories of learning that help teachers, students, parents, and others vested in the educational enterprise better describe and assess the complex learning that happens through the open-ended projects characteristic of studio learning.

In our research, we gathered evidence for learning in the habits of mind by observing and documenting changes in students' art work, their working process, and the way they talked about their work and working process. Teachers can similarly document students' learning. In collaboration with the preschools of Reggio Emilia, Italy and other schools in the United States, researchers at Project Zero have been investigating methods of documenting the learning that goes on in collaborative projects in early childhood classrooms (Project Zero & Reggio Children, 2001; Project Zero et al., 2003). Teachers observe and then create visual and textual narratives of student working processes including records of what children say, photographs of their work and working. This process makes the learning visible to the teachers, as the process of documenting often gives them greater insight into children's learning and how to support it. It also creates compelling portraits of learning. For instance, students at a Reggio Emilia school were trying to depict the game of "ring around the rosy" in a drawing. The documentation shows children's initial drawings that solve the problem in one way (e.g. drawing the circle of children from a bird's eye view, making a line of children rather than a circle, drawing very long arms to complete the circle), their reflections on the limitations of their drawings, and then their methods for developing what they believed to be a more accurate representation, and their revised drawings (http://www.pz.harvard.edu/mlv/documentation/index.cfm). Documenting their struggles with the problem, their multiple approaches to the drawings, and their thinking behind it gives a more accurate and compelling vision of their learning than just hanging their final drawings on the wall.

Addressing the Needs of Diverse Learners

The types of studio learning described here are open-ended and flexible; studio problems can be solved in many ways. One of the key advantages of this flexibility is that it addresses the needs of diverse learners.

There are many forms of diversity in an early childhood classroom. Children may have different intellectual strengths and interests; they may be at developmentally different levels, and their cultural backgrounds may provide different experiences that prepare them for the classrooms. In his Theory of Multiple Intelligences, Gardner identifies 8 ½ intelligences which reflect different human potentialities valued by our culture: linguistic, logical-mathematical, spatial, bodily-kinesthetic, interpersonal, intrapersonal, musical, naturalistic, and (possibly existential) (Gardner, 2006). Research on assessing multiple intelligences showed that even young children aged 3-5 showed different patterns of strengths and weaknesses on assessments of multiple intelligences. While they did not make the claim that these differences were permanent attributes of the children, providing experiences in the preschool classroom that draw on the full range of intelligences allows each child experiences in areas of relative intelligence (Gardner & Krechevsky, 2006).

Similarly, arts integrated approaches allow concepts to be explored in verbal and visual modalities. This is a richer exploration for everyone, but also lets students who have relative strengths in one or the other modality both experience success in a modality of relative strength while simultaneously working in a modality of relative weakness.

Thoughtful visual arts integration may be a particularly useful approach in classes with linguistic diversity. For example, I worked with a teacher who had a large group of students in her class who were learning English as a Second Language (ESL). She had found that the visual arts allowed these students to express their ideas nonverbally, and gave her and their other classmates insight into their thinking, ideas, personalities and interests. Students with limited English speaking and writing skills were able to express their intelligence and feel more confident and engaged in the classroom.

The Arts and 21ˢᵗ Century Literacies and Skills

A key justification for integrating visual arts into early childhood education, is that it is reflective of the worlds children currently live in, and develops the ways of thinking they will need to thrive in the future. To be sure, the visual arts have been an important part of human culture since the earliest cave paintings, but a feature of much of the current socio-cultural context is that more information is being communicated visually and more people are involved in projects requiring design and creative expression. In a 2005 report from the Pew study of Internet and American life, researchers found that ½ of all teens had created some form of media content, many on a regular basis and much of it visual (Lenhardt & Madden, 2005). Henry Jenkins (2006) has been documenting the evolution of this pattern, describing a shift towards increased involvement in what he terms, *participatory cultures*, which are cultures that, among other features, encourage its members to engage in artistic and creative expression. This increased involvement in artistic and creative endeavors is not limited to hobbies. As Daniel Pink (2005) argues in his book, *A Whole New Mind,* our economy is shifting from an information age to a conceptual age, where the kinds of thinking developed through arts and design is the kind of thinking that is in greater demand. The economist, Richard Florida (2002), empirically documents the importance of the *creative class* in the current economy. Given these cultural shifts, beginning the earliest stages of education with a thoughtful, arts-integrated approach seems not only a way to engage students, but is important preparation for their futures.

Conclusion

With any pedagogical approach, teachers must think through why they would spend their time with this focus rather than others. In this case, why should a teacher integrate the arts into the early childhood classroom, and highlight the types of thinking involved in the arts. I have argued that the visual arts are already present in many early childhood classrooms, and that taking a "studio thinking" approach to these arts activities does not necessarily add more time, rather it makes those art experiences more thoughtful and able to be connected in meaningful ways to other areas of learning. Open-ended arts experiences can provide engaging and important learning experiences for students with diverse intelligences, linguistic backgrounds, skills, experiences and learning styles. Incorporating more visual and creative thinking helps students to be better able to function in the evolving world that requires learning to interpret and express in multiple media and modes.

References

Atkinson, D. (1991). How children use drawing. *Journal of Art and Design Education, 10*(1), 57-72.

Baghban, M. (2007). Scribbles, labels, and stories: The role of drawing in the development of writing. *Young Children, 62*(1), 20-26.

Barrett, T. (2003). Interpreting visual culture. *Journal of Art Education, 56*(2), p 6-12.

Bransford, J. D., & Schwartz, D. L. (1999). Rethinking transfer: A simple proposal with multiple implications. *Review of Research in Education, 24,* 61-100.

Bransford, J.D., Brown, A.L., & Cocking, R.R. (Eds.) (1999). *How people learn: Brain, mind experience and school.* Washington, DC: National Academy Press.

Burningham, J. (1970). *Mr. Gumpy's outing.* New York: Henry Holt.

Davis, J. (1997). The "U" and the wheel of "C": Development and devaluation of graphic symbolization and the cognitive approach at Harvard Project Zero. In A. M. Kindler (Ed.), *Child development in art* (pp. 45-58). Reston, VA: National Art Education Association.

Eisner, E. (2002). *Arts and the creation of mind.* New Haven, CT: Yale University Press.

Florida, R. L. (2002). *The rise of the creative class and how it's transforming work, leisure, community, and everyday life.* New York: Basic Books.

Freedman, K. (2003). *Teaching visual culture: Curriculum, aesthetics, and the social life of art.* New York: Teachers College Press.

Gardner, H. (1982). *Art, mind and brain*. New York: Basic Books.

Gardner, H. (1990). *Arts education and human development*. Los Angeles: Getty Center for Education in the Arts.

Gardner, H. (2006). *Multiple intelligences: New horizons*. New York: Basic Books.

Gardner, H., & Krechevsky, M. (2006). Nurturing intelligences in early childhood. In H. Gardner (Ed.), *Multiple intelligences: New horizons* (pp. 89-112). New York: Basic Books.

Heath, S. B. (2001). Three's not a crowd: Plans, roles and focus in the arts. *Educational Researcher, 30*(3) 1-7.

Heath, S. B. (with A. Roach) (1999). Imaginative actuality: Learning in the arts during non-school hours. In *Champions of Change*, 19-34. Washington, D.C.: The Arts Education Partnership and The President's Committee on the Arts and the Humanities.

Hetland, L., Winner, E., Veenema, S., & Sheridan, K. (2007). *Studio thinking: The real benefits of visual arts education*. New York: Teachers College Press

Jenkins, H. (2006). Confronting the Challenges of Participatory Culture: Media Education for the 21st Century. Occasional paper for the MacArthur Foundation. Retrieved from http://digitallearning.macfound.org/site/c.enJLKQNlFiG/b.2029291/k.97E5/Occasional_Papers.htm on January 27, 2006.

Kendrick, M., & McKay, R. (2004). Drawing as an alternate way of understanding young children's constructions of literacy. *Journal of Early Childhood Literacy, 4*(1), 109-128.

Lenhardt, A., & Madden, M. (2005). *Teen Content Creators and Consumers*. Washington, DC:Pew Internet & American Life Project. Retrieved January 23, 2008 from http://www.pewInternet.org/PPF/r/166/report_display.asp

McKay, R., & Kendrick, M. (2001). Children draw their images of reading and writing. *Language Arts, 78*(6), 529-533.

Perkins, D. (1992). *Smart schools: From training memories to educating minds*. New York: Free Press/Macmillan.

Perkins, D., Jay, E., & Tishman, S. (1993). Teaching thinking: From ontology to education. *Educational Psychologist, 28*(1), 67-85.

Perkins, D. N., Tishman, S., Ritchhart, R., Donis, K., & Andrade, A. (2000). Intelligence in the wild: A dispositional view of intellectual traits. *Educational Psychology Review, 12*(3), 269-293.

Piaget, J. (1962). *Play, dreams and imitation in childhood*. (C. Gattegno & F.M. Hodgson Trans.) New York: Norton.

Pink, D. (2005). *A whole new mind: Moving from the information age to the conceptual age*. New York: Riverhead Books.

Project Zero, Cambridgeport Children's Center, Cambridgeport School, Ezra H. Baker School, & John Simpkins School. (2003). *Making teaching visible: Documenting individual and group learning as professional development*. Cambridge, MA: Project Zero.

Project Zero & Reggio Children. (2001). *Making learning visible: Children as individual and group learners*. Reggio Emilia, Italy: Reggio Children.

Ritchhart, R. (2002). *Intellectual character: What it is, why it matters, how to get it*. San Francisco: Jossey-Bass.

Ritchhart, R., & Perkins, D.N. (2000). Life in the mindful classroom: Nurturing the disposition of mindfulness. *Journal of Social Issues, 56*(1), 27-47.

Ritchhart, R., & Perkins, D.N. (2005). Learning to think: The challenges of teaching thinking. In K. Holyoak & R.G. Morrison (Eds.), *Cambridge handbook of thinking and reasoning* (pp. 775-802). Cambridge, MA: Cambridge University Press.

Soep, E. (2004). Visualizing judgment: Self-assessment and peer assessment in arts education. In E. W. Eisner & M. D. Day (Eds.), *Handbook of research and policy in art education* (pp. 667-687). Mahwah, NJ: Lawrence Erlbaum.

Vygotsky, L. (1962). *Thought and language* (E. Haufmann & G. Vankar, Eds. and Trans.). Cambridge, MA: MIT Press.

Winner, E., & Hetland, L. (Eds.). (2000). The arts and academic achievement: What the evidence shows [Special issue]. *Journal of Aesthetic Education, 34*(3/4).

Wilson, B. (2004). Child art after Modernism: Visual culture and new narratives. In E.W. Eisner
    & M. D. Day (Eds.), *Handbook of research and policy in art education* (pp. 299-328). Mah-
    wah, NJ: Lawrence Erlbaum.

Kimberly Sheridan
George Mason University
Fairfax, VA   USA

Dr. Kimberly Sheridan is an assistant professor of educational psychology and art education at George Mason University. Prior to 2006, she was a research specialist at Harvard University's Project Zero, and she continues collaborations there. She is a co-author of the book, *Studio Thinking: The Real Benefits of Visual Arts Education* and has authored articles on arts and cognition. She has experience teaching in early education settings, designing art programs for early education, and working with teachers to use the arts to promote high-level thinking.

Part Two
Contexts and Layered Texts

Chapter 5
The In-Depth Approach:

Young Children's Artistic Learning in the Context of Museum Environments and Other Cultural Settings

Eli Trimis and Andri Savva

Abstract In this chapter, we explore children's art learning in different museum environments (archaeological, contemporary, craft) using the in-depth approach. Basic elements of this approach include the child, *chorotopos* (space/place), the teacher, and time. Our research involves teachers and young children from Greece (area of Thessaloniki, Northern Greece) and Cyprus (Lefkosia) and suggests that children's contact with a range of art exhibits in museums and other cultural settings is an important part of children's educational meaning making experiences if appropriate approaches and methods are used.

Keywords in-depth approach, museum experiences, artistic learning, early childhood settings, pre-service teachers

Theoretical Framework

This chapter draws attention to a broad theoretical framework of art education arguing that knowledge is constructed through interaction with objects and people, emphasizing learners' prior experiences, interests and motivation. Thus, an individual's knowledge and understanding of the world is in a continual state of

Aristotle University of Thessaloniki, Greece and European University, Cyprus

University of Cyprus, Cyprus

M. J. Narey (ed.), Making Meaning.
© Springer 2009

change as new experiences, mediated through social contexts are encountered and interpreted by the learner (e.g., Gergen, 1995; Lave & Wegner, 1991). Philosophers, cognitive scientists and educators (e.g., Dewey, Piaget, Vygotsky) have agreed that the mind creates knowledge in response to the world as it creates and recreates itself (Freedman, 2003). Vygotsksy focused on the impact of the cultural settings in which a student learns and argued that learning not only occurs in context but is driven by context (Freedman, 2003). The theory of creative representation corroborates the above views and highlights the significance of giving opportunities to young children to approach real objects, people and places in enhancing their thinking in and about art (Hohmann & Weikart, 2002). The importance of creating and observing visual representations and the ability to reflect on them distinguishes humans from other species. This becomes even more important considering young children's age group where the foundations are set for a complete and fulfilling adulthood.

We argue that situated knowledge, the conceptions and misconceptions about art and culture, can begin during the early childhood years. According to recent brain research, the environment is crucial in the development of the brain. More over, we have learned that there are windows of opportunity where children absorb and develop specific knowledge and skills (e.g., language, music, art) (Stephens, 1999), suggesting that in becoming literate in visual symbolic code involves the ability to both produce and perceive art (Gardner & Perkins, 1989). We support this perspective and suggest that such opportunities and experiences during the early years are essential for children's social, cognitive, emotional and aesthetic development. Thus, the significance in studying young children's art learning in specific socio-cultural contexts (chorotopos) (Trimis, 1996), focusing on the full complexity of their experiences (Thompson, 2005), is highlighted in the research presented in this chapter.

Experiences focusing on emotional engagement through artistic activities based on the exploration of the child's *chorotopos* (place/space) enable individuals to relate to their cultural environment (natural and man made), and to discover that they can affect it by enhancing their visual/aesthetic sensitivity (Savva, Trimis, & Zachariou, 2004). Although there is a widespread acceptance among researchers of the cognitive, affective, and social aspects of the learning experiences of visitors in museums and other places of cultural interest (Hooper-Greenhill & Moussouri, 2002), few studies have considered or described the impact of *chorotopos*, including museums, on young children's art learning through their own voices and perspectives and attempted to link this with school based art curriculum (Trimis & Savva, in press). With a few exceptions (e.g., Anderson, Piscitelli, Weier, Everett, & Tayler, 2002; Piscitelli & Anderson, 2000; Savva & Trimis, 2005a, 2005b; Trimis & Savva, 2004) there is an absence in the literature of studies examining young children's learning in specific settings (such as different type of museums) focusing particularly on how they approach art objects and exhibits. Similarly Hooper-Greenhill & Mousouri (2002) suggest that much research need to be done in the area of history and archaeology museums and heritage sites including children's learning and experiences. Such research would inform museum and school communities as well as art educators about the experiential aspects that children find most interesting and rewarding and assist in the developmental aspects of exhibitions and educational programs in museums and schools. It might also provide opportunities for teachers and museum educators to become aware of how they might integrate and link different kinds of cultural visits to everyday classroom artistic activities and produce relevant pedagogical materials.

The In-depth Approach

As new programs in art education are developed and implemented, teachers often try to understand how an art museum experience can enhance and enrich children's art learning. Recent literature refers to the significance of incorporating stimuli gained from visits to museums and other places of cultural interest. Hooper-Greenhill (1991) considers it to be one component of a three-part unit consisting of a preliminary preparation, a museum visit, and follow up work. Trimis & Savva (2004) suggest an in-depth approach: an art instruction method in which children have opportunities to explore and transform materials, and produce art before visiting cultural places, to see how similar art activities are carried out in the real world (e.g., art gallery, craft shop, artist's studio, folk museum). This approach emphasizes constructive learning based on children's viewing and making that gradually develops from the simple to the complex, from the known to the unknown. Cultural places such as monuments, craft shops, archaeological places, museums and artworks are considered an important part of this process.

Trimis (1996), Trimis & Manavopoulos (2001), and Epstein & Trimis (2002) report programs based on the in-depth approach, where *chorotopos* (space-place) is considered an important factor, provide and enhance young children's knowledge in making and viewing their own and others art and culture. The in-depth approach (Trimis, 1996) based on the previous broad theoretical framework of art education, suggest that:

> ...children must directly experience objects, places or events and the art materials they use to represent them, through their senses and actions. Representations often begin when children accidentally recognize the similarity between something in their lives and an attribute of the medium they are working with. (Epstein & Trimis, 2002, p.42)

The in-depth approach is a method that promotes children's investigation of materials and techniques in depth. The ultimate goal of the in-depth approach programs is for children to experience materials encountered in a variety of environments. Learning takes place in real situations and is not limited to the classroom as children engage in thinking in, and thinking about, art.

The Material

The in-depth approach uses closely related experiences in similar media. Through the continuous exploration of similar art media children's art experiences progress from the simple to the more complex. This process helps children exploit the aesthetic properties of these materials and raises awareness of the aesthetic as well as the functional qualities inherent in them. It also enables children to recognize the materials' origins and relation to their environment (natural, man-made, cultural) and to develop cognitive concepts such as spatial concepts (durability, resistibility, variety of size, volume, shape, and consistency). In this sense, artistic activities emphasizing familiarity and explorations of art mediums, as well as reflection opportunities on the creative process in various contexts (e.g., natural parks, monuments, religious places, shopping malls, buildings, workshops, museums etc), enable young children to understand the origins of the materials and their role in their life and view art as part of their culture (Savva & Trimis, 2005a, 2005b; Trimis, 1996).

Basic factors in implementing the in-depth approach include the child, the teacher, time, and *Chorotopos* (space/place), young children's age group and social-cultural background along with their previous experiences and knowledge should be considered. Special attention is given to the role of the teacher: Teachers should posses the qualities of flexibility, enthusiasm, the joy of discovery and they should be open to learning from children, in other words be able to co-construct their knowledge along with children. Time is also an essential factor: children should be given sufficient time for exploration, creation and reflection. The length of activity is determined by the child's interest. So it can last as long as the interest of the children lasts. The last factor but not least, in the in-depth approach is the *chorotopos*[1]. *Chorotopos* is linked to the school itself and its surrounding area meaning the space inside and outside the school. It starts from the inside of the classroom and extents to the neighbourhood, the village, the community, and the town. In a broad sense it refers to the place, the landscape, the neighbourhood, the region, the area, the village, the city where the school is situated, and the human factor. Thus museums are considered to be part of children's *chorotopos* and in a broad sense include archaeological, prehistoric and sites of cultural heritage.

The structure of the in-depth approach programs progresses through a sequence of four stages as children think in and about art: Preliminary, Enrichment, Production, Reflection (Trimis, 1996). The stages are flexible and the boundaries between them are not fixed. Often one stage overlaps with another. This method

---

[1] The term chorotopos (originates from the Greek language meaning the choros - space and topos - place). It is linked to the school itself and its surrounding area meaning the space inside and outside the school. In a broad sense it refers to the place, the landscape, the neighbourhood, the region, the area, the village, the city where the school is situated and the human factor. It refers to the natural and man-made environment of the immediate place-space of the school.

uses closely related experiences in similar media in order to enable children evidence a growth and satisfaction that is missing in more fragmentary area approaches (Epstein & Trimis, 2002; Trimis, 1996; Trimis & Savva, 2004; Trimis 2004 a, b). These stages are analyzed below:

1. *Preliminary:* This is the stage in which children first encounter a material or artistic concept - a period of getting acquainted that is characterized by playing with materials, tools and ideas, or a visit to a workshop, park, or any other place of cultural interest. During this stage the children's natural curiosity may be stirred and extended by the teacher posing open-ended questions or setting up games and problem solving situations.

2. *Enrichment:* This stage refers to every experience - media that expands a child's curiosity and knowledge, skills and aesthetic sense of a medium or an artistic concept. Enrichment is a continuous process, it occurs at every stage of the encounter with artistic materials and ideas. It happens through visual, auditory, kinesthetic and other sensory stimulation. A child's experience with a medium can be enhanced in many ways: through complementary materials and tools, stories, poems, photographs, music, riddles, games, visits and re visits to man-made and natural environments etc, museums, galleries, workshops, sites of cultural heritage.

3. *Production:* It is the making of art - the culmination of the child's preliminary and enrichment experiences. While production occurs at any previous point, this stage is noteworthy for the child's intention to produce something concrete and visible. Making intentional choices of materials, tools and techniques to proceed and give form to ideas that are meaningful to him or her.

4. *Reflection:* It is a very important stage that takes place during each of the previous stages of the in-depth program, and also at the end of the program. Children are encouraged to look, observe carefully, express their opinions, be evocative, try to remember initial intentions and talk about future plans in relation to the end product. They are encouraged to express their views about the work of their peers and make suggestions. Children are helped by the teacher to recall the process from the preliminary stage to the last stage, to reflect on the steps that laid them to their creations, the concepts and ideas that laid them to the end results, to reexamine their actions, choices and connections they made. They compare their creations to the creations of others and are led to the realization of the results of their actions. This process helps enhance their critical thinking. Their arts' experiences become sources of communication with others in an interactive environment while exchanging ideas, making decisions, and exercising their descriptive language skills.

The Rationale and Context of the Studies

Both European cities, chosen for the purposes of this research (Lefkosia, Cyprus and Thessaloniki, Greece) have a long history, a rich cultural background and numerous cultural sites. Their location has influenced their social-political and cultural development apparent in many cases in their natural and man-made environment. Thessallonikis' (Greece) cultural heritage includes Pre-Historic, Greek — Hellenic, Macedonian Hellenistic, Roman, Byzantine, Ottoman, and Jewish influences. In Lefkosia (Cyprus) are also apparent influences from pre historic, Greek-Hellenic, Roman, Byzantine, Frankish, Venetian, Ottoman and English-Colonial periods. In both cities a large multicultural heritage is evident. Although both are modern cities, with historical centres and a very intense visual culture with theme parks, shopping centres, billboards, etc., they offer opportunities for visits to numerous museums that are Historical, Archaeological, Folk, Byzantine, Contemporary and places of cultural interest with monuments, religious places, and ruins found in different sites.

In Thessaloniki and Lefkosia, visual art programs for young children usually emphasize experiences in making art with two-dimensional materials. Most of the time, art appreciation is done with reproductions and is not linked to art making (Trimis & Savva, 2004). In contrast pre-service teachers participating in the following studies implemented programs that followed the in-depth approach and incorporated activities with scrap materials and clay that were linked to actual experiences of viewing and discussing works of art with children in archaeological, contemporary, and folk museums.

In recent times, museum educators have attempted to reach out to first time visitors, particularly young children, who constitute an important and large part of present and future audiences. Studies indicate that museums as well as other cultural settings are places of learning (Falk & Dierking, 2000; Savva & Trimis, 2005a). It is asserted that there is much to be gained from a broadened canon in art education and particularly from acknowledging the great number of out of school domains (Trimis & Savva, in press). Thus we adopt the tendency for the importance of expanding the educational process outside the school environment in the neighbourhood and to the larger *chorotopos*, for more meaningful learning experiences. Our interest in researching young children's artistic learning derives from the theoretical foundations and principles of the in-depth approach that incorporates all the above (Trimis, 1996). The examples of in-depth programs presented below are part of a larger study focusing on artistic learning in the context of museum environments and other cultural settings. These in-depth programs enable children to become familiar with their own world, to see them selves as part of it, and validate their experience in it. It is suggested that artistic activities[2] in re-

---

2 Artistic activity is defined as a type of making activity, in which interactions of various symbol systems (e.g. language, drawing) are involved. Special emphasis in the present study is given to visual arts activities with which children through medium (materials) represent their feelings, actions and ideas.

lation to their own place could make children feel closer and more situated to their own environment, help them to understand their local and global cultural heritage, and the world around them (Trimis & Savva, in press).

We argue that exposure to settings, images and visual artifacts related to children's environment inside and outside school has a strong impact on them and based on this view we sought to: 1) introduce to pre-service teachers ways of implementing art programs based on the in-depth approach and in the context of museum and other cultural environments. 2) promote children's learning by incorporating making and viewing experiences in various settings.

Pre-service teachers were asked to document and report on the young children's responses and making by taking observation notes and photographs before, during and after the museum visits and audio taping reflective discussions with children during the implementation of each program (during making, viewing and reflective activities).

Examples of In-depth Programs in Early Childhood Settings

In-depth Program 1: Paper Scrap Materials

The implementation of the program with scrap materials was applied in a pre-school setting near the centre of Thessaloniki (region of Kalamaria). The pre-school is located next to the sea. As an extension to the main building there is a large yard (like a big balcony) paved with concrete tiles and with a view to the sea. The school interior is spacious with plenty of light coming through the windows. The implementation of this program involved twenty children (twelve girls, eight boys), aged 4-6. Even the youngest group of children had acquired the skill to tear, cut, crumple, paint with brushes and make collages. Children had already worked with drawing and painting, collage with paper and fabrics but had never worked with scrap materials.

The program was implemented end of March. Taking into consideration the consumerism, the contact of young children with scrap materials and their connection to ecology, recycling and environment as well as the children's minimal experiences in using them to make art, it was essential to give them the opportunities to expand their concept of art and environment by focusing on the use of these materials (Trimis & Savva, 2004). The scrap materials used were restricted to mainly paper scrap material (e.g., different sizes of paper boxes, shoe boxes, match boxes). The variety and the size of boxes were sequentially introduced to the children. As visual aids the program included posters, photographs and reproductions. The type of the material let the children to investigate the concept of house (Ikea). This was not used as a theme to restrain the imagination but to open new possibilities of approaching the symbol house, through perception, observation and representation of a familiar symbol. Children were free to work with other themes if they chose.

Taking into consideration the *chorotopos* of the school the pre-service teacher along with the researcher decided to include in the in-depth program a visit to a supermarket near the school, a walk in the neighborhood, a visit to the folk museum and a visit to the Vellidio Cultural Centre[3] where there was a non permanent exhibition of modern architecture. The program was based on making and observing art, emphasizing exploration with materials that children experience in their everyday life and that offer themselves ideas. It highlights aspects gained from manipulating, combining, assembling constructions and thus enhancing children's spatial awareness (Trimis, 1996).

Phase 1: Preliminary

The first acquaintance was when this material was placed in different areas and levels in their classroom to surprise the children and give them the opportunity to work with the material in different spaces of the room, alone or in groups. Children's first responses as they enter the room were:

"What is that trash?"

"The room is full of boxes and rubbish."

"It is not rubbish, these are boxes."

"We also have at home these type of boxes."

"All of us have these, since we drink juices and buy matches."

The teacher explained that these have multiple uses and encouraged them to play with those boxes. The curiosity of the children to touch and to choose one or more boxes and express their views was apparent.

"I will take this box and I will draw on it."

"Yes, that is a good idea."

"Look, this box looks like a little house."

"Mine looks like a skyscraper."

These responses helped some of them to form groups.

"If I stick these two boxes together I will make a coach and then I am going to paint it."

"Oh! Look, this box has a beautiful color."

"Yes, this is very pretty, what are you going to do with this?"

---

[3] A cultural centre situated in the historical centre of the city in Thessaloniki

Another group not interested to construct anything initially, gave advices, observed the constructions of other children and finally got involved.

"Look I made a house."

"This is not a house, and there is no roof."

Still another group was selling and buying things and some others carried boxes to the dollhouse. The next day they discussed with their teacher their constructions and talked about the connection of the material with the environment and ecology and their every day life. They decided to visit the big supermarket in their neighborhood, to investigate on the origins of the material and collected many more boxes and cartons. They observed and discussed the variety of packaging, wrapping and the way they are carried.

"They are the same boxes in the same area."

"... they are all in a row."

"... if they were mixed they would be nice."

"... plastic does not melt like paper"

They observed houses on the way back to school were surprised when they saw a house called "haunted."

Phase 2: Enrichment

The material was enriched by bigger sized boxes collected by the children and the teacher from supermarkets and elsewhere (in their *chorotopos*). The bigger sized boxes (cartons) gave new ideas and incentives to the children who worked in different areas alone and in groups. Some measured and tried to enter in the boxes, sitting inside them. A boy talked to himself, tried a box on his head and went around the room wearing the box. He cut some openings, announcing all his operations and finally he wore the box, became a robot and started walking pretending and making sounds around the room, while children watched and admired him. Another child announced that he was making a bed, a chair and a broken frame and shouted: "Yes! This is a haunted house with ghosts". He painted it with different colors to make it look old and haunted. Other children decided to paint their houses. The next day while observing and discussing their creations one child proposed to draw his house on a piece of paper. The teacher enhanced this idea, by provoking all children to draw their three dimensional constructions and thus increase their perceptual awareness through their own observation of a familiar, meaningful object (Trimis, 1996). All the children followed the idea, watching their creations carefully and drawing them with marking pens. They discussed and described their creations and decided to take a walk in their neighborhood in order to observe houses, buildings, residencies, condominiums, etc. While walking, they observed, compared and connected present and previous experiences with housing compounds and buildings: "There is no such an old house not even in the village of my grandparents!" and, "This is a two-story house like our house." Children then sat in the park and talked about what they observed: railings, balconies, verandas, doors, gardens, windows, etc. They sprawled on the grass and drew. Back in the school the next day the material is enriched; children discussed their experiences and proceeded into representing them:

"A village and a factory..."

"I will make a star for the neighborhood."

"Why do you put the sun down?"

"During the daytime is on the sky but it appears also on earth!"

Children recalled previous experiences in their *chorotopos*: "Let's draw something to remember it...as we did in the classroom and the excursion that we had in our neighborhood." They continued discussing, problem-solving, dealing with space-concepts and environmental issues, while they stabilize, sticking them to bases, or taking decisions concerning the positioning of the houses, observing from different angles... The teacher enriched further the activities and the concept "house" hanging posters, photographs and other visual aids with various buildings. Finally, they all decided to visit the Folk and Ethnological Museum of Macedonia-Thrace (Fig. 5.1).

During the visit, the teacher took the children to the section of the museum with the traditional houses (village houses or other). They observed and discussed the maquette constructions:

"We do not have an oven in our yard, we buy bread from the store."

"Our building has many floors, these have only two."

"This house is made all with grass."

They continued to enrich their experiences by visiting Vellidion Cultural Centre, where drawings, designs, and maquettes (i.e., scale models) of internationally well-known architects were exhibited. After having a tour by the curator, observing contemporary house constructions, they discussed and asked questions about the job of an architect and made comparisons of the houses they saw in the folk museum with the houses in the Centre.

"These are completely new."

"They have verandas and they don't have roofs."

Children also had the opportunity to observe a house of their own choice and make a drawing of it.

Fig. 5.1 Children explore the concept of houses at the museum

Phase 3: Production

Enrichment of material (e.g., big boxes from supermarkets, large papers, different quality of paper etc) enabled children to work in different spaces of their school (inside and outside) and in a more complicated way. They went in and out of the boxes; they pulled them and turned them around by helping each other. They stabilized them on the ground, choosing a different side of the box each time. They felt free to improvise and transform, give new meanings to materials and objects. For example, they exercise force and movement by pulling and pushing the boxes. They cut windows and doors by asking the help from their teacher; they joined together their boxes to make bigger constructions. They interacted and transformed the material into different types of constructions.

"My box is bigger than yours."

"If I turn it this way, mine will be taller."

"We both fit in this one."

"I will make a house which will have a window on the top instead of a roof."

They decorated their boxes (homes) with colored papers and in some cases they painted them. Finally, they took the big boxes into the school yard, put one box next to the other to make a neighborhood, and they role-played, acting scenes from their everyday life, while one boy decided to construct a boat, stepped onto his colored boat, and announced to the others that he was going to travel.

Phase 4: Reflection

Although several reflections preceded the concluding one, the final reflection included a slide projection showing all the stages of the program (Trimis, 1996).
Some children enthusiastically made comments and some of them (the younger
ones) didn't want to speak at all. After the slide projection, the teacher asked the
children to bring their own work and talk about it. Some of them enjoyed talking
about their own work and some of them preferred to talk about the work of others.
Most of the children referred to the material used, the techniques they employed to
put together and decorate their construction. They reflected upon the process and
their initial ideas, and recalled experiences in their museum visits.

In-depth Program 2: Working with Clay

This second program was implemented in a school situated in the outskirts of the
Lefkosia (Cyprus). It is a big school with large inside and outside spaces. There is
an anteroom where children usually work along with their teacher in visual arts.
The classroom where the program was implemented was a large, comfortable
space with lots of stimulations that is decorated with children's work. Three pre-
service teachers implemented this program during their initial training in art education. They had an extensive experience in making art using clay and observed
clay artifacts in the archeological museum in Lefkosia along with the researcher.
They visited again the museum to study in-depth the areas that they were going to
visit with the young children. While the Cyprus Museum in Lefkosia
(http://www.mcw.gov.cy/mcw/da/da.nsf/All) is a very important archeological
museum with exhibits ranging from the Neolithic to the Roman period, for this research study, three main museum rooms where chosen, along with a supplemental
small hall for the following reasons:

1. They had mainly exhibits made from clay, from Neolithic to Roman age (stone
   utensils, pottery, figurines, figure idols, clay containers and jars) and
   representations of ancient tombs). In the entrance of the first hall there were
   very large photographs representing ancient dwellings and archeological sites.
   Some of the photographs were showing origins of some of the artifacts and
   others ways of excavation.
2. The main material of the artifacts was clay.
3. The halls were connected and they were easily accessible by children.
4. Many of the exhibited artifacts had common characteristics with children
   works –simplified forms (realistic and abstract).
5. The supplemental area was chosen because it was easily accessible and because it contained authentic representations of excavated tombs, and archeological findings. These were helpful in facilitating the children to perceive the
   time and the place in relation to the artifacts.

The visit to the museum was organized at a time with the least visitors. Sixteen children (eight boys and eight girls), aged 5-6 were involved in the program. Almost all the children had no experience with clay, in making three-dimensional constructions and had never visited a museum. However, they had created an exhibit area, in their school to show their artwork.

Phase 1: Preliminary

The children initially played with clay and then discussed issues concerned with the origin and the consistency of the material. Children continued exploring the material in groups or alone, creating balls, joining small pieces of clay together putting them one next to the other. One child made a figure with all the facial characteristics. Other children made a machine, a tank, jewelry, a farm, and a snail. Most of their creations were flat, except for a few three-dimensional ones. The pre-service teachers reported that they tried to enhance children's ability to construct by assisting and showing them new techniques with clay. Afterwards, the teachers showed the children selected artifact photographs from the museum to introduce them to the idea of the archeological museum. They let the children imagine and ask questions about the museum, and eventually make the decision to visit it.

Phase 2: Enrichment

In small groups of four, the children toured the three museum halls. In the entrance of the hall, children had the opportunity to observe large photographs. In this phase children were left to move around freely, ask questions and to respond to artifacts of their choice. It was evident, as pre-service teachers reported, that children had faced difficulties in approaching some of the artifacts due to the ways these were exhibited (far above the eye level of children).

The first tour was followed by a more careful observation of selected items. The pre-service teachers provoked children's interest, enhanced their curiosity by asking questions and giving opportunities to express their likes and dislikes. In most cases they linked the museum artifacts with their immediate experiences and their every day life:

"This looks like an animal."

"It is like a bowl where you put cornflakes."

"It is a pig, and I like pigs, because in the farm that I have visited there are pigs."

"It has the shape of a cross and I also have one in my house."

Most of the children believed that people constructed the museum exhibits many years ago. The authentic representations of excavations facilitate children to be aware of the time and place in relation to artifacts:

"They are very old... from the ancients."

"They found them deep in the earth."

"There are people who dig the earth and they find them."

In most cases they recognized the material and the artistic process of making of the objects, saying, "Look all these holes...I think the ancients made these holes with pointed tools" and "...they have used a lot of clay...look how huge it is!" When they were asked about the function of their choices. (How do you think this was used? What is the reason of making such a....) children reported:

"This jar was probably to put inside something to drink from, something like water but maybe they used it as a censer to burn incense..."

"This is a clay pot... probably they put food or even their little toys."

"It is a human and animal. I like it. They made it many, many years ago... They gave it to their children to play with."

Many children referred to the size of the museum exhibits and felt impressed by the large sized ones, "It is big and round on the top, it becomes thin underneath...may I see in it?" A small number of children also referred to the decoration and colors of the clay pots. "I like it because it has flowers and designs."

In many cases, the teacher enriched the vocabulary of the children. For example, she introduced the word, *Kentavros*, for the human-animal artifact. Children then had the opportunity to make a drawing of their choice in the yard of the museum (Fig. 5.2).

Phase 3: Production

After returning to school, children recalled their experiences during the museum visit. They were particularly impressed by the tombs and continued to discuss the process of excavation. "They dug and found a lot of things....", "...they even found people in the earth." Other children referred to the material of the objects observed in the museum "there were lots of clay items," "there were clay objects that people were making them, them selves in the old times... and they were some made from stone". During the process of working with clay some of the children recalled their experiences in the museum: "Do you remember those animals made of clay?" and "My jug will be bigger ...when I will put more clay...." It was apparent that as the children were experimenting with the clay, they responded to the transformation and the remodeling of the material. Only some of the children were intentionally deciding to make clay pots, and asked the teacher to show them how.

Fig. 5.2 Children draw museum objects

Children needed more time to explore the characteristics of the material and its possibilities to be transformed from one state to the other; to discover its inherent qualities, physical properties, and plasticity (Epstein & Trimis, 2002). Exploring and creating with the art materials should not be limited and the length of the activities should be determined by their needs (Trimis & Savva, 2004). Other in-depth programs focused on clay and other materials in order to enhance children's thinking in art do provide more time for exploration and transformation of materials and the production of artworks (Epstein & Trimis, 2002).

Phase 4: Reflection

After finishing their constructions, the children exhibited their work (Fig. 5.3) and discussed their experiences and impressions from their visit to the museum and their work with clay. The children recalled their experiences, from the very beginning of the program (e.g. the initial play with clay, the representations and discussion of photographs, the visit to the museum and the interpretation of artifacts, the drawings in the yard of the museum and finally their work with clay). It was obvious during the reflection process that children easily recalled their experiences by referring to their own given titles and the material used for the artifacts (Savva & Trimis, 2005b).

Fig. 5.3 Children's clay work

In-depth Program 3: Found Materials

This third program was implemented by two pre-service teachers in a public early childhood setting, part of a school compound, near the center of Thessaloniki (Greece). The large classroom had no organized space for making art. The large yard is shared by another pre-school and an elementary school. The building is located between two narrow streets; the view from the windows of the classroom is one of high condominiums, shops, and cars. The school is close to the museums in the centre of Thessalloniki. Twenty children (9 boys, 11 girls), aged 4.5-6 years, took part in the program. Almost all the children had minimal experience in making art with found materials and only one child had visited previously a museum. Thus, the pre-service teachers decided to apply a program using found materials and to incorporate repeated visits to the Macedonian Contemporary Art Museum in order to enrich children's experiences according to the in-depth program.

The Macedonian Contemporary Art Museum (http://www.mmca.org.gr) is a large museum that hosts prestigious national and international exhibitions and collections with libraries, theatre, shops, educational workshops, and artists' residential complexes. The choice of visiting this museum was based on the fact that it hosts artwork collections with found materials in its permanent exhibit and that it is only twenty minutes walking distance from the school location (*chorotopos*).

Although the pre-service teachers, as part of an art education course, have been well informed about modern art, they had visited the museum with the researcher to acquire knowledge on specific exhibit artifacts as well as information concerning the museum space and the art collection. They revisited the museum to enrich their information on the space and the procedures.

Phase 1: Preliminary

The pre-service teachers discussed the concept "museum" with the children before the actual visit. They invited children to recall previous experiences and beliefs (Hooper & Greenhill, 1991). Children's responses included:

"In a museum one can find pottery."

"It must be very nice there."

"There are painters in there."

"My aunt makes beautiful paintings with her brushes."

"Museum...what is that?"

"There are statues in there... Haven't you seen?"

"If I draw something will you take it to the museum?"

When the pre-service teachers announced the planned visit to the museum children appeared enthusiastic and happy. The visit was planned to stimulate the interest of children. The pre-service teachers chose two areas located in the basement and one area in the first floor of the museum, hosting part of the permanent collection. The areas were easily accessible and connected. Children were left free to make their own choices during the visit, by exploring the place and responding to the art works. Children approached mostly large constructions, colorful artworks and artworks depicting a familiar or favorite subject matter (Fig. 5.4). These findings are consistent with other research studies in museum settings (e.g. Anderson et al, 2002; Savva & Trimis, 2005a, 2005b). In most cases they experienced the three dimensional space of the artwork and the placement of forms in relation to each other (Savva & Trimis, 2005). In some cases their preferences for large-scale exhibits was associated with kinesthetic or tactile experiences (Anderson et al, 2002). For example children had approached and shown their interest for the works: *Gong* by Takis (1978), *Development in Four Elements* by Giannis Boutea (1992), *Danse Macabre* by John Tinguely (1969), and *Condolences* by Jean Pierre Raynaud, (1963) (see http://www.mmca.org.gr). Comments made about Takis' *Gong* included:

"It is a slide and it goes very high."

"It's a large street... an uphill road"

"I am sliding and I fall on the sand"

"I am on the mountain and I am skiing"

Phase 2: Enrichment and Production

Back to the school, the next day, the pre-service teachers enriched the program with various found materials; they discussed with the children the functions, origins and properties of the materials, linking them to everyday life. The children observed, compared, selected and grouped a variety of found materials. Following this, they were encouraged to play with the materials and use their senses (touch, smell, hearing). They started talking about the properties and characteristics of the materials and their intentions to use them:

"I have the bigger box...bigger than yours."

"These bottles of Coca Cola can be the huge ears for my bunny."

"I will use grass, shells and stones to make designs."

They started working mostly individually and a few in groups, and talked about their choices in relation to artists' work and choices of materials in the museum. This was an opportunity for the children to reclaim, transform, and recycle found materials into something useful, the ordinary into something special and meaningful. They worked with enthusiasm and announced their intentions, although many of them changed these during the process. It was apparent that children were fully engaged in the process of making and responded with great interest to the materials.

Fig. 5.4 Children explore the works of art

Phase 3: Reflection

The children's constructions were exhibited, and children were encouraged to look, observe carefully, describe their work and others' works, express their opinion, and try to remember initial intentions (Trimis, 1996). They talked about the artistic process, technical difficulties and they created their own stories and titles about their artworks: "I put the bottle in order to make a tower where fairies live" and "I painted the shell red in order to give a gift to the fairy."

Phase 4: Enrichment

The pre-service teachers decided that a second visit to the museum might provide children with the opportunity to be more acquainted with the museum environment and to look at and interact with artworks intimately (Trimis & Savva, 2004). The children recognized immediately the *chorotopos* of the museum as soon as they approached in the vicinity. Inside the museum they seemed better oriented and familiar with the place. Although they revisited artworks that they had found interesting during their first visit, they also observed artworks that at the first visit were not noticed. For example, they noticed and carefully observed *Wings* by Dionysopoulos Pavlos (1970), made of poster paper and plexiglass. The artwork provoked their imagination and interest:

> *"These are wings which were made in the old times."*

> *"Maybe Dedalos and Icarus made them."*

> *"They fell from a huge bird."*

> *"These are fairy or angel wings."*

They closed their eyes and pretended to enter the artwork saying:

> *"The wind is blowing me."*

> *"I feel as though I am flying very high"*

> *"it is perfect to be among the clouds."*

> *"I am wearing them and I am flying to my village."*

Children approached many artworks that they had observed during their previous visit. However, this time they found an opportunity to observe these same artworks more closely and in different ways. Also, in this second visit, children were more expressive and engaged in approaching artworks. For instance, they were leaning, moving, kneeling, lying on the floor, and pointing with their finger, extremely attentive and very interesting to observe the details. In many cases, they interacted with each other, adding onto each other's comments. For example, they started moving and improvising stories when viewing John Tinguely's (1969)

Danse Macabre. They observed other elements and details of the artwork that they did not notice the previous time. "Oh…here is again my little skeleton…I am taking him by the hand and we dance together." The pre-service teachers commented that they didn't expect the second visit to last so long, since the children knew about the place and the exhibits, and they were surprised for their unending interest and their positive disposition to observe the artworks in-depth. It appears that the repeated visits help children familiarize with the museum environment, the *chorotopos*, and to get better acquainted with artworks (Savva & Trimis, 2005a, 2005b; Trimis & Savva, in press). This apparently could play a significant role in understanding art (e.g. Hein, 1998; Silverman, 1995).

Phase 5: Production

The pre-service teachers motivated the children to recall experiences during their museum visit by asking them to refer to what they remembered or impressed them. They expressed positive views about the museum and the artworks. In many cases they described the artworks by referring to the materials (e.g. the "wings made of glass") or to specific details or elements depicted on the artworks. Then, they proposed to children to proceed to work with found materials in order to create their own constructions. The materials had already been enriched by the pre-service teachers and the children with more natural and man-made materials. In many cases the explorations of new materials suggested the theme (Trimis, 1996; Trimis & Savva, 2004). During the process children commented on the work of artists in the museum. A group of children decided to make wreaths like the ones in the museum (see Jean Pierre Raynaud's (1963) *Condolences*), and since the found material was considered inappropriate by them, they suggested a malleable material. Thus the pre-service teachers provided children with flour and water to produce dough with which the children made a wreath decorated with flowers. Although pre-service teachers helped whenever asked by children, this time the children were much more acquainted in handling the materials, working with them while using different techniques and approaches.

Phase 6: Reflection

The artworks of children were exhibited so that children could have the opportunity to talk about them. They discussed their art works, described the process and commented on the work of their peers. In some cases it was apparent that there was an influence of what they observed in the museum with what they have made in the class "It is not like the table in the museum that squeezes olives ….its for eating our dinner." It was also obvious that the three dimensional material enabled children to express more complex situations and themes. The next day, while the artworks were still exhibited children from the neighboring kindergarten classroom were invited to observe them. In a playful environment, the visiting children were introduced to the exhibits. They expressed their views and discussed with their classmates the exhibited constructions trying to guess the themes and the materials used. They were very much interested and they wanted to create their own, so they borrowed found materials while more materials were added by their teacher to make their constructions in their own school setting.

After a few days, the pre-service teachers engaged the children in a discussion in order to have a final reflection starting from the very beginning of the program and the first day of the visit to the museum, to the last day of the exhibition and the visit of their classmates. Children tried to remember all the procedures. They discussed their first visit to the museum and remembered the name of the museum, mentioned their preferences of the exhibited work in the museum, the materials used by the artists and they gave their own titles to the artworks. "...these materials are taken for recycling and from there, they take them new." "Artists in the Museum of Contemporary Art, they are *contemporized* and make artwork." Children's preferences were focused on particular artworks which were mentioned by their given titles.

The arrangement of exhibits and the open space appeared to be a significantly positive influence for children's experiences in the museum. It gave them opportunities for examining closely the exhibited work. The second visit enabled children to observe not only the external characteristics of the artwork but focused on the creations of imaginative stories inspired by the theme of the artwork, giving meaning to the exhibited work. They were extremely engaged in approaching specific artworks and in the meanwhile their experiences were creative and enjoyable. It was observed that the children elaborated upon their verbal responses non verbally by acting and visual representing actions observed in the exhibits (e.g., by observing an airplane on an artwork they imitated the sound of it, or the movement of the human figure). They felt familiar with the place and consciously made their choices, focused on the artwork that they were interested in, enabling them to closely observe details and thought through the artwork. The opportunity to visit again the museum made them feel comfortable and familiar with the place.

Conclusions

These research studies explored 1) how the pre-service teachers implemented in-depth programs incorporating museum visits, 2) how children respond to art in different museum environments, and 3) how the in-depth approach facilitated the children's artistic learning.

The pre-service teachers' participation in the studies was facilitated by the in-depth approach. It gave them a framework to organize and implement their program, linking making with observing (thinking in, and about, art). They felt positive and more confident in planning similar future programs incorporating various visits in museums and other cultural settings. It provided them with an opportunity to plan and implement sequential and constructive art activities in contrast with fragmented art activities that usually take place in early childhood settings. In all studies, making and observing art (preferably authentic art) was found to be an essential part of the educational programs, a finding consistent with research studies applying in-depth programs (Savva & Trimis, 2005a, 2005b; Trimis, 1996; Trimis & Savva, 2004; Trimis & Savva, in press). Some pre-service teachers who implemented the program, suggested that time was a constraint (see Program 2, 3). For example, in Program 2, they observed that children needed more time to explore and experiment with materials (clay) and revisit the museum. However, as it is suggested, children's time in exploring and creating with art materials should not be limited when using the in-depth approach; rather, the length of activities should be determined by their needs (Trimis & Savva, 2004). Pre-service teachers reported that their experience was extremely significant and that the constraint of time was mainly due to the fact that they were implementing the program in schools were the curriculum followed by the in-service teacher did not allow them to extend their program. It is also evident that in all cases pre-service teachers were extensively trained and educated before applying the in-depth program. Their role was crucial in providing "special scaffolding to further the exploratory process in discovering and problem solving situations" (Trimis & Manavopoulos, 2001, p. 21) as well as in questioning, introducing activities to children, supporting children's active and interactive process of learning, recalling and reflecting. Thus, evidence from in-depth art education programs corroborates the views of constructivist learning theorists (e.g., Gergen, 1995; Lave & Wagner, 1991; Phillips, 1995) who argue for meaningful learning in authentic contexts and the fundamental role of the teacher.

These studies highlight several significant findings regarding children's thinking in and about art. Through in-depth programs, when considering the responses to artworks and the artistic creation of children, evidence suggests that:

- Children made meaning of exhibited artifacts based on their previous experiences and interests. In most cases they created their own stories and titles of the observed artworks and their creations and thus corroborating the views of those who believe that programs in museums emphasizing construction of meaning may deepen and expand children's artistic experiences (e.g. Durrant, 1996; Savva, 2003; Savva & Trimis, 2005a).
- Although their responses were varied depending on the type of museum, and the artworks exhibited, it was observed that, in many cases, children approached mostly large constructions, colorful artworks and artworks depicting a favorite and familiar subject. In some cases their preferences for large artworks were associated with kinesthetic or tactile experiences (see Program 3). They also described the artworks by referring to the materials or to specific details or elements depicted on the artworks. The findings are consistent with research regarding the responses of young children to painting reproductions as well as to other art objects in authentic contexts (e.g., Gardner, Winner, & Kircher, 1975; Parsons, Johnston, & Durhum, 1978; Piscitelli & Anderson, 2000; Savva, 2003; Savva & Trimis, 2005a, 2005b; Taunton, 1984; Trimis & Savva, 2004).

- It appears that the repeated visits to museums especially when these provide visitors with a friendly milieu (see Program 1, 3) help children familiarize with the museum environment, the *chorotopos*, and to get better acquainted with artworks, therefore, corroborating the view of those who assert that learning to look at art requires time and effort (Durrant, 1996).

- In some cases visits to museums (viewing artworks) seemed to enrich children's ways of representing their topic. For example in Program 1, their observations of buildings in their neighborhood, and artifacts in museums which was apparent in their constructions. In other cases (Program 2, 3) the children's making was based on the aesthetic properties inherent in the materials and their potential transformation (Epstein & Trimis, 2002; Trimis, 1996).

- The exploration of materials is considered to be significant in enabling children to represent their ideas and enhance their creative representational abilities. In all studies children linked their experiences with the material, with the process of creation of an artifact observed in museum or other cultural settings and thus they enriched their viewing and approach to artworks. They became able to understand the potential expressiveness of materials, their inherent meaning, their functions and their role in art and their everyday life (Savva & Trimis, 2005a, 2005b; Trimis, 1996). Engagement in activities such as constructing with found materials, drawing three dimensional constructions enhanced their observational skills and enabled children to experience spatial awareness and concepts like stability, balance, size etc (see Program 1, 3). Through making and observing they integrated visual arts experiences with content in other curriculum areas (environmental issues, dramatic play, and language).

- Through observations, descriptions, interpretations and reflection of their own and others' art works and in an interactive environment of learning, children increased their perceptual awareness, acquired new vocabulary, and strengthened their descriptive language power. The integration of literacy into arts experiences is supported by many educators, such as Danko-McGhee (2006) and Kerlavage (1995). In many instances, and especially during viewing contemporary artworks (Program 3), children used their imagination to move beyond concrete situations by giving new meanings to artifacts observed (Duffy, 1998; Savva & Trimis, 2005a, 2005b).

- Making meaning about art (whether archeological, contemporary or architecture), and in relation to their environment, appears to be significant in constructing children's views about art. Children became culturally sensitized and their learning enhanced. In all cases they realized that art is more than a painting, and that many materials and many ways can be used to visualize experiences, ideas, and feelings. Recent literature refers to the expanded concept of art suggesting that "our daily interactions involve learning through images and objects that represent knowledge and mediate relationships between creators and viewers" (Freedman, 2003, p. 89).

Considering the responses and artistic creation of children, evidence suggests that their everyday habits and customs are powerful mediators when linked with their experiences and the creation of objects (Savva & Trimis, 2005). These studies support the constructivist learning theories, and demonstrate personal meaning making can be very influential in young visitors' responses and follow trends in aesthetic development that state that familiarity with art can play a significant role in understanding art (Hein, 1998; Housen, 1987; Silverman, 1995). Thus we assert that children should be allowed to construct personal knowledge from places, people and objects and through interactions between object, properties and their own previous experiences and thoughts in an interactive environment of learning (Trimis & Savva, in press). It is suggested that repeated visits to art museums and to other places of cultural interest (contact with a range of visual art forms) in their *chorotopos*, along with provisions for rich and lasting opportunities for material exploration, invention and transformation are important components for art learning and are central to an in-depth visual art program.

References

Anderson, D., Piscitelli, B., Weier, K., Everett, M., & Tayler, C. (2002). Children's museum experiences: Identifying powerful mediators of learning. *Curator, 45*(3), 213-231.

Danko-McGhee, K. (2006). Favorite artworks chosen by young children in a museum setting. *International Journal of Education through Art, 2*(3), 223-235.

Duffy, B. (1998). *Supporting creativity and imagination in the early years.* Buckingham: UK: Open University Press.

Durrant, S. R. (1996). Reflections on museum education at Dulwich picture gallery. *Art Education, 49*(1), 15-24.

Epstein, A. S., & Trimis, E. (2002). *Supporting young artists: The development of the visual arts in young* children. Yipsilanti, MI: High Scope Educational Research Foundation.

Falk, J. H., & Dierking, L.D. (2000). *Learning from museums: Visitor experiences and the making of meaning.* Walnut Creek, CA: AltaMira Press.

Freedman, K. (2003). *Teaching visual culture. Curriculum, aesthetics and the social life of art.* New York: Teachers College Press.

Gardner, H., Winner, E., & Kircher, M. (1975). Children's conceptions of art. *Journal of Aesthetic Education, 9*(3), 60-77.

Gardner, H., & Perkins, D. (1989). *Art, Mind and Education. Research from Project Zero.* Champaign, IL: University of Illinois Press.

Gergen, K. J. (1995). Social construction and the educational process. In L.P. Steffe and J. Gale. (Eds.), *Constructivism in education* (p. 17-39). Mahwah, NJ: Lawrence Erlbaum.

Hein, G. E. (1998). *Learning in the Museum.* London: Routledge.

Hohmann, M., & Weikart, D. P. (2002). *Educating young children: Active leaning practices for preschool and child care programs.* Ypsilanti, MI: High Scope Press.

Hooper-Greenhill, E. (1991). *Museum and gallery education.* Leicester, UK: Leicester University Press.

Hooper-Greenhill, E., & Mousouri, T. (2002). *Researching learning in museums and galleries 1990-1999: A bibliography review.* Leicester, UK: University of Leicester Research Centre.

Housen, A. (1987). Three methods for understanding museum audiences. *Museum Studies Journal, 2*(4), 41-50.

Kerlavage, M. (1995). A bunch of naked ladies and a tiger: Children's responses to adult works of art. In C. Thompson (Ed.), The visual art in early childhood learning (pp. 56-62). Reston VA: National Art Association.

Lave, J., & Wenger, E. (1991). *Situated learning: Legitimate peripheral participation*. Cambridge: Cambridge University Press.

Parsons, M., Jorhnston, M., & Durham, R. (1978). Developmental stages in children's aesthetic responses. *Journal of Aesthetic Education, 12*(1), 83-104.

Piscitelli, B., & Anderson, D. (2000). Young children's learning in museum settings. *Visitor Studies Today, 3*(3), 1-20.

Philips, D. C. (1995). The good, the bad and the ugly: The many facets of constructivism. *Educational Researcher, 24*(7), 5-12.

Savva, A., Trimis, E., & Zachariou, A. (2004). Exploring the links between visual arts and environmental education: Experiences of teachers participating in an in-service training programme. *International Journal of Art & Design, 23*(3), 246-255.

Savva, A. (2003). Young pupils' responses to adult works of art. *Contemporary Issues in Early Childhood Education, 4*(3), 300-313.

Savva, A., & Trimis, E. (2005a). Responses of young children to contemporary art exhibits: The role of artistic experiences. *International Journal of Education and the Arts, 6*(13). Retrieved from http://www.ijea.org/v6n13/.

Savva, A., & Trimis, E. (2005b). Linking children's museum experiences with art educational programmes in pre-primary schools: The case of Cyprus Archeological Museum. *Educational Review, 39*, 115-132. (In Greek).

Silverman, L. (1995). Visitor meaning-making in museums for a new age. *Curator, 38*(3), 161-170.

Stephens, K. (1999). Primed for learning: The young child's mind. *Child Care Information Exchange, 3*, 44-48.

Taunton, M. (1984). Aesthetic responses of young children to the visual art: A review of the literature. *Journal of Aesthetic Education, 16*(3), 93-109.

Thompson, C. M. (2005). Images of the child in art and art teacher education. *Art Education, 58* (2), 18-24.

Trimis, E. (1996). A developmental art program for pre-school education based on the principles of holistic an in-depth approach method. O.M.E.P (In Greek). *Researching the Child's World, 2*, 137-151. (In Greek)

Trimis, E., & Manavopoulos, C. (2001). Promoting the creative abilities of young children through a visual art program with seemingly scrap materials. In Kouth, E. (Ed.) *Research in the pre school educational, instructive methodology* (pp. 115-132). Athens: Tipothito. (In Greek)

Trimis, E., & Savva, A. (2004). The in-depth studio approach: Incorporating an art museum program into a pre-primary classroom. *Art Education, 57*(6), 20-36.

Trimis, E., & Savva, A. (*in press*). Artistic learning in relation to young children's chorotopos: An in depth approach to early childhood visual culture education. *Early Childhood Education Journal*.

Eli Trimis
Aristotle University of Thessaloniki
Thessaloniki Greece
and
European University
Nicosia   Cyprus

Eli Trimis is a visual artist and associate professor at the Faculty of Education, School of Early Childhood Education Sciences, Aristotle University of Thessaloniki. She also taught in the Fine Arts School at the same university and as a visiting professor in the Department of Education, University of Cyprus. Presently, teaches at European University in Cyprus. She is the coordinator of the educational programs at Telloglio Arts Foundation (affiliated with Aristotle University of Thessalloniki).

Andri Savva
University of Cyprus
Nicosia   Cyprus

Dr. Andri Savva lectures on courses related to art and aesthetic education in the Department of Education, University of Cyprus. She has worked as a teacher in primary schools and as a curriculum development officer in the Cyprus Ministry of Education and Culture. Her research interests are concerned with the role of artists in education, the development of art education programs in early childhood settings, and teachers' training in arts education. She has published on aspects of arts education in national and international journals.

We express our special thanks to the pre-service teachers for their contribution to the above studies (Maria Loukovitou, Kefala Anna, Tasiouka Alexia, Zimara Pavlina, Kasini Maritsa, Kostea Panayiota), and the children who offered us an enormous amount of images and icons full of joy and knowledge.

Chapter 6
A Circle of Friends:

Re-envisioning Art Learning and Individual Difference in the Classroom

Paula G. Purnell

Abstract Two critical aspects of providing equity and excellence in education for all children are 1) how we perceive individual differences and 2) how we assess students' talents and abilities. In this chapter, I will provide an overview of the historical antecedents that have shaped our current policies and practices related to art learning and individual difference, and suggest that a fundamental shift in perception is needed; away from the deficit model toward an asset model; away from a culture based on perceived limitations toward a culture of presumed competency.

Keywords Art learning, individual difference, differently-abled students, curriculum, instruction, assessment, deficit model, asset model, presumed competency, inclusive classrooms

> Happy are they who see beautiful things in modest places where others see nothing. Everything is beautiful. The whole thing is knowing how to interpret. (Camille Pissarro, (as cited in Maloon, 2005. p. 18).

Painter Camille Pissarro (1830-1903) was an ardent observer of life. Despite harsh criticism from an arts establishment obsessed with realism, Pissarro continued to interpret his world of dappled light and vibrant color until, eventually, others embraced his new way of seeing. In teaching, as in art, perception is everything. What we see, what we expect to see, and how we interpret what we see influences every decision that we make in the classroom each day. Ironically, however, it is as impossible to examine one's perceptions objectively as it is to look into one's own eyes. Yet, it is unreasonable to assume that we can teach and not simultaneously transmit our expectations, values, beliefs, and ideals to our students. How we perceive each student's cognitive acuity, creativity, and potential for learning and participation is constantly being processed through the lens of our own experiences and background knowledge. Most of us have been indoctrinated, first as

---

Point Park University and Indiana University of Pennsylvania, USA

M. J. Narey (ed.), *Making Meaning.*
© Springer 2009

students and then as teachers, in an educational system that values individual achievement in language and mathematics and is based on the hierarchical categorization of students' abilities to perform specific tasks. The potential success of students whose abilities fall outside of the expected norms, or whose talents lie beyond the subjects that we test and measure, often goes unrealized.

The practice of assessing students' abilities according to their perceived limitations instead of recognizing their inherent potential is reflected in the terminology that pervades our profession. In fact, the main criterion for eligibility for special education services is "proof of intrinsic deficit" (Harry, 2007, p. 16). Certainly, it's naïve to suggest that we don't need a common lexicon to measure, assess, discuss, and address students' areas of strength and weakness. A common language is necessary in order to communicate effectively. However, the belief system that underlies the terminology – including words such as at-risk, learning challenged, special needs, disabled, and handicapped – are stigmatizing labels, rooted in the ignorance of the past, that still have the power to undermine students' sense of worth and wholeness, stunt youthful enthusiasm for self-exploration and discovery, and reinforce students' misconceptions about their differently-abled peers.

The purpose of this chapter is to critically examine some of the fundamental presumptions that we, as educators, have internalized concerning students' cognitive and creative abilities, and to explore the possibility of broadening our perceptions, definitions, and practices to include aptitudes and talents that are not adequately addressed by our current system of assessment and instruction. This discussion will include the following questions.

- What are the historical antecedents that have shaped curriculum, instruction, and assessment practices in the United States, and how do they continue to influence our perceptions of art learning and individual difference in the classroom?
- How have research and recent advances in technology broadened our understanding of ability and creativity, and what alternative educational approaches have they inspired?
- What role do individual teachers play in establishing a new model for education based on students' assets rather than deficits, and on the presumption of competence rather than projected limitations?

Just as the well-established arts schools of Pissarro's day were suspicious of new ways of seeing and interpreting the world, the educational establishment purveys a certain skepticism when theorists suggest that there is a more democratic, optimistic, respectful, and responsible way to invite students to participate fully in the construction of their own knowledge. In *The Arts and the Creation of Mind*, Elliot Eisner (2002) describes a painting lesson in which an art teacher invited his students to look at common objects in a variety of new and unique ways. Eisner concludes with a statement that we, as teachers, will do well to remember "The larger point of the lesson is that perceptual attitude is a choice, that there is more than one way to see" (p. 59).

Perceiving Possibilities

Sometimes even the smallest exchange can profoundly impact our perceptions. A few years ago I was conducting an artist residency in a fourth grade classroom. The students were preparing for the culminating event of my residency and the room buzzing with activity. Children were rehearsing their lines, trying on costumes, painting backdrops and taking up every bit of available space. In the midst of the ruckus I noticed an aide standing behind a young girl seated in a wheelchair and looking confused. Just then the teacher, a wonderful 20 year veteran, waved toward an open corner of the room and called to the aid, "Just put her over there."

I have thought of that moment and those five words, spoken in haste and without any intended malice, many times since. I have wondered what this objectifying statement revealed about the teacher's basic beliefs about the student's social status, her capacity for decision-making, and her potential for participating in classroom activities. I was reminded of Paulo Freire's warning that "Any situation in which some men prevent others from engaging in the process of inquiry is one of violence. The means used are not important; to alienate men from their own decision making is to change them into objects" (1968, p. 73). I have wondered what effect this comment might have had on the student's feelings of self-worth and competence, and how it might have influenced her classmates' perceptions of her ability to function independently.

I realize that similar statements are made by caring, dedicated, well-meaning teachers across the country each day, and while such statements may seem inconsequential to a casual observer, I believe that comments such as these are evidence of our deep sense of ambiguity about our differently-abled students. Taken collectively, these comments serve to propagate an educational culture based on limited definitions of ability and an attitude of presumed incompetence. The fact that this statement is so unextraordinary is why it begs our critical examination – because ultimately, *nothing* that a teacher says or does in the classroom is inconsequential. "To a great extent, students develop expectations for competencies for themselves and others based on the teacher's public evaluations of classroom performance" (Lotan, 2006, p. 38). The influence over attitudes that teachers can unwittingly wield is why it is so important to critically examine the foundations of our beliefs and question the criteria on which we base our evaluations of each student's classroom performance.

Curriculum and Instruction

If I were to draw a diagram representing our current practices in curriculum and instruction it would look like a target. The center, or bull's eye, would include reading, writing, mathematics, and to some degree, science. Also occupying the center of the target would be those students whose physical and cognitive abilities fall within expected norms. Everything else – all of the other subjects like history, geography, art, music, and physical education; and all of the students whose tested abilities measure above or below the norm – would lie somewhere in the outer rings of the target. Throughout our nation's history the target's center in proportion to the outlying rings has expanded and constricted according to the current political and social trends (See Table 6.1). The traditional target model, however, has remained basically unchanged.

Table 6.1. Historical Antecedents related to Art Learning and Individual Differences in Education in the United States

Time Period	Art Learning	Individual Difference
Prior to the 1800's	The New England School Model emphasizes practicality, religious obedience, and economic self-reliance. The arts were not considered "academic" coursework.	No social programs exist to address the medical or educational needs of children with physical or cognitive disabilities.
Early 1800's	Noah Webster's Elementary Spelling Book (1783) extols the nationalistic themes of respect for honest work, the value of money, and the virtues of industry. Over a million copies are sold by 1875 (Webb et al, 2007).	Public institutions are created, usually at a great distance from the general population, to house and educate children and adults with disabilities. Early institutions include the Connecticut Asylum at Hartford (1817), the New England Asylum for the Blind (1829), and the Asylum for the Idiotic and Feebleminded (1848).
Mid 1800's	Friedrich Froebel (1782-1852) develops the concept of Kindergarten founded on child-centered learning and creative play. The first Kindergarten in the United States opens in 1856.	
Mid 1900's	Progressive Education Movement describes art learning "not as a decorative addendum to the school day, but as the very embodiment of education" (Wakeford, 2004, p. 89).	Public opinion recognizes the individual's worth and dignity. Public schools begin to offer segregated educational programs for children with disabilities.
1950's	The launching of the unmanned Soviet satellite Sputnik incites "a counterrevolution against Progressive education" and a return to basic, core subjects in the classroom (Berube, 1999, p. 2).	Brown v. Board of Education enforces the federal constitutional principle of "equal protection of the laws" and recognizes segregation as inherently unequal.
1960's	New Social Contracts lead to the establishment of The National Foundation for the Arts and Humanities. New education bills provide indirect assistance for arts educators, ranging from supplemental education centers to special programs for the disadvantaged.	Concept of mainstreaming is introduced with few specific guidelines for application or enforcement. Identification and implementation is generally described as haphazard and inconsistent.
1970s	The philanthropic community publishes *Coming to Our Senses: The Significance of the Arts in American Education* arguing a social imperative for engaging students in arts-based learning across the curriculum (Quinn & Hanks, 1977).	Before 1975, children with disabilities could be denied an education solely on the basis of their disabilities. The Education for All Handicapped Children Act (EAHCA), along with some key supreme court cases, mandates all school districts educate students with disabilities.

Table 6.1 (continued)

1980s	A controversial report, A Nation at Risk: The Imperative for Educational Reform (1983) blames America's education system for the nation's failure to dominate the global economy. The "Back to Basics Movement" is rejuvenated (Bracey, 2003).	Under EAHCA (now IDEA) and Section 504 children with disabilities must be educated in the least restrictive environment, and provided free, individualized, appropriate education.
1990s	President Bush and the National Governors' Association established the first national goals in education; the arts are not mentioned. Clinton administration Education Secretary, Richard Riley, advocates for the arts in education. Goals 2000: Educate America names the arts as a core subject for the first time.	IDEA is reauthorized and calls for students with disabilities to be included in state and district-wide assessments. Regular education teachers are required to be members of the Individualized Education Program (IEP) teams.
2000s	No Child Left Behind Act of 2001 sets academic accountability measures evidenced through standardized test scores in English, math, and science. Pressure on schools to raise test scores results in a reduction of time devoted to arts instruction in schools across the country and a narrowing of the curriculum.	NCLB calls for all students, including students with disabilities, to be proficient in math and reading by the year 2010.

Note. Compiled from Berube (1999); Rothstein (2000); Wakeford (2004) and Webb, Metha & Jordan (2007)

The historical antecedents of this model can be found in the ascetic religious beliefs of the Puritans, the pragmatic needs of the early Colonists, and the limited resources of a burgeoning American society. The Puritans' anti-aestheticism and austere religious beliefs led them to reject all forms of ornamentation and embellishment. The Puritans did not deem the arts necessary to sustain colonial life and, therefore, learning in the arts was not considered serious academic coursework. Following the Revolutionary War, universal education became the new democratic ideal. Resources, however, were severely limited. Most public schools were poorly staffed and equipped, and only taught the basics of reading, writing, and arithmetic. In the early 1800s, public schools provided regimented lessons and factory-style classrooms that were designed to be cheap and efficient and to instill the virtues of obedience, orderliness, and industriousness (Webb, Metha, & Jordan, 2007). By the early 1900s national economic growth and industrialization demanded a new American educational model. Educators suggested that instruction should be child-centered and based on discovery rather than rote memorization. John Dewey (1934) and the Progressive Education Movement considered the arts, and the act of making art, a vital tool for exploring and understanding the world. The declaration of World War II in 1941 dramatically impacted public opinion and altered the nation's educational goals. During the post-war era progressive education was criticized and deemed responsible for a general decline in educational standards. In 1959 James Conant led the movement for increased academic rigor and a return to the basics in the curriculum; returning the arts to its peripheral educational role. Since the 1960s, despite abundant research indicating the social and cognitive benefits of arts-rich learning, consecutive administrations have oscillated between embracing and discarding arts education policy. This lack of consistency caused Eric Jensen (2001) to protest, "A federally mandated basic arts education policy does not exist. That's not just embarrassing and inexcusable; it's irresponsible" (p. vi).

The path toward equitable education for differently-abled students has been difficult and circuitous. Prior to the 1800s the birth of a child with physical and/or cognitive disabilities was considered a private, often shameful, family matter – not a social issue. In the early nineteenth century educational reformers began to develop segregated programs designed to teach children with disabilities basic life skills so that they could become more independent and, eventually, productive citizens. Children whose abilities did not align with the limited educational opportunities available, however, often languished in isolation. It is remarkable to note that as late as the 1975 more than half of the children with disabilities in the United States were still receiving either inappropriate, segregated educational services or were not attending school at all (Rothstein, 2000).

Art learning and individual differences share a history of inconsistent policies and practices in the United States. The lack of a common vision has resulted in narrow definitions of ability and academic achievement, which form the basis of our in-class evaluations of individual student's performance. The narrow scope of our perception is reflected in our current assessment methods and is also evidenced in our students' attitudes about their own talents and abilities, as well as the talents and abilities of others.

Assessment

My writing is informed by my experiences as a faculty member, a professional development instructor, and years of being a teaching artist and an outreach presenter for an organization serving children with disabilities and their families. Recently, I visited a third grade class for a workshop on disability awareness. Following a skit illustrating some of the challenges that a child with a learning disability might confront in school, one skeptical student raised his hand and asked "How can you be smart and still not be able to write your own name?" "That's a good question." I answered. "Let's try something." I invited the students to each hold a piece of paper on their forehead and write their name on it. When my dubious, young friend looked at his paper he was surprised to see that he'd written most of the letters in his name backwards. "So," I asked, "Are you still smart?"

Like this student, it can be hard for us to conceive of a kind of smart that exists outside of our own limited experiences. A child with Dysgraphia or autism may have a very difficult time proving his "smarts" to teachers and fellow students who believe that cognitive abilities are mirrored by the student's writing and speaking skills. In the same way, it is unlikely that a child's visual acuity or musical sense will be recognized by administering traditional paper and pencil tests. Janet Olson (1992) examined the plight of visual learners whose unique strengths, abilities, and talents continue to be overlooked by our verbal-centric assessments. Visuals learners process information and create meaning through images rather than words. Olson considered the growing number of children being diagnosed with learning disabilities and wondered "Could it possibly be that many, if not most, of these children are visual learners and they simply do not respond to the traditional verbal approach to learning?" (p. 114). Assessing students solely on their verbal-linguistic skills has created a system that labels verbal learners "normal" while visual learners are thought to be are somehow "defective." A child might demonstrate excellent spatial perception, visual memory skills, and the ability to reproduce exact detail but still be diagnosed as having minimal brain damage (MBD). Olson asks, "If a child cannot learn to draw, play the piano, or dismantle and reassemble an engine, shouldn't they also be considered brain damaged?" (p. 114). The majority of our current assessment practices, however, are designed to serve the "uniform approach" to education, in which the same narrow subject matter is conveyed in the same way to all of the students. By ranking students according to their ability to perform on a narrow set of subject-specific tasks, our assessments validate the perception that the most important subjects are those which can be quantified using normed instruments, such as mathematics and science, while "Those disciplines that prove most refractory to formal testing, such as the arts, are least valued" (Gardner, 1993, p. 165). Remediation for visual learners under this one-size-fits-all system of assessment usually consists of teaching the same material, just presented at a slower pace. "More words," Olson laments "words, words, words" (1992, p. 115).

Educational assessment hasn't always been the one-dimensional, monolithic, multibillion dollar industry that we know in the 21st century. In the apprenticeship model of assessment, an apprentice worked under the tutelage of a master, and assessment was immediate, authentic, and simple: the master gave the apprentice a task and when it was completed to the master's satisfaction the student moved on to a new set of skills. In a somewhat similar manner, students attending early American one-room school houses brought learning materials from home and worked to improve their academic skills independently under the teacher's guidance. It wasn't long, however, before educational reformers decided that education needed to be more structured and that the curriculum should follow a hierarchical sequence, moving logically from simple to more complicated tasks. Efforts to create a sequential scheme that could move students through the curriculum in an organized way resulted in a public school system shaped like a pyramid. The large base represented all of the children attending common schools. Each level of the pyramid became increasingly narrow, as the academic content became more advanced and successful students were passed onto the next grade level. Those who were less academically successful either stayed behind or left school altogether. Each consecutive grade level naturally resulted in a more concentrated grouping of students with strong academic abilities and also, not coincidentally, greater economic resources. Privileged students generally excelled and matriculated while the majority of working-class students left school to join the job force after completing 8th grade.

This process of student classification was self-determining, albeit weighted in favor of those with higher social status. Then, in 1904, French psychologist, Alfred Binet, developed research investigating a scientific method for measuring human intelligence._ He had hoped that his research would help to identify children whose low performance skills indicated a need for special education. Instead, Intelligence Quotient (IQ) testing was implemented en masse to determine which students would succeed in school and which were most likely to fail. IQ testing aligned perfectly with the industrial zeitgeist of the day, and soon mass testing dominated the educational field – with far reaching ramifications. In 1993 Howard Gardner voiced concern that the United States had "embraced formal testing to an excessive degree" (p. 161) and was in danger of becoming a "complete testing society" (p. 164). Eight years later, the No Child Left Behind Act of 2001 (NCLB) reauthorized the Elementary and Secondary Education Act (ESEA) and implemented new academic accountability measures to be evidenced through standardized test scores in English, math, and science. Pressure on schools to raise test scores, along with other social and political factors, has resulted in the further alienation of students with limited verbal and writing skills (Rabkin & Redmond, 2006), a decline in the amount of time devoted to arts instruction in school districts across the country (Chapman, 2007), and a serious narrowing of the curriculum (Laitsch, 2006). Teachers, therefore, must maintain vigilance in order to recognize and support students' strengths and abilities that are not measured or valued in the current climate of testing. Recent research and evolving technologies are providing exciting, new tools to help us broaden our understanding of intelligence, creativity, and the human experience.

Research and Technology: Knowing What We Don't Know

The first step to knowledge is to know that we are ignorant. (Lord David Cecil, as cited in Peter, 1977, p. 279).

Because of my limited perception, I almost missed meeting a remarkable student. I was conducting an artist residency at an elementary school in northwestern Pennsylvania. My presence was a disruption to the normal classroom routine and this was of special concern to a boy named Teddy. Teddy was taller than his classmates and he did not speak. When I would begin moving desks to make additional space, or the class would burst into a loud cacophony on their homemade instruments, Teddy would edge closer to the door, rocking. If the noise became too great he'd slip into the hall with a member of his therapeutic support staff (TSS) and watch us intently through the window. I'd smile welcomingly when Teddy returned to class, and wave understandingly to his TSS when he would leave, but that was the extent of my one-on-one interaction with Teddy. On the last day of my residency the teacher invited the students to draw pictures of their favorite residency activity. I am sorry to admit that my reaction to Teddy's drawing was one of surprise. I was surprised by the deliberate lines and the accurate sense of perspective evident in his drawing, both of which were more advanced than his peers'. I was also surprised to see that he had chosen to draw the Native American Unity Dance: a picture of smiling children, holding hands, standing in a close-knit circle. I realized that I had made many erroneous assumptions about Teddy. I had assumed, imagined, and projected what I believed he had seen, felt, and experienced during my residency.

I am glad that as teachers we are able to learn from our mistakes. I can't reclaim the lessons that Teddy might have taught me or the artistic skills and emotional depth that he might have shared with his classmates. I can, however, recognize how much we, as educators, still don't know about the internal lives of our students. I can listen closely to the researchers, theorists, students, and fellow teachers who are trying to develop more equitable teaching approaches and strategies; and I can remember Howard Gardner's words "Education that is geared toward fostering understanding cannot be readily achieved but is the only education worth striving for" (1993, p. 160)

It's heartening to know that while art learning and individual differences may have historically occupied outlying areas in our educational system they are currently at the core of exciting, new research and technologies that are expanding our understanding of the human experience. Like keys opening previously locked doors, they allow us to communicate in ways that were previously impossible. Consider, for example, an article coauthored by Douglas Biklen and Jamie Burke (2006). As part of a research project thirteen years earlier Biklen had observed Burke who, at that time, was a nonverbal preschooler. In the intervening years, Burke had become an articulate young man and was able to type and simultaneously speak words using an electronic communication board. In this remarkable encounter, Biklen asked Burke to describe his early school experiences.

> When I was growing up, speaking was so frustrating. I could see the words in my brain but then realized that making my mouth move would make those words come alive, they died as soon as they were born. What made me feel angry was to know that I knew exactly what I was to say and my brain was retreating in defeat. I felt so mad as teachers spoke in their childish voices to me, mothering me, but not educating me (p. 169).

It's painful to realize that any one of us could have easily played the role of the overly maternal teacher; but we can forgive our own ignorance. The bigger issue is: how do we change our practices in light of new evidence indicating a level of intellectual competence that we did not previously recognize in students with limited verbal abilities? Biklen suggests,

> In short, the outside observer (e.g., teacher, parent, diagnostician, associate) has a choice; either to determine that the person is incompetent (i.e., severely mentally retarded by APA definition) or to admit that one cannot know another's thinking unless the other can reveal it. The latter is actually the more conservative choice. It refuses to limit opportunity; by presuming competence (p. 167).

   Biklen and Burke remind us that perceptual attitude is a choice. Jamie Burke's story underscores the consequences of a system in which students can be placed in diagnostic categories, such as severe mental retardation, not because their task performance indicates a specific intellectual capacity, but because of the students' inability to provide written or verbal evidence of his or her true cognitive abilities. Janet Olson (1992) recognized the impact that the narrow categorization of students has had on the lives of visual learners, and admonishes us to be more responsive to students' distinct modes of communication. "Art is actually a kind of language and a form of communication that gives form to personal ideas, feelings, and experiences that can be shared with others" (p. 150). The internationally acclaimed Reggio Emilia preschools, which were developed in the 1940s in Northern Italy, also recognize that it is imperative that children find the form of communication that best suits the child's individual style, personality, and preferences. Children in Reggio Emilia programs are encouraged to explore and demonstrate linguistic concepts through arts-based experiences including graphic arts, music, drama, and puppetry. Children's diverse modes of self-expression, including painting, dancing, sculpting, or singing, are referred to as the many "languages" of children. "These various forms of representation strengthen the development of mental schemas and allow every child a voice" (Fawcett & Hay, 2004, p. 236).

   Many educators understand through empirical evidence that there is a wonderful diversity in how children learn and how they communicate their learning to others. Current brain research concurs and supports an individualized, multiability approach to assessment and instruction. Scientists and neuroscientists are mapping the mind/body connection and discovering an integrated cognitive system which incorporates physical, sensory, and emotional components to create meaning. These recent discoveries have important implication for learning in and through the arts. Participation in the visual arts, for instance, draws on the frontal lobes for processing, occipital lobes for visual input, the cerebellum for movement, and the mid-brain for emotional response (Jensen, 2001). Researchers are also documenting the brain's powerful interaction with musical experiences and recording the changes it affects in emotion, respiration, and heartbeat (Reimer, 2004). Research reveals a great diversity among human brains; not only is there variation in the specific neural processes utilized by individual brains, but the life experiences of individuals may actually impact the physical development of the brain (Johnson, 2004).

   The uniform school approach and industrial school model have validated the development of curriculum and assessment materials designed to address the needs of the mythical "average student." Brain research is helping us understand that there simply is no such animal. Teachers are regularly encouraged to modify and adapt existing materials to accommodate students identified as having "special" needs. In reality all children have special learning needs that spring from their individual interests, talents, abilities, and life experiences. The question we need to ask is not how can we tweak our current practices to better accommodate a small number of "special" students, but rather, how can we fundamentally change curriculum, instruction, and assessment to accommodate our expanding understanding of human intelligence and art learning and to best serve the learning needs of all students? Perhaps the most appropriate response is a sort of radical optimism; an educational framework built on the presumed competence of all students.

Rachel Lotan (2006) offers a practical approach to this challenge. She suggests that "teachers create curriculum, instruction, and assessments deliberately and purposefully to address the range of previous academic achievement and academic skills, the linguistic variability, and the intellectual diversity found in heterogeneous classrooms" (p. 33). In other words, discard the mass produced, one-size-fits-all approach and instead make the most of the wonderful array of talents and abilities that exist in every classroom. She proposes a systematic approach to building equitable classrooms based on equal-status interactions, a reconceptualization of intellectual competence, and an inclusive pedagogy utilizing multi-ability tasks. The multiple-ability orientation invites students to solve complex problems using a wide range of intellectual abilities in addition to traditional reading, writing, and calculating, such as drawing, model building, and role-playing. Students' artistic talents, creativity, leadership qualities, and critical thinking skills become valued classroom assets as students learn to use their own individual strengths and, at the same time, recognize the abilities of others, as they work to discover solutions together.

In the traditional educational model the potential successes of students whose abilities fall outside of the expected norms, or whose talents lie beyond the subjects that we currently test and measure, are simply off the map. New strategies are now being developed that take advantage of recent advances in research and technology and offer a more democratic, balanced approach to education. Effectively implementing these strategies, however, will require a fundamental shift in perspective: from the deficit model and the presumption of incompetence, toward an assets model and presumed competency for all students; from a narrow curriculum and hierarchical assessments, toward an equitable pedagogy and multiple-ability orientation; and from a classroom social structure of exclusion and alienation, toward a democratic system that recognizes the unique and important contributions of each member.

Joining the Circle Dance

How we define and address students' cognitive and physical differences; and how we define and address individual students' talents and abilities are two critical components in providing equity and excellence in education for all children. These issues, however, have not traditionally occupied a central role in the evolution of educational practice and policy in America's public schools. The general lack of focus surrounding these issues has left many teachers feeling unprepared to effectively address student diversity and art learning in their classrooms. One investigation found that only 40% of the general classroom teachers surveyed felt competent and prepared to include students with disabilities in their classrooms, and more than 90% reported that they "do not have adequate knowledge about the specific characteristics and health care needs of students with various disabilities" (Singh, 2001, p. 22).   Similarly, teachers have resoundingly acknowledged low self-efficacy in their own creative abilities and in their ability to teach the creative arts to their students (Burton, Horowitz, & Abeles, 1999; Conway, Hibbard, Albert, & Hourigan, 2005; McKean, 2001). At the same time, many teachers are finding that the demands of meeting the needs of an increasingly culturally and linguistically diverse student population, along with the day-to-day realities of documenting and processing the growing number of students identified as needing learning support services, are simply overwhelming. One teacher told me recently "Each day we're given more to do, but they never take anything away!" I have met teachers who have decided to wait-out the implications of NCLB, knowing that a new administration will bring a new batch of policies and legislation. Recognizing that they can't control national politics or social trends, many teachers choose, instead, to focus on the things that they can control. They strive daily to be the most responsive, nurturing, well-informed teacher that they can be. There is certainly logic and merit to this approach, but there is also a danger. The danger is that until teachers affect policy, administrations will continue to come and go and nothing will fundamentally change. The educational value of learning in the arts has been described as effective but not efficient (Jensen, 2001). In other words, the evidence of higher standardized test scores that politicians need to prove the effectiveness of policy changes can't be produced between election cycles. Policy is written from term to term, while teachers and students are in it for the long haul.

Essential change won't come from policy makers. Researchers have provided clear data indicating that our current approaches to curriculum and assessment are outdated and out of step with our student population's contemporary needs – but real change, the revolutionary kind, begins when teachers critically examine and fundamentally change their own perspectives, beliefs, and attitudes. Research, policy, and practice are like three cities built on different mountain tops, and only the most intrepid traveler is able to traverse the distance between them. I believe that only the meaningful transformation of teachers' perceptions will portend real changes in classroom practices – and that significant changes in policy will eventually follow evidence of successful practice.

The good news for teachers is that this kind of revolutionary change doesn't require that they spend their weekends on Capitol Hill, become experts on every type of learning or physical difference, or take painting or violin lessons. Changes in perception result when teachers closely observe their own classroom practices, dialogue with their students and colleagues, examine their belief systems, and cultivate an attitude of presumed competency. Paulo Freire (1968) reminds us that teachers have a responsibility to "respect the dignity, autonomy, and identity of the student" acknowledging that such educational practice demands "permanent, critical vigilance in regard to the students" (p. 62).

Transforming education from the inside out won't be easy. We will need a new vision and a new model – not a pyramid, a ladder, or a target. I would like to suggest the model so eloquently illustrated in Teddy's drawing: a circle dance. The circle dance is probably the oldest and most ubiquitous form of dance in the world. It can be found in Greek, African, Middle Eastern, Eastern European, Celtic, and North and South American indigenous cultures. Its imagery evokes qualities of interconnectedness, harmony, brother/sisterhood, and balance. In a circle dance all of the participants stand shoulder-to-shoulder and eye-to-eye. The circle expands to accommodate and welcome all who wish to join. It is not a static form, but instead changes and evolves according to shared experiences and the perception of a common rhythm.

Conclusion

> All our knowledge has its origins in our perceptions (Leonardo da Vinci, as cited in Peter, 1977, p. 280).

Inculcated by the traditional, uniform school approach, we continue to assess and instruct students according to their perceived deficits rather than their presumed competencies and potential for learning; and we continue to define academic achievement according to the hierarchical categorization of students' performance on a narrow range of specific tasks, often ignoring students' unique talents, experiences, and ways of knowing. An overview of historical antecedents illustrates that there has been little consistency or direction in educational practice and policy related to the role of art learning and individual differences in the classroom. The lack of a common vision has perpetuated a culture of testing and an ever-narrowing curriculum. Recent research and the development of new technologies, however, are expanding our conception of human intelligence and ability. In response, some educators are suggesting that what is needed is a fundamental shift in perception: away from the deficit model, toward an asset model; away from a culture based on perceived limitations to a culture of presumed competency. Revolutionary change, however, won't come from policy makers or mass produced curriculum materials. The onus of change lies with individual teachers who are willing to critically examine their belief systems, reconceptualize limited definitions, and implement more equitable and inclusive classroom practices.

Cynics may contend that perceiving possibilities is unrealistic – that it is just an effort to view the harsh realities of free, public education through rose colored glasses. But I contend that cynics have never launched a revolution. A revolution begins when one person acknowledges an injustice and takes personal responsibility for making fundamental changes to the status quo. When a system subjugates the role of art and creativity in the lives of children, and continues to define individual differences as pathologies, I believe that a great injustice is being served, not only to individual children, but to our culture and society as a whole. Revolution begins with an individual making a conscious decision to change his or her perceptions and practices; in this case, a teacher choosing to perceive the possibilities rather than the deficits, and to create a culture of inclusion rather than segregation. Teachers wield great power to influence individual lives; by inviting students to join together in a circle of friends, teachers have the power to change the world.

References

Berube, M. R. (1999). Arts and education. *Clearing House, 72*(3), 150-153.

Biklen, D., & Burke, J. (2006). Presuming competence. *Equity & Excellence in Education, 39*, 166-175.

Bracey, G. W. (2003). April foolishness: The 20th anniversary of A Nation at Risk. *Phi Delta Kappan, 84*(8), 616 622.

Burton, J., Horowitz, R., & Abeles, H. (1999). Learning in and through the arts: Curriculum implications. In E. Fisk (Ed.), *Champions of change: The impact of the arts on learning* (pp. 36-46). New York: Center for Arts Education Research, Teachers College, Columbia University.

Chapman, L. (2007). An update on No Child Left Behind and national trends in education. *Arts Education Policy Review, 109*(1), 25-36.

Conway, C., Hibbard, S., Albert, D., & Hourigan, R. (2005). Professional development for arts teachers. *Arts Education Policy Review, 107*(1), 3-9.

Dewey, J. (1934). Art as experience. New York: Perigee Books.

Eisner, E. W. (2002). *The arts and the creation of mind.* New Haven, CT: Yale University Press.

Fawcett, M., & Hay, P. (2004). 5x5x5= Creativity in the early years. *JADE, 23*(3) 234-245.

Freire, P. (1968). *Pedagogy of the oppressed.* (M.B. Ramos, Trans.). New York: Seabury.

Gardner, H. (1993). *Multiple intelligence: The theory in practice.* New York, NY: Basic Books.

Harry, B., & Klingner, J. (2007). Discarding the deficit model. *Educational Leadership, 64*(5), 16-21.

Jensen, E. (2001). *Arts with the brain in mind.* Alexandria, VA: Association for Supervision and Curriculum Development.

Johnson, L. (2005). How am I smarter? Using intelligence measures to describe arts education benefits. [Review of the article *Music lessons to enhance IQ*]. *Teaching Artist Journal, 3*(10), 270-277.

Laitsch, D. (2006). *Assessments, high stakes, and alternative visions: Appropriate use of the right tools to leverage improvement.* Tempe, AZ: Education Policy Studies Laboratory. Downloaded March 5, 2008 from http://epsl.asu.edu/epru/documents/EPSL-0611-222-EPRU.pdf

Lotan, R. (2006). Teaching teachers to build equitable classrooms. *Theory to Practice, 45*(1), 32-39.

Maloon, T. (2005). *Camille Pissarro.* Sidney, Australia: Art Gallery of New South Wales.

McKean, B. (2001). Concerns and considerations for teacher development in the arts. *Arts Education Policy Review, 102*(4), 27-32.

Murphy, M. (2006). *The history and philosophy of education: Voices of educational pioneers.* Upper Saddle River, NJ: Pearson.

Olson, J. (1992). *Envisioning writing: Toward an integration of drawing and writing.* Portsmouth, NH: Heinmann.

Peter, L. J. (1977). *Peter's quotations: Ideas for our time.* New York: Bantam Books.

President's Committee on the Arts and Humanities. (1998). *Eloquent evidence: Arts at the core of learning* (3rd. ed.). [Brochure]. Murfee, E: Author.

Quinn, T., & Hanks, C. (Eds.). (1977). *Coming to our senses: The significance of the arts for American education.* New York: American Council for the Arts.

Rabkin, N., & Redmond, R. (2006). The arts make a difference. *Educational Leadership, 63*(5), 60-64.

Reimer, B. (2004). New brain research on emotion and feeling: Dramatic implications for music education. *Arts Education Policy Review, 106*(2), 21-27.

Rothstein, L. (2000). *Special education law* (3rd ed.). New York: Longman.

Singh, D. (2001). *Are general classroom teachers prepared to teach students with physical disabilities?* Paper presented at the Annual Convention of the Council for Exceptional Children, Kansas City, MO. (ERIC Document Reproduction Service No. ED455635)

Spring, J. (2005). *The American school, 1642-2004* (6th ed.). New York: McGraw Hill.

Wakeford, M. (2004). A short look at a long past. In N. Rabkin & R. Redmond (Eds.), *Putting the arts in the picture: Reframing education in the 21st century* (pp. 81-106). Chicago, IL: Columbia College Chicago.

Webb, D. L., Metha, A., & Jordan, K. F. (2007). *Foundations of American education* (5th ed.). Upper Saddle River, NJ: Pearson Prentice-Hall.

Paula G. Purnell
Point Park University
Pittsburgh, PA USA
and
Indiana University of Pennsylvania
Indiana, PA USA

Dr. Paula G. Purnell teaches at Point Park University and at Indiana University of Pennsylvania. She is an award winning musician, and a rostered artist with the Pennsylvania Council on the Arts' *Artists in Education* program. Paula teaches arts-based professional development classes and presents disability awareness workshops in the greater Pittsburgh area. For the past fourteen years she has worked with students, parents, teachers, community arts organizations, and school administrators to advocate for the arts in education.

Chapter 7
Multiple Modes of Communication of Young Brazilian Children:

Singing, Drawing, and English Language Learning

Sharon Cecile Switzer

Abstract A series of home visits with a group of Brazilian immigrant families of three and four year olds refutes the premise that financially disadvantaged immigrant children do not receive support for their learning at home. Parents and other family members participate in developing their children's literacy skills, and were observed engaging in a variety of communicative practice, such as singing, drawing, or dramatic play. In this qualitative study approximately 60 home visits were conducted to observe the focal children in their daily home environments. Observed communicative events were coded for type of modality, such as dramatic play, singing, drawing, video, photographs, and art. Data derived from observations of multimodal literacy events revealed that the greatest frequency of such literacy events occurred in dramatic play. In addition, themes identifying the purpose of the multimodal literacy events, often related to relationship building between parent and child, as well as themes related to maintaining relationships and connections to the homeland. Implications for practitioners involve recognizing the numerous multimodal literacy experiences children experience at home before formal schooling, as well as the need for sensitivity on the part of teachers regarding the importance of extended family relationships and connections to the homeland.

Keywords literacy, Head Start, young children, family literacy, emergent literacy, early childhood, immigrant children, immigration, early literacy, ethnography

East Stroudsburg University of Pennsylvania, USA

M. J. Narey (ed.), Making Meaning.

Language and the communicative skills associated with its symbolic representation grow and develop out of a context that includes culture, history, and socioeconomic influences. Paulo Freire emphasized the critical connection between language and the socio-cultural and historical context in which communication takes place. "The language that we use to talk about this or that and the way we give testimony are, nevertheless, influenced by the social, cultural, and historical conditions of the context in which we speak and testify" (Freire, 1998, p. 58). Language influences and constitutes the spoken context of communication, even as the context of communication, including its social, cultural, historic, and economic aspects, influences language. Indeed, all learning arises from, and is dependent on, the context. It is for this reason that my study of the literacy practices of a group of young Brazilian children examines the home context, as well as the cultural, historical, and socioeconomic background of the families in which they live.

Existing evidence indicates that the beginning of children's literacy and language development occurs through oral language interactions with the adults around them (Bissex, 1980; Chall and Snow, 1982; Heath, 1983; Scollon & Scollon, 1981; Taylor; 1983; Taylor & Dorsey-Gaines, 1988). Parents, in playing and talking with their children, provide valuable language and pre-literacy experiences for them (Butler and Clay, 1987; Dickinson, 1994; Larrick, 1982; Morrow, 1993). Existing research, however, has focused primarily on monolingual families, and on print-based modes of communication.

The purpose of this study was to examine the symbolic communicative and language-based activities observed in homes of Head Start children where Brazilian Portuguese was the home language. In analyzing this data, other modes of communication in addition to print were of particular interest.

Communicative Practice and Literacy

What does literacy mean? It is more than decoding and answering comprehension questions. Recent literature sets it in a larger sphere. Literacy events are defined as occasions in which literacy is an integral part of the activity (Barton, 1998; Street, 1987, 1997). This research draws from a study of the uses of print in the home environments of young Brazilian children. Analysis of the data from that study revealed that children engaged in a variety of modes of communication, in addition to verbal expression. I, therefore, re-examined these data using a broader definition of literacy to include multiple modes of meaning-making in the communicative practices observed in the homes.

Grillo (1989) uses the term *communicative practices* to refer to the "social activities through which language or communication is produced" (p. 15). Grillo, then, views literacy as one type of communicative practice within a larger social context, de-emphasizing both reading and writing (together or separately) as the sole indicators of literacy. It is clear that recent trends in research have focused on understanding the broader context in which literacy develops. The broader view of literate activities as forms of communicative practice would also include drawing, singing songs, dancing, or even creating musical sounds to convey and/or evoke feeling or emotional response.

All learning takes place within the context of a situation or activity. During the child's emergent literacy phase, the family's culture has a significant influence on the child's literacy development. Literacy is linked to the institutions and settings in which it is developed. Therefore, it is important for educators to understand the cultural context of children as they develop their language and literacy skills.

Context of Language Acquisition and Literacy

If we accept the tenet that language and literacy develop, not as isolated skills, but as part of a broader context and culture, then the question that is likely to follow is: What are the ways that language and literacy develop within that context? In recent years the concept has taken hold that literacy is an emerging process that unfolds gradually and continually from birth. This is an important concept, and it is one that has framed my study of the literacy practices observed in the homes of five Brazilian immigrant families.

The development of literacy is a process that begins from the time that language begins to develop in infancy. As children develop their ability to communicate through the interactions with the adults and caregivers around them, they begin to internalize the structures and conventions of the language spoken around them. At the same time as they develop their ability to communicate effectively in that language, they are creating the foundations for the ability to communicate through the symbolic representations of that language.

In-home Practices Affecting Literacy Development of Children

The emergent literacy paradigm has brought to the forefront the pivotal importance and impact of the home and family on children's literacy. Thus, a study of the language and literacy development of young children needs to take into account the home environment because this is the context in which the language and literacy development of these children is taking place.

Multiple Modes of Literacy

In extending the understanding of literacy to encompass the multiple variations in which children make meaning and communicate their thoughts and emotions, I have broadened my understanding of the activities and interactions observed in the homes of these young children. Similar to studies conducted by other researchers, for example Johnson (2003), I sought to uncover what might be the multiple modes of literacy in this group of immigrant children.

Until recently most literacy research has focused primarily on linguistic and print-based sources of communication (Johnson, 2003; Kress, Jewitt, Ogborn, & Tsatsarelis, 2001). By looking at literacy and learning through the wider lens of multiple modalities (Hamilton, 2000; Kress, 1997; Kress et.al, 2001; Kress & Van Leeuwen, 2001; Stenglin & Idema, 2001), I hope to provoke a more thoughtful analysis and understanding of the rich literacy background that immigrant children, especially children of non-English speaking parents or non-native English speaking parents, bring to the classroom.

I have framed the analysis of data reported in this chapter within a theoretical approach that integrates sociocultural and activity theory (Rogoff, 1997; Wertsch, 1991) with a multimodal theory of language, literacy, and communication (Kress, 1997; Kress & Van Leeuwen 2001; Kress et. al, 2001).

Sociocultural and activity theory is founded on the notion that thought and the construction of meaning is by necessity situated in the cultural, historical, and institutional setting in which it occurs (Johnson, 2003; Wertsch, 1991). Thus in my research I focused on what children did, with whom they did it, and what message they communicated in the event.

Such an approach acknowledges that a solely verbocentric approach to understanding communication is limited to the ability of the participants to speak, read, and write using words (Stein, 2000), a particular barrier to participants who are neither fluent nor culturally grounded in that language. In fact, Kress posits that "what is most significant . . . is that the substance of the lesson – the curriculuar content – is represented in the *image* [italics added], not in the language" (Kress, 2000, p. 338).

In using the term multimodal texts, we are referring to those texts through which meaning is conveyed through multiple means that may or may not include the spoken or written words (Walsh, 2006). Thus multiple modalities of meaning include images such as photos, pictures, and drawings. They include audio texts such as sound effects and music. They also include kinesthetic "texts" such as dance, dramatizations, theatre, and dramatic play.

Since the discipline of semiotics examines how meaning is made through all kinds of signs, visual as well as verbal, we have seen an expansion in our understanding of literacy as multimodal to include "images, gestures, music, movement, animation, and other representational modes on equal footing with language" (Siegal, 2006, p. 65).

The body of research investigating the use of multimodality in classrooms, presents a picture of youth who are demonstrating success in learning, thinking, and understanding, despite the fact that previously they had been identified as "struggling" or "learning disabled" by practitioners viewing their learning and literacy through a solely linguistic lens (Siegal, 2006, p. 73). If we accept the position that drawing and writing are two forms of symbol-making that are equally valuable in young children's meaning-making (Dyson, 1993), then we would not view drawing merely as a pre-writing activity.

"If students live within communities and cultural contexts that value spoken language, performance, dance, craft, and music more than writing, then how can the worldview of the school integrate these multiple modes of representation to give students the best opportunities to demonstrate their abilities" (Stein, 2004, p. 112)? This brings to forefront the importance of recognizing the multiple modalities of meaning-making that are prevalent in the cultures of many children. According to Archer "To be 'literate' then does not simply mean having acquired the technical skills to decode and encode signs, but having mastered a set of social practices related to a set of signs which are inevitably plural and diverse. . . . Literacies are therefore understood as multiple, socially situated and contested" (Archer, 2006, p. 450).

Observations of In-Home Literacy Events

It is critical that researchers keep the study of literacy within the context of the everyday lives of the people around them (Szwed, 1981). Through in-home observations, I have attempted to learn the stories of my informants as suggested by Bateson (1984) because they are intrinsically worthy (Seidman, 1991). In order to further a deep understanding, my intent was to work with a small group of participants (5 families) with whom I could maintain extended contact over a period of time (Merriam, 1988; Miles & Huberman, 1994). Therefore, I relocated to an island off the coast of New England where a community of Brazilians resides, and I remained there for the duration of the data collection.

As an ethnographer, I immersed myself in the Brazilian culture and home-life of the families in my study. I drew upon my past experience of having lived three years as an American in Brazil. This was aided my understanding of cultural issues my participants might confront. I conducted an average of ten home visits per family during the 6 months of data collection. Home visits lasted from one to two hours and took place at times when the parents could conveniently be available. During the study, I was able to see families at several different times of the day and different days of the week, including weekends.

Virtually all aspects of the daily lives of the families were of interest to me in the early stages of the research. It was my intention that by the setting of such broad boundaries the data-gathering process would not be distorted or restricted by any preconceived notions. One aim of the initial visits was to allow the families to become familiar with the research process and comfortable about my presence. When the family members no longer treated me as a visitor and I had ascertained that performance behaviors for my benefit had subsided (between visits 2 and 5), the subsequent field notes were treated as real data.

Following the procedures of other researchers who have studied uses of language (Heath, 1983) or literacy (Purcell-Gates, 1996; Taylor, 1983; Taylor &

Dorsey-Gaines, 1988; Teale, 1986) in the home, I noted and recorded all materials in open view in the home that were related to literacy, including such items as books, printed notices, bills, signs, environmental print on household products, television guides, and writing materials. I also noted conversations that occurred about literacy related activities, such as an inquiry by the parent about what the child did in school that day. In addition, literacy events engaged in by family members on excursions outside of the home, such as paying bills by check, reading labels during grocery shopping, or filling out a form to be on a waiting list for a post office box were also recorded. I also included in my field notes additional modes of communication, such as, singing, dramatic play, drawing, painting, and object-building, such as block building. In short I included all aspects related to children's attempts to convey meaning through symbolic representations or creative activities.

Description of Context and Participants

All of the participants in this study were Head Start participants, living on an island off the coast of New England. The length of time parents had been in this country when the project began varied, ranging from ten years to six months. Thus some parents had lived in this country for some time prior to the birth of the focal child. Others had arrived more recently, bringing their children with them from Brazil.

The focal children of the study were those enrolled in a home-based Head Start program. Therefore, it did not include a pre-school for the children to attend. The central role of the Head Start program was to provide support services for families, parent education, home visiting, as well as assistance in placing children in existing pre-school programs in the community.

Four of the five children were females. Four of the five were four years old at the time of the observations. Four of them had siblings, either older or younger; and one sibling was born during the period of data collection. Because all of the families qualified for Head Start by income eligibility, they all would be considered of low socioeconomic status by the standards of the local community. All of the participants in this study were year-round residents of the island, despite the fact the central economic base was summer tourism.

Length of time in this country varied. Two children had been here less than one year. Two children were born in the United States. One child, Tatiana, had been here about one and a half years. Parents' ability to speak English coincided with their length of time in the United States. For example one parent who had lived in this country for 11 eleven years, was very fluent in English. Other parents spoke virtually no English. Those who did not, such as Augosto's and Maria's parents, studied English with tutors and/or with books and tapes at home. The two children who were born in the U.S. spoke both English and Portuguese and often combined the two when speaking to me.

The dearth of available and affordable English classes made it very difficult for parents to take formal classes in English. The principal language spoken in the homes of all participants was Portuguese.

Parents' educational background in Brazil also varied. One of the mothers had been a teacher in Brazil. Another had been a journalist. One of the fathers had been an accountant. Another said he had done clerical work for an airline. However, the economic situation in Brazil had made it impossible for them to find employment. In this country the fathers were primarily laborers in the construction and landscaping industries. The mothers worked in restaurants and hotels as cooks and housekeepers. Rosa's mother and father owned a Brazilian store that sold foods, cosmetics, and household items from Brazil.

Evidence from the Study: Making Meaning through Music and Singing

Activities involving music and singing abounded in these homes, albeit in different ways and different amounts. The use of music and singing for making meaning was directed by the parents, depending on the value they placed on this mode.

For Augosto's family, music came in the form of toys that could be used to teach skills. He had a musical "alphabet" toy. Although this toy was primarily meant to teach children the letters of the alphabet and the phonetic sounds connected to them, it also played music. The toy consisted of buttons to press. Each button was in the shape of a letter of the alphabet and each had a picture of a word that started with that letter. As he pressed the button, a voice could be heard, for example, "This is the letter 'x'." Choices for the game could be set to "Learn the letters," "Learn the sounds," or "Find it," to direct the user to the correct letter. However, in this home the importance of music was secondary to that of reading and writing.

In Janaina's home, there were no expensive musical toys; but singing was a natural part of the day. During my visits, Janaina typically walked around the house singing songs she had learned in her preschool. The ABC song was a favorite. Her parents encouraged this singing, and joined in with her. Janaina's father was fluent in English, and he sang the English songs with her. Her mother, who could not speak English, sang in Portuguese or Spanish or listened and encouraged Janaina to sing in English. Excerpts from my field notes of observations on different days illustrate this.

Then Father and daughter pretended to be strumming guitars. She sang "Old MacDonald" in English, and he sang the "E-I-E-I-O" with her.

Later she pointed to the letters "ABC. Then she broke into the ABC song followed by "Twinkle, Twinkle Little Star."

On another occasion her mother was doing dishes when I arrived.

All at once she and Janaina began to sing the Christmas song, "Feliz Navidad." They sang it together in both English and Spanish.

Then her father asked Janaina to sing the song of the months of the year. She said to him in English, "I don't know how to start it. You start it." He started it in English for her. Then they sang the song together in English. After that she sang "Charlie[sic] Old St. Nicholas". She wanted her father to sing with her, but he said he didn't know it. Then she sang it to him, and he hummed along.

In this family music and singing was used as a way for family members to connect with one another by joint engagement in a joyful activity. However, music and singing were not predominant activities in either Tatiana's or Maria's homes except in occasional instances when they listened or sang along with religious songs from TV or videotapes.

This was not the case in Rosa's home. Music and singing were major influences in her family. Both her father and her older brother, George, were musicians who played in their Brazilian church services. Their musical instruments, a Yamaha synthesizer and a guitar, were placed prominently in the living room, the central part of the home.

In addition to singing religious songs in Portuguese, Rosa sang to her dolls. She became the singing voices of her dolls in her dramatic play with them. All of the singing in this pretend play was in Portuguese despite the fact that Rosa spoke English as easily as any three year old native English speaker.

Similar to Janaina's home, singing together was as natural as talking together; and singing appeared to be a vehicle for family members to build and maintain relationships with one another. Rosa, her mother, and her older brother frequently interjected their conversations with songs. The following quotation from my field notes exemplifies this.

George, her older brother, had stopped in to talk to their mother. As he left the room, he was singing in Portuguese. A short time later Rosa took a stuffed bear; and her Mother said in English, "Oh, I just love that bear." Then they sang a Portuguese song together. It was a song about a bear.

Then Rosa took a rag doll, and she wound the key on the back of it. It was a music box. Rosa and her mother sat silently, reverently, as they listened to the music box play.

It was clear that music and song were very important in their lives.

Evidence from the Study: Making Meaning through Video and Photographs

During my home visits I observed several instances in which children, as well as parents, used images in the form of video and photographs to interpret their world. In all five homes the television was on during some of my visits. Usually it was tuned to children's programming, such as *Teletubbies*. Sometimes a video of a children's story, such as *Pinocchio* was being played. In Maria's and Tatiana's homes, the television was almost always playing in the living room where the children were engaged in various art or dramatic play activities. In those instances, the television was largely ignored. In Janaina's and Augosto's home, the television was always tuned to closed captioning when available. The parents explained to me that this was to help them learn and improve their English. Television was rarely used in my presence at Rosa's home.

Video

Videos were used as digital narratives in much the same way that story reading or story telling could occur. On one of my visits, Augosto watched the video *Pinocchio*; and he excitedly explained and interpreted to me (only in Portuguese) a description of everything that was happening in the video representation of the story. In effect, Augosto became the narrator of the story to me as he explained and interpreted every detail. On another occasion when he was watching *Teletubbies*, he performed the same role as narrator and interpreter of the story to me.

> *Augosto laughed at the cartoon and then repeated to me in Portuguese what he was laughing at. He laughed at the music and dancing in the cartoon. He made comments in Portuguese about what was happening in the video. For example, he told me when the goldfish went to bed and when Jiminy Cricket wiggled his bare toes. He talked about Pinocchio; and he noted the hat on his head, the clothes he wore, and the color of his shoes. He also talked about the whale. "He looks so big, and look at the cat and the goldfish in the bowl." Neither would he let me forget the umbrella Jiminy was holding, nor the leaves on Pinocchio's nose.*

On another occasion, I noted in my field notes:

> *Augosto was watching "Teletubbies". He narrated the story for me, and he hummed along to the melody of "Twinkle, Twinkle Little Star". He chattered along in Portuguese about what was in the video, commenting on "their big stomachs," and the "antennae coming out of their heads." At times he got up and acted out what he saw on the video.*

Janaina was the only other child who watched television on a regular basis in my presence. However, the context was very different from Augosto's. Janaina only watched children's videos with her father at her side, and with the closed caption option turned on. These instances were also treated as narrative. However, the experience for Janaina was one in which she cuddled closely to her father, as they whispered comments about the story to each other. On one visit I observed the following:

> *Janaina was engrossed in the story and was snuggled up to her father. The two dinosaurs in the video talked about their fear of never finding their lost little boy dinosaur. Then the scene went to the little dinosaur who was crying, and Janaina looked really intently with her eyes wide and piercing. She had a very serious expression on her face. A song played, and Dad patted Janaina gently on the arm in time with the rhythm of the music.*

> *Then the scene changed to a beautiful sky at night, star studded as a beautiful song of hopefulness played. Janaina whispered to her father in Portuguese, "It's beautiful."*

> *Then Dad cuddled up to Janaina again. When the movie got scary, Dad would turn to look at Janaina; and he would talk to her very quietly, almost in a whisper.*

This TV watching was an intimate moment between parent and child. I think the fact that her father was as interested in the video as Janaina was made the moment special. He didn't think it beneath him to watch an animated video, and I think the message to his daughter about the importance of story was a significant one. The interactions between them were very quiet. Although I was only a couple of feet away, I couldn't hear what he said to her. I think this was intentional, that this was meant to be private between the two of them. I understood this to be a close and intimate experience between them.

In Tatiana's family, the children watched a video only once during my visits. This was because the fuse was blown in the living room and the children's room, and they did not have lights to see. The only room with electricity was their parents' bedroom, so their mother set the TV to show a video for them to watch from their parents' bed. The video was one of several biblical stories for children that they received from their church. It was the story of Joseph who had been sold to foreigners and lived in a foreign country, and it carried deep meaning for the family.

> *Then Tatiana's mother explained that the children love this story; and she loves it, too, because it is the story of Joseph in a foreign land. He learned the language and became close friends with the king; but he still had a hunger for his homeland and for the chance to speak his own language; and he missed his father very much.*

It was clear that the theme of this video, longing for home and loved ones, held deep meaning for Tatiana's mother, as well as for her children.

Photographic Images

Both Augosto and Tatiana, along with their mothers, demonstrated this theme of connection to the homeland and distant family by showing me the cherished photos of their homes and families in Brazil. As recorded in my field notes:

> There were photos of past birthdays and vacations, as well as photos of friends, cousins, aunts, and uncles.

The photographs of home were used to keep alive their memories of home. This was especially important for the children, whose memories of Brazil were fading.

Evidence from the Study: Making Meaning through Dramatic Play

As would be expected of three and four year olds, dramatic play consumed a large amount of children's time during my visits.

Augosto's dramatic play took the form of engaging his Ninja Turtles and Tarzan dolls in carrying out warfare with one another. He added accessories, such as toy airplanes, trains, cars, and roads to extend the stories he enacted through them.

> There was a ramp for cars to go down a plastic road, many matchbox cars and trucks, a tollbooth, police station, bank, a MacDonald's Playland, highway signs, parking lot, and an auto service center.

Meanwhile as Augosto performed his narrative, he explained the organization of the setting he created for his narrative; and he embellished with sounds and gestures, as necessary.

> Augosto explained the cars and the layout to me; and when he put a tree on the set he told me what he was doing. He showed me how various accessories, such as the tree or the toll gate worked; and he moved them to different places on the board to demonstrate this. He also made noises like an ambulance and a fire truck when he moved those vehicles along the roads on his set.

For Maria, Tatiana, and Rosa, dramatic play was manifest through their play with dolls, stuffed animals, and puppets. For Maria, a great deal of her imaginative play revolved around her Barbie dolls and her extensive collection of accessories. Maria's parents, who usually sat near Maria as she played, made comments and asked questions about what she was doing. Maria's mother often got down on the floor with her and became a partner in her play.

At this point in time, Maria had been in the U.S. approximately 6 months, and her experience of international travel was still in her memory. One day Maria brought out a suitcase for her Barbie doll. Maria's mother took this opportunity to find out what Maria remembered about Brazil.

> *Mother engaged her in a conversation, asking her if she wanted to go to Brazil. She asked Maria about her grandmother and grandfather. She wanted to know if Maria missed them. Then Maria's mother named one family name after another, asking if Maria remembered them. She answered "mais ou menos" (more or less), to each name. (Maria's mother had previously disclosed to me her fear that Maria would forget her family in Brazil.) Then she asked Maria if she missed "Robo". Maria asked who that was, and her Mother said "Cachorro" (dog) to help her remember. Again, Maria replied, "mais ou menos."*

Once again the theme of missing Brazil arose, and once again it was initiated by the parent rather than the child.

While Maria's play had centered on Barbie dolls, Tatiana had a large variety of dolls and accessories to extend her dramatic play. In addition, Tatiana's older sister engaged in imaginative play with her. Helena, Tatiana's mother, was only occasionally involved, though she was always within earshot of their activities. The two girls used a variety of "little people", as well as, their dollhouse to dramatize their "stories", which involved coming and going and living in their house. Although Tatiana's sister was in first grade in school and could speak English, the two girls primarily spoke Portuguese to each other.

Tatiana also had Barbie dolls that she dressed and undressed. One of the dolls was dressed like a Bahian Brazilian woman. She wore a large colorful hoop skirt and a bandana on her head. Tatiana also dramatized her play through her stuffed animals that she caused to growl and "scare" me. The girls also engaged in a variety of dress up that involved jewelry and ponytail bands. On one occasion:

> *The children were playing in the living room at the coffee table. They adorned their hair with elastic ponytail holders, and they had several pairs of earrings. One set was shaped like flowers. Another one was shaped like a leaf. Two more were shaped like half loops, and another was a pair of red love knots. There also were two brooches. One was of a brightly colored toucan, and another was of a parrot. They had a pair of copper-colored elongated "diamonds", which the older child, Thaissa, wore. She had plastic bracelets and more ponytail holders. She went out of the room, and moments later returned with a rectangular mirror with a Currier and Ives print, about 24" by 12" in size. She stood it in place on the coffee table, and the two girls took turns adorning themselves and looking at themselves in the mirror.*

Rosa's dramatic play was influenced by a big playhouse in her room, a child-sized piano, and an extensive collection of stuffed animals and puppets. In her play and in her conversations with me, she switched back and forth from Portuguese to English. I responded to her in the language she used to address me. Rosa used her playhouse for dramatic play scenarios in which she was the mother, and her stuffed animals and puppets were children and guests. One day during one of my home visits

> *Rosa went into the playhouse and invited me in with her, but I told her I couldn't come in because I'm too big. Then she took more stuffed animals into the playhouse with her, where there was a little kitchen. She closed the door to the playhouse and said, "Wait right here." I heard dishes clanking. Then she opened the door and said, "Here's some food," and she offered me a child-sized saucer. I joined in her dramatic play, and I pretended to eat from it.*

Evidence from the Study: Making Meaning through Creating Objects and Images (Drawing, Painting, Building)

All of the children were involved in constructing objects and images in various ways. In fact the Head Start home visitor often brought paints, paper, glue, paste, and other materials to the homes when she visited.

Augosto had a special box that contained chalk, and the cover of the box was a chalkboard. He regularly used it to draw and create pictures that he interpreted to me. One example was the day he made a ship, and he carefully pointed the sails that he made. He explained that they were necessary to make the ship go.

Drawing was an important part of Janaina's routine. According to her mother, Lena, "Janaina draws all day long." Then Lena explained that "Janaina only makes pictures of family. She labels the people in her drawings with the names of family members." An example was one of Janaina's drawings that was displayed prominently in the kitchen. Lena explained that Janaina had drawn a picture of their family and pointed it out to me.

> *On the wall was a dry erase board with a drawing of a lady, a man, and a very small person. A heart and a star were also drawn into the picture.*

Lena proudly showed me pictures of Janaina's drawings as examples of her "creative imagination." One picture was a child on a skateboard. Lena, who had not finished high school in Brazil, was very proud of Janaina's artistic ability; and she encouraged her.

> *Lena showed me a large book of newsprint that she bought for Janaina's drawings. While I visited, Lena and Janaina sat together as Janaina made pictures.*

This was a regular scenario during my visits. Her father, also, encouraged Janaina in her drawings.

Then she and her father talked together in Portuguese. He gave her a marker. She went and took the dry erase board, and he wiped it clean for her. She took it back to the kitchen table and began to draw on it. She drew a circle, and then added what looked like hair to it. Then she added a body.

Maria also liked to make creations by drawing pictures and coloring them. She had her own set of materials to work with.

After lunch Maria went to her room and brought out a book that had blank pages where she could draw her own pictures. She showed them to me. Then Maria drew a simple picture of a tree with apples or some sort of fruit hanging from it. She drew a big heart next to it. Her mother proudly explained that Maria loves books and always has a book in her hand. She also told me that Maria loves to draw and color. Then Maria went to her room and came back with a case full of crayons, colored pencils, and colored felt tip markers. She began coloring the picture she had drawn.

The home visitor, Marisa, made weekly visits to the homes of these children. One day she visited when I was there, and she brought a recipe for homemade play dough as a project for the day.

Marisa gave Maria the ingredients. She helped Maria with the measuring cup, and then Maria poured the ingredients into a bowl as they made the play dough. Then Marisa piled the play dough on the counter in front of Maria who immediately began patting it and working with it. Marisa got involved. She showed her how to flatten it, how to roll it in a ball, and how to roll it into a cylinder. Then Maria's mother came over and got right next to Maria and watched her work with the " masa" (dough).

Tatiana engaged in a variety of artistic creations, often with the help of her older sister. The two girls had a basket of colored pencils, construction paper, and glue that they kept in their bedroom. They often brought the basket into the living room, their play area. One day when I arrived, the girls decided to paint in the living room.

The children brought out paints, water, pencil, and paper. Tatiana had the paints. Thaissa drew a picture of a tree with apples on it. Then she gave the picture to Tatiana who painted the tree, the apples, and the tree trunk. They worked on a towel that had been placed as a cover on the coffee table . . . After a while, Thaissa also began painting her drawings. All the pictures were of apple trees with tree trunks, a mass of green leaves above. All the trees were covered with red, round fruit. The whole background was against a blue sky.

Their mother, who had been a few feet away at the open counter, which was her kitchen work area, came over to see what they were doing. She commented on the blue color of the sky that Thaissa painted. Then their mother started to draw a tree on the paper, and Tatiana began painting it. Then Thaissa put drops of red water paint on her paper. She took a sipping straw, and she blew a design on the paper.

Thaissa and Tatiana also had a variety of construction toys (tinker toys, blocks, etc.). The girls often played together building a structure or a city. Sometimes each built her own, as they worked side by side. They also had a set of red construction blocks. Sometimes their mother participated in their constructions as she had in their painting. During one visit, I made the following observation.

The girls sat down on the floor and took out the box of colored construction blocks that they used before. Tatiana laid out a square with her blocks. Then she asked her mother what it was. Helena told her it looked like a person with arms and legs and a body. Then Helena showed her how to separate the "legs" and make it look more like a person. Then Tatiana played with changing the shape and trying different ways of putting the blocks together.

The girls also had an extensive racetrack that they had constructed on the floor of their bedroom. They, then, used the cars and racetrack as they played out their narratives.

I observed Rosa engaging in a communicative event focused on drawing on only one of my visits. It was a very cold winter's day, and Rosa discovered that she could breathe on the window and make a fog slate. Then she could draw an image on it. Rosa and her mother breathed on the window together. Then they drew a cross on the fog slate. This demonstrated to me that thoughts of their Christian faith were a routine part of their daily lives.

Multiple Modes of Making Meaning and Literacy

While the previous discussion of evidence from this study has focused on modes of communication other than verbal expression, these families did show that they value the skills that they have been taught are necessary for success in school. In addition to the multiple modes of literacy that were evident in these homes, the children were encouraged to prepare for school. There were numerous instances in which parents taught their children to write letters of the alphabet or numbers. One day

Helena, Tatiana's mother, was teaching three-year old, Tatiana, how to make her letters. Tatiana made her letters in caps on a lined, spiral-bound tablet. She filled the space between the two lines and formed the letters very perfectly. Helena stayed by her side and encouraged her, saying, "That's right," "That's very good," and "That's perfect." This was all in Portuguese.

Augosto had a toy computer, and a box of letters and numbers; and his mother used these to teach the letters and numbers to him, in Portuguese.

Then he took the chalk out and closed the lid. He drew a picture of a "5" and she praised him. A few minutes later he was looking for a number "1", and he

took a "J". His mother explained, "'J' is a letter, not a number." Then she helped him find the "1".

A favorite activity of all the children was to attempt to "write" or "read" their names and the names of their family members. Rosa made a game of reading and writing and tracing letters of the alphabet to represent important people in her life. One day she induced me to trace the shapes of some styrofoam letters that she brought to me.

Then Rosa ran out and came back with a foam letter "R". She said, "Write my name," (in Portuguese). I took the letter R and traced it on my paper. Then she got excited and said, "Do another!" She repeated this, until I had made the letter "R" four times. She pointed to each and said, "Rosa." Then she brought more letters, and she asked me to trace "E" because it is for her Grandmother, Eloisa.

Parents also counted toys, and other household objects with their children to teach them to count. They shared with me their desire for their children to do well in school. They also expressed their wish to read to their children, but they did not have access to Portuguese children's books; and so they could not do this. Janaina loved books, and she discovered that I could read to her in English. During one of my visits

She brought me one book after another, in English, to read to her; and we talked about the pictures and the colors. Then she went to her box of books, and she kept bringing me books, one after another, to read to her.

While parents may have viewed many of the activities described above as diversions, I believe that these activities demonstrate that children were using the objects and materials available to them in their play to construct meaning of the world around them, as well as to communicate meaning to others in much the same way that people use linguistic tools to do so.

For example, children in their drawing and painting activities created representations for themselves and those around them that related to family relationships, such as Janaina's drawings of her family. Rosa, in drawing the cross with her mother, was demonstrating her understanding of the importance of this symbol in the life of her family. She did not need special tools to convey her reverence for this object, which was undoubtedly important to this family who provided a ministry of music to their church. Indeed, music itself was a powerful expression of meaning in this family who sang to one another throughout the day, and who placed their musical instruments in the center of the living room.

The use of video in the homes was one way to provide traditional stories to children whose parents were unable to read such stories in English and who did not have access to these stories in Portuguese. Thus the use of video became a story-telling medium. The description of Janaina and her father watching videos together conjures up images that might be associated with parental storybook reading to children, in which cuddling and touching and whispering are engaged in by parent and child.

Longing for Extended Family and the Homeland

A powerful theme that presented itself again and again as I observed the communicative events in these families was the importance of family and a longing for loved ones at home.   As previously discussed, Janaina's drawings were all of family members, which shows how important her family was to her; and Rosa's "game" of naming and writing letters for all the people in her family was another example of this.

The poignant conversation with Tatiana's mother regarding the favorite video depicting the Biblical story of Joseph, the photos of home and family displayed by Augosto's and Tatiana's mother, and the conversation initiated with Maria by her mother regarding traveling to Brazil and remembering family members show that thoughts of home and Brazil are not far from the minds of the parents.

Implications for Practitioners

The understandings derived from this study can provide important messages for practitioners, teachers, and administrators of programs for immigrant children, families, and English language learners.

Literacy and Communication Occurs in Multiple Ways

The children in this study were regularly engaged in activities that involve rich meaning-making and understanding, sometimes in traditional linguistic venues, to be sure, but often such activities involved video, drawing, painting, imaginative play, and music.   As teachers and practitioners we need to broaden our understanding of literacy to include these multiple modes of communication. We need to consider ways to open avenues for meaning-making in the classroom so that all children, regardless of linguistic English ability and background, have opportunities to engage in meaningful activities.   For example students who do not yet have sufficient English language literacy to write a narrative could be allowed to represent their narrative through video, drawings, paintings, or other representational media.

Importance of Faith, Family, and Homeland

A second implication for practitioners is to recognize the powerful role that faith, family, and homeland hold in the lives of these families. Talk about extended family in Brazil occurred frequently in these homes, and the pain and anxiety of loved ones was apparent when news of their illness was received. Photos of home were brought out regularly. However, all of these occurrences were initiated by the parents who also voiced concerns that their children would forget Brazil and their beloved family members who were there.

This deep attachment to family may seem strange to Americans who pride themselves on their independence from their parents. However, I believe that this attachment to the homeland on the part of these families emphasizes the courage and determination that it took for them to move so far away from their loved ones for the sake of giving a better life to their children, as well as the family members they left behind. All of these families told stories of sending money back to family in Brazil, as well as saving money to bring parents and loved ones here.

In addition, all of the families were, to a greater or lesser degree, involved in a local Brazilian church. These churches provided fellowship and support for these and other immigrant families. It is my belief that as practitioners we need to revere and respect the strong emotional bond that immigrant families have for their homeland. "Children learn what is important within the cultures of the communities in which they operate through the interactions with more experienced members of those cultures or communities" (Anning, 2003, p. 8). These relationships are part of the culture and identity of the parents, and also of the children. I believe that the important role of faith, family, and homeland is an essential part of the cultural context of these children and their parents. I believe that as practitioners, administrators, and teachers of children of immigrants such as these Brazilians, we need to accept the cultural context that has formed them, so that we can find avenues with which they can connect our culture to theirs.

Literacy and English Language Learning

Contrary to what some may believe, many immigrant parents are educated and literate in their native language. Their difficulty with literacy in the U.S. is due to their inability to read, speak, listen, and understand the English language adequately. Despite their strong desire, which Helena referred to as her "passion", to learn English, immigrant parents often work long hours and are thus unable to participate in programs for English language instruction that can be expensive. Unfortunately funding for public programs has diminished considerably in the past few years, and when programs do become available there are long waiting lists.

The children and parents in this study showed that they value narrative. This was evident in children's dramatic play, in their art work, their block construction, and their use of video. Yet the limited English proficiency of the parents made it difficult, if not impossible, for them to read stories to their children.

Clearly, as practitioners, we need to assist parents in accessing English language instruction on the one hand; while encouraging and recognizing the value of the alternate modes of literacy and communicative practice found in these homes.

The multiple modes of literacy used by these children to construct narrative illustrates their adeptness at making meaning through the arts. Indeed, the presence of such multiple modes of literacy appears to be especially important in families where linguistic ability in English is limited.

References

Anning, A. (2003). Pathways to the graphicacy club: The crossroad of home and pre-school. *Journal of Early Childhood Literacy, 3*(1), 5-35.

Archer, A. (2006). A multimodal approach to academc 'literacies': Problemitising the visual/verbal divide. *Language and Education, 2*(6), 449-462.

Barton, D. (1998). *Literacy: An introduction to the ecology of written language.* Cambridge, MA: Blackwell Publishers Ltd.

Bateson, M. C. (1984). *With a daughter's eye.* (1st ed.). New York: William Morrow & Company, Inc.

Bissex, G. (1980). *GNYS AT WRK: A child learns to read.* Cambridge, MA: Harvard University Press.

Butler, D., & Clay, M. (1987). *Reading begins at home.* (2nd ed.). Portsmouth, NH: Heinnemann Educational Books, Inc.

Chall, J., & Snow, C. (1982). *Families and literacy: The contribution of out-of-school experiences to children's acquisition of literacy.* Cambridge, MA: Harvard University Press.

Dickinson, D. (Ed.). (1994). *Bridges to literacy: Children, families, and schools.* Cambridge, MA: Blackwell.

Dyson, A. H. (1993). The social worlds of children learning to read and write in an urban primary school. New York: Teachers College Press.

Freire, P. (1998). *Teachers as cultural workers.* (D. Macedo, D. Koike, & A. Oliveira, Trans.). Boulder, CO: Westview Press.

Grillo, R. (1989). Anthropology, language, politics. In Grillo, R. (Ed.), Social anthropology and the politics of language (pp. 1-24). Cambridge: Cambridge University Press.

Hamilton, M. (2000). Expanding the new literacy studies: Using photographs to explore literacy as a social practice. In D. Barton, M. Hamilton, & R. Ivanic (Eds.), *Situated literacies: Reading and writing in context* (pp. 16-34). London: Routledge.

Heath, S. (1983). *Ways with words: Language, life, and work in communities and classrooms.* New York: Cambridge University Press.

Johnson, D. (2003). Activity, theory, mediated action and literacy: Assessing how children make meaning in multiple modes. *Assessment in Education, 10*(1), 103-129.

Kress, G. (1997). *Before writing: Rethinking the paths to literacy.* London: Routledge.

Kress, G. (2000). Multimodality: Challenges to thinking about language. *TESOL Quarterly, 34*(2), 337 340.

Kress, G., Jewitt, C., Ogborn, J., & Tsatsarelis, C. (2001). *Multimodal teaching and learning: The rhetorics of the science classroom.* London: Continuum.

Kress, G., & Van Leeuwen, T. (2001). *Multimodal discourse.* London: Edward Arnold.

Larrick, N. (1982). *A parent's guide to children's reading.* Philadelphia, PA: Westminster.

Merriam, S. (1988). *Case study research in education: A qualitative approach* (1st ed.). San Francisco: Jossey-Bass.

Miles, M., & Huberman, A. (1994). *Qualitative data analysis: An expanded sourcebook.* (2nd ed.). Thousand Oaks, CA: Sage Publications.

Morrow, L. (1993). *Literacy development in the early years: Helping children read and write.* (2nd ed.). Needham Heights, MA: Allyn & Bacon.

Purcell-Gates, V. (1996). Stories, coupons and the TV guide: Relationships between home literacy experiences and emergent literacy knowledge. *Reading Research Quarterly, 31*(4), 406-428.

Rogoff, B. (1997). Observing sociocultural activity on three planes: Participatory appropriation, guided participation, and apprenticeship. In J. Wertsch, P. Del Rio & A. Alvarez (Eds.), *Sociocultural studies of mind* (pp. 139-164). Cambridge: Cambridge University Press.

Scollon, R., & Scollon, S. (1981). The literate two-year-old: The fictionalization of self. In R. Scollon & B. Scollon (Eds.), *Narrative, literacy, and face in interethnic communication* (pp. 57-98). Norwood, NJ: Ablex.

Seidman, I. (1991). Interviewing as qualitative research: A guide for researchers in education and the social sciences. New York: Teachers College Press.

Siegal, M. (2006). Rereading the signs: Multimodal transformations in the field of literacy education. *Language Arts, 84*(1), 65-77.

Stein, P. (2000). Rethinking resources: Multimodal pedagogies in the ESL classroom. *TESOL Quarterly, 34*(2), 333-336.

Stein, P. (2004). Representation, rights and resources: Multimodal pedagogies in the language and literacy classroom. In K. Toohey & B. Norton (Eds.), *Critical Pedagogies and Language Learning* (pp. 95-115). Cambridge, UK: Cambridge University Press.

Stenglin, M., & Idema, R. (2001). How to analyse visual images: A guide for TESOL teachers. In A. Burns & C. Coffin (Eds.), *Analysing English in global context* (pp. 194-208). London: Routledge.

Street, B. (1987). Literacy and social change: The significance of social context in the development of literacy programs. In D. Wagner (Ed.), *The future of literacy* (pp. 55-72). Oxford, UK: Pergamon Press.

Street, B. (1997). The new literacy studies. In B. Street (Ed.), *Cross-cultural approaches to literacy* (pp. 1-21). New York: Cambridge University Press.

Szwed, J. (1981). The ethnography of literacy. In M. Whiteman (Ed.), *Variation in writing: Functional and linguistic-cultural differences* (pp. 13-23). Hillsdale, NJ: Lawrence Erlbaum.

Taylor, D. (1983). *Family literacy: Young children learning to read and write.* Exeter, NH: Heinemann.

Taylor, D., & Dorsey-Gaines, C. (1988). *Growing up literate: Learning from inner-city families.* Portsmouth, NH: Heinemann.

Teale, W. (1986). Home background and young children's literacy development. In W. Teale & E. Sulzby (Eds.), *Emergent literacy: Writing and reading* (pp. 173-206). Norwood, NJ: Ablex.

Walsh, M. (2006). The 'textual shift': Examining the reading process with print, visual and multimodal texts. *Australian Journal of Language and Literacy, 29*(1), 24-37 .

Wertsch, J. V. (1991). *Voices of the mind: A sociocultural approach to mediated action.* Cambridge, MA: Harvard University Press.

Sharon Cecile Switzer
East Stroudsburg University of Pennsylvania
East Stroudsburg, PA   USA

Dr. Sharon Switzer is an assistant professor in the Early Childhood and Elementary Education Department at East Stroudsburg University. She teaches in the K-12 ESL Specialist program, as well as Language Arts in Childhood Education.

Chapter 8
The Heart of the Arts:

Fostering Young Children's Ways of Knowing

Patricia T. Whitfield

Abstract The education of young learners has become a casualty of *No Child Left Behind* (2001). While the mandates of this law have led to an intensively structured, narrow, teacher-driven academic curriculum accompanied by high stakes testing for all children, its exclusion of the arts has been particularly calamitous for children who do not come from White, middle-class homes. Literacy has been defined as acquisition of text through a limited number of programs reliant on printed symbols. Yet, children come to know in a multitude of ways and those whose roots lie in oral, visual, or kinesthetic cultures are placed at a disadvantage when their first experiences with schooling are bereft of joy and individual expression related to their cultural roots. This chapter will address children's meaning making in culturally responsive settings.

Keywords No Child Left Behind Act, apartheid curriculum, creativity killers, mulisensory learning, culture

"I found I could say things with color and shapes that I couldn't say in any other way – things I had no words for" (O'Keeffe, as cited in Drokojowska-Philp, 2004, pp. 214-215). With these words, Georgia O'Keeffe, one of America's best-known artists gave poignant voice to a significant way of knowing. Unfortunately, America's young children are currently being deprived access to such multimodal ways of knowing through the implementation of the *No Child Left Behind Act*. The *No Child Left Behind Act of 2001 (NCLB)* reauthorized the *Elementary and Secondary Education Act (ESEA)* and was signed into law on January 8th, 2002. Though its title signals concern for all children, the harsh reality of its implementation is its almost total abandonment of the arts as an integral part of the curriculum for young learners. *NCLB* has engendered curriculum that overlooks the importance of providing opportunities for children to explore the world through their many intelligences -- especially those intelligences that enable them to negotiate between and among symbol systems as they learn to read and write. Although the

Professor Emerita, Lyon College, USA

M. J. Narey (ed.), *Making Meaning.*
© Springer 2009

arts are considered a core subject under *NCLB* there is "no quest for balance among studies in the arts, sciences, and humanities" (Chapman, 2005, p. 7) and it tends to "impose a discipline-based model on schools, with clear disdain for social studies and other interdisciplinary approaches to teaching and learning" (Chapman, 2007, p. 25). The effects of this imbalance may be harmful to children who are from culturally diverse backgrounds or whose families who have yet to achieve middle class status in the United States by limiting children's access to alternate ways of understanding that may be more relevant in their lives. Curricula driven by *NCLB* often perpetuate deficit views of children whose strength may be in the arts rather than the areas most heavily targeted by the act and it works to deprive teachers of autonomy in responding to diverse children's learning needs. Further, it removes from young children the spontaneity and joy they bring to learning that is particularly brought about through the arts.

Under *NCLB*, literacy learning, a key educational accomplishment of the early school years, has been reduced to an emphasis on direct instruction and repetitive systematic phonics. Further, learning to read has been decontextualized, (i. e. removed from a relevant context and taught in isolation). Such an approach to the teaching of reading is "especially harmful to those children coming from homes that may be viewed as 'literacy deprived' " (Whitfield, 2005, p. 44). Although culturally diverse and bilingual homes are often rich with literacy opportunities, when there is a disconnect between the home and the school, it is more difficult for those who do not belong to the dominant culture to become literate (Blackledge, 2000) in the way schools define literacy.

In an interview with Nagel and Guest (2007), Jonathan Kozol, a long-time advocate for the children of poverty, made the following statement in regard to the effects of the No Child Left Behind Act:

> In the so-called 'low performing' inner-city schools …it has introduced a reign of terror, a state of siege …principals tell me they're forced to handle education in a way they personally abhor … turning their schools into virtual test-prep factories where teachers are forced to spend half the school year or more not presenting educational content with the rich cultural depth that is familiar in the suburbs, but drilling children in test-taking strategies so that their school can meet its [annual yearly progress]. …even the best teachers use a 'drill and grill' curriculum …Allowing children to ask interesting and discerning questions will get them in trouble with the curriculum cops' … (p. 4)

Kozol added that a teacher can no longer teach a beloved poem if he or she can't cite the standard it meets. He noted, "A first grade teacher recently said to me, 'What's beauty got to do with it?' [concluding]…we're not dealing with apartheid schools, but apartheid curriculum" (p. 4). John Holt (1995) made similar observations in his book, *Freedom and Beyond*. He described a system in which schools not only present obstacles to poor children but also are actually designed to keep children living in impoverished areas from being successful in school, while convincing the children that they are to blame for their own failure. Susan Ohanian

(1999) has also written prolifically and passionately about the detrimental effects of standardized testing on all children, but especially on those living in poverty. She provides evidence of an industrial, utilitarian attitude toward the arts that has been fostered by business and government and has devalued the role of the arts in American schools and society, depriving children access to meaningful arts learning. She notes that the city of Berlin provides more funding for the arts than does the entire U.S. government, and that France "devotes vast expenditures to the arts ... because French politicians believe that the public needs culture" (p.127).

Offsetting these passionate concerns for underserved children in our schools are many examples of individual teachers who strive to include the arts in their work with young children. Gardner (1994) identified exemplary teachers who helped children in inner-city schools learn to "express themselves directly, imaginatively, and often lyrically... [noting that the child] should be encouraged to play, to 'be crazy', to experiment" (p. 289). Gallas (1994) worked with students who would, under other circumstances, be considered academic failures and found that they "produced powerful works of art that somehow defied mainstream assumptions about their potential as thinkers ... children who could think more deeply and push the boundaries of their own learning through the arts – that the arts offered a new definition of the language of learning" (p. 112).

While *NCLB* currently targets children in third grade and up for testing, its ramifications of are now being felt in early childhood classrooms as well. In my own experiences working with teachers of young learners, I have found many to be near despair over the impact of NCLB. One kindergarten teacher recently described how popular dramatic play areas in their preschool had been removed from individual classrooms and placed in a much less accessible space in order to allow the children to concentrate more fully on their "academic" work. At an early childhood conference that I attended I listened as preschool teachers commiserated and bemoaned the fact that, instead of introducing young children to the joys of books and reading, the academic curriculum of elementary schools was being been "pushed down" into their preschool classrooms. There is a growing demand for early childhood teachers to provide increasingly "academic" lessons -- heavy on direct teaching and testing, with fewer and fewer opportunities for exploration and discovery. In fact, kindergarten teachers must now instruct learners how to "bubble in" so that they can complete answer sheets correctly when testing day arrives. A daunting task for children whose fine motor skills are still developing!

In short, NCLB has resulted in academic programs nationwide characterized by the type of learning that many believe is inappropriate for developing young children's creativity: "inflexible schedules, intense competition, reliance on extrinsic rewards, and lack of free time" (Jalongo, 2002, p. 8). The effects on young children, so eager to learn, have been deleterious and stultifying. In direct contrast to programs designed to cultivate young children's capacities for imaginative thinking and artistic self-expression these programs are the embodiment of what Amabile (1986) described as "creativity killers."

The Role of the Arts

Dewey (1934) identified the role of the arts in the human psyche and described their ability to bring humans together. He believed that art "strikes below the barriers that separate human beings from each other … Art renders [people] aware of their union with one another in origin and destiny" (p. 272). The arts comprise an important element in all cultures and provide a way to express what it means to belong to the human family and societal groups. Numerous acclaimed theorists and experienced teachers have recommended that all children, and specifically children from culturally diverse homes or low socio-economic backgrounds, should be provided opportunities to learn utilizing alternative symbol systems and a variety of intelligences (Gardner, 1994, 1999). Premier among these alternative systems and ways of knowing are the arts: music, dance, drama, and the visual arts.

Gallas (1994) presents a strong and credible rationale for according the arts a premier role in curriculum, maintaining that art experience "fills a number of roles: (1) the arts as representing a methodology for acquiring knowledge; (2) the arts as subject matter for study, in and of themselves; and (3) the arts as an array of expressive opportunities for communicating with others, or art as story" (p. 116). Jerome Bruner (1996, 1999, 2004) has written extensively about the power of narrative in learning, examining the impact of culture in establishing self-identity, and the role of narrative in the individual's construction of reality. To omit the arts from young children's learning experiences deprives them of the opportunity to transmediate, (i.e. develop a repertoire of strategies to use across symbol systems). The arts serve, then, as an essential component in children's ability to make meaning of their world.

The Role of the Teacher

Susan Ohanian (1999) has declared, "a teacher's individual curriculum choices become increasingly vital as our society devalues its children" (p. 3). In Ohanian's words, "…we teachers, particularly those of us in elementary school, teach who we are. We are the curriculum" (p. 9).

James Banks (1994) has emphasized teachers' transformational role in children's education but cautions that

teachers are human beings who bring their cultural perspectives, values, hopes, and dreams to the classroom. They also bring their prejudices, stereotypes, and misconceptions …The teacher's values and perspectives mediate and interact with what they teach and influence the way that messages are communicated and perceived by their students. … Because the teacher mediates the messages and symbols communicated to the students through the curriculum, it is important for teachers to come to grips with their own personal and cultural values and identities in order to help students from diverse racial, ethnic, and cultural groups … (p. 159)

For teachers to work effectively and compassionately with children, they must first respect children's cultures and acquire deep learning about them. They must do as Bernstein (1972) suggested, "If the culture of the teacher is to become part of the consciousness of the child, then the culture of the child must first be in the consciousness of the teacher" (p. 149).

In Paley's (1986) study of fantasy in children, she emphasizes the significance of a teacher's "learning who children are...since the subject I most wish to learn about is the children, I must concentrate on this play, for they will teach me who they are by the fantasies they explore" (p. xiv).

The Role of the Visual Arts

More specifically, children make meaning in a multitude of ways as they seek to understand their worlds. Sidelnick and Svoboda (2000) maintain, "young children frequently interchange the terms draw and write as they discuss their work" (p.177). Vygotsky (1978, as cited in Sidelnick & Svoboda, 2000) explains, "children's drawings capitalize on the narrative impulse that emerges in their earliest representational drawings, on their tendency to create stories in drawings, and on the talk that surrounds and supplements drawing events" (p. 174).

Howard Gardner's (1994) theory of multiple intelligences has significant implications for children's ability to make meaning through manipulating symbol systems. He maintains the use of symbol systems is the major developmental event of the early childhood years and that "within a short period, the world of the child becomes a world of symbols" (p. 129). Of special importance to teachers of young children is Gardner's identification of the early childhood years as being a "crucial time for the "reorganization of a child's developing systems" (p. 131) as it is during this period that the child learns to "put his (sic) acts and perspectives into words or pictures" (p. 135).

The Influence of Music

We must also recognize music's importance in the curriculum, not only for its aesthetics but also for its power as a way of knowing. Research studies have suggested a correlation between music participation and improved academic performance, particularly for children from culturally diverse and/or economically disadvantaged schools (Catterall, 2002). Geneva Gay (2000) indicates improved academic performance in African-American students by the incorporation of music and movement into the curriculum. Perret and Fox (2004) point out that the results of a Harvard University's *Project Zero* meta-analysis of the relationship between the arts and academic learning has indicated a possible causal relationship between performing and listening to music and improved spatial-temporal reason-

ing. Adding further support to this potential relationship, Perret and Fox go on describe an innovative music program for elementary school students who are academically challenged that was started in the 1990s in Winston-Salem, North Carolina. In this innovative program, musicians from the city's symphony visited the
school several times a week for 30 minutes per visit and taught lessons designed to
integrate music with subjects taught by the classroom teachers. Children were introduced to music concepts and terminology, such as rhythm, meter, and high and
low pitch, as well as to the "story elements like character, setting, conflict, and
resolution" in musical pieces (Perret & Fox, 2004, p.3). The program resulted in
improved attentiveness of the children as well as improved test scores over a
three-year period. Given that early years of schooling are devoted to acquiring
written literacy, Perret and Fox are quick to point out the similarities between language and music.

> Language and music share ... important characteristics in the brain. The separate parts of
> music ... are processed in different parts of the brain and reassembled to make what we
> experience as music. Similarly, language is broken up into the perception and processing
> of phonemes and meaning and comprehension. Music and language both rely on
> perception and processing of assembled units with temporal and tonal features that are
> associated with unique symbols – notes in the case of music, letters in the case of
> language. Both music and language are multisensory. (p. 120)

Multisensory learning is the purview of the young learner. While schools in the
United States have tended to emphasize logical-mathematical and linguistic approaches to pedagogy, entire potential repertoires of teaching and learning have
languished and many otherwise bright and eager-to-learn children have been left
behind.

The Role of Dramatic Play

Children at play are actually engaged in serious learning. Through play, they reenact real-life or imaginative situations, solve problems, explore and resolve relationships with others, and experiment with new roles.

Acknowledgment of the significance of play has deep roots in early childhood
education. Pestalozzi (1915) viewed play as important in developing children's
imaginations, a significant factor in their growth as learners. In the 1930's Susan
Isaacs (as cited in Smilansky & Shefatya, 2004), reported that "dramatic play enables the child to progress in the socialization process while, at the same time, it
projects him (sic) into situations where he (sic) must think, explore, and strive at a
much higher level than...would be expected at his (sic) chronological age"
(p.139). According to Blatner (1995), role reversal in role-playing not only develops empathy, but also promotes risk-taking, a necessary component for creativity,
by encouraging comfort with making a mistake.

Vygotsky (1962) has expounded prolifically on the sociocultural importance of
play in the development of higher mental functions in children. Rea (2001) com-

ments on children's adaptive-creative thinking during play. Further, there is considerable evidence that play during early childhood can predict later facility in divergent thinking (Russ, Robins, & Christiano, 1999). Children are very aware of social situations and can reenact them with considerable accuracy in their dramatic play.

Paley (1988) found this to be true in her work with four-year olds as she observed what she called their "fantasy play." In *Bad Guys Don't Have Birthdays*, Paley (1988) chronicles three themes that pervade the creative play in her preschool classroom: bad guys, birthdays, and babies. She explains her interest in children's dramatic play as her belief that it is their most significant way of making meaning.

Novelty is an intriguing and attractive aspect of play for children and, thus, highly motivational as a learning strategy in the classroom. Roskos and Christie (2002) emphasize that "much of play's delight is in the unfamiliar and unexpected ...children are challenged by surprising facts and puzzling, even shocking, ideas that invite adaptation and clarification of existing knowledge" (p. 47). Again, the emphasis here is on the fostering of creative and fluid thinking or, as Roskos and Christie so eloquently described it, "Play, in other words, is a dynamic knowledge system that fluctuates at the edge of children's capabilities" (p. 47).

The Role of Movement and Dance

Anyone who has ever worked with young learners is well aware that they are not stationary figures. They move! Sitting still for extended periods of time is not only alien to children, but it might appear that it is virtually impossible. Therefore, it is evident that movement can be an age-appropriate and effective educational tool.

For instance, it has been previously noted that Gay (2000) cites several research studies showing that music and movement enhanced the academic performance of African-American students. These activities included not only dance but also clapping and other movement activities. Further, acquiring spatial reasoning assists children in the study of geometry and other aspects of higher mathematics, and as Perret and Fox (2004) note, "learning to dance improves spatial reasoning" (p. 45).

Integration of movement and dance with other subject areas has proven to be an important means of helping all children learn. Smith (2002) writes of teaching narrative writing through dance. She worked with first graders using dance integrated with lessons across the curriculum. She maintains, "every child learns by moving... In dance, children interpret ideas and feelings through the use of their bodies in an open-ended search for a unique movement vocabulary" (p. 91). Smith, among others, advocates the use of a drum to assist in children's movement activities. Klug (Klug & Whitfield, 2003), who has worked extensively with children of poverty in both urban and rural settings and is committed to culturally relevant pedagogy, has found that moving to the beat of a drum has enhanced the listening skills of Native American children. Gallas (1994), who incorporated the whole spectrum of the arts with learners, found that using movement helped children to understand science concepts, as in dramatizing the life cycle of the butterfly.

Leaving No Child Behind: Integrating the Arts for Successful Learning

The Reggio Emilia program, founded in Italy after World War II, emphasizes a variety of forms of expression and symbol systems to foster children's intellectual growth. Reggio Emilia's key concept is that of the *competent* child (Edwards, Gandini, and Forman, 1998). This belief, emerging from the chaotic destruction accompanying World War II in Italy, saw children as the future and perceived children as equipped to construct their own knowledge of the world. Among other key concepts, the Reggio approach focuses on what children can do, rather than what they cannot. This perspective contrasts dramatically with the lingering American educational perspective of deficit attributed to children of poverty or from non-dominant cultures. Further, a significant component of any Reggio Emilia school is the belief that children and artists are discoverers of new ways of seeing the world and that learning goes beyond words. Reggio students document their learning through music, dance, and dramatic play interwoven with project learning in small groups emphasizing problem solving. The program offers a model for those populations of children who are underserved and frequently left behind in American schools.

Working with Native American Children

In this section I will focus briefly on one underserved population of students in America's schools that has been part of my research (Klug & Whitfield, 2003), Native American children. Unfortunately, in the United States, teachers tend to design teaching and learning experiences for their students with little attention to their children's communities or cultural backgrounds, and the teaching of Native American children is no exception. Like in many other cultures and communities, the arts, rather than the printed word, play a significant role in these children's lives. Music, especially the drum, which "represents Mother Earth's heartbeat and accompanies both singing and dancing in rituals" (Klug & Whitfield, 2003, p.124) is a particularly important language across many Native American cultures. Visual art also is a form of expression in weaving, cradleboards, baskets, etc.

I draw upon my research (Klug & Whitfield, 2003) to relate the following experiences of two pre-service teachers who learned to integrate the arts in their teach-

ing of Native American children. In the first example, Ben (pseudonym) worked
with a mentor teacher whose classroom abounded with stuffed animals. She was
using the toys to connect with the children's traditional cultural belief that animals
are our brothers. Ben cites as his most memorable teaching experience reading
Hawk, I'm Your Brother by Byrd Baylor (1976). To accompany the story, Ben had
the children create their own hawks. When he had to leave for two weeks, he had
the children put their hawks in cages until his return. When he returned, he asked
the children to retell the story up to the point he had left and was astounded when
children could do so virtually word for word. As descendants of an oral culture,
their skill is not surprising, but for a teacher from another culture it was an unexpected and much appreciated feat. At the end of the story, Ben gave the children
the opportunity to either set their hawks free or keep them. Most chose to set them
free.

Ben found that the children in his mentor's classroom performed significantly
better academically than those in another room whose teacher used more traditional methods in which the learning activities were teacher-directed and scripted.
His experience both motivated him to change his own teaching methods and to
work with Native American children in the future.

A second example is a pre-service teacher who strove to provide cultural experiences in her students' learning by incorporating music, art, and dance into the
curriculum. She and her colleague teachers further established Friday afternoons
as a time for the children to demonstrate their dancing, drumming, and flute playing for their parents and elders of the community. These times of sharing not only
enhanced the students' knowledge of their own cultures, but also gave them the
opportunity to share what they had learned, dressed in the regalia made for them
by their elders, garments that were in themselves artworks. And, the Friday performances built a bridge between the school and the community, resulting in a re-
spectfully shared culture, similar to the fundamental tenets of the Reggio Emilia
program.

Other Programs that Make a Difference

Perret and Fox (2004) describe a how a program involving collaboration between
the Winston-Salem, North Carolina Symphony and Bolton Elementary School en
gaged children in active participation in and understanding of music. Students at
Bolton came predominantly from lower SES homes with nearly 70 percent on free
or reduced lunch, living with a single parent, other relative, or in foster homes, and
many were homeless or transient. More than 60 percent underperformed on state-
wide, standardized tests. The program consisted of the symphony's woodwind
quintet visiting the school two to three times a week for half hour lessons that they
coordinated with the classroom teachers. Each lesson was designed to build upon
a previous lesson and before long the children attained academic benefits. The
musicians understood that they themselves already used multiple intelligences

(Gardner, 1999) and incorporated those strategies into their own instruction. The musicians and teachers drew parallels between types of intelligences used in both music and academic subjects. For example, according to Perret and Fox,

> Reading music is a linguistic task … while rhythm involves logical-mathematical intelligence, Playing an instrument draws on bodily-kinesthetic ability; and ensemble playing is both a spatial and an interpersonal challenge. For these skills to add up to something pleasing and meaningful requires musical intelligence. (p. 43)

A further example of programs that are attempting to meet the needs of all children through the arts is one initiated by Tucson (Arizona) Unified School District. The district has developed a successful program called Opening Minds to the Arts (OMA). Inspired by a presentation at the National Symphony Association in 1994 about the Winston-Salem music integration program, the then-Tucson symphony president led the initiative to bring a similar program to Tucson. In collaboration with the University of Arizona School of Music and Dance and the Tucson Symphony, the program now serves nearly 2000 students, 700 teachers, and 44 schools in the Tucson Unified School District (2008). This exemplary program has been recognized by the Arts Education Project in Washington D.C. as a national model. From 2001-2004, the research group WestEd conducted a comparison study between six Tucson elementary schools with high percentages of children who were living in poverty, second language learners, and/or moved frequently. Three schools participated in the OMA curriculum, which incorporated music, opera, dance, theater, and visual arts into reading, writing, math, and science, while the other three schools used "standard" teaching methodology. The study found that OMA significantly improved students' test scores in reading, writing, and math as well as improving teachers' effectiveness.

These large-scale examples must also be supported by the work of individual teachers who are committed to ensuring that all children learn and who recognize the role of the arts in facilitating that learning. For instance, Klug, mentioned previously, has incorporated a variety of arts into her work with Native American elementary school children on a reservation in the West. Strongly committed to culturally relevant pedagogy, she encourages students to express their understandings of literacy materials through their drawings. Because Native American children often come from cultures that value oral tradition, storytelling, drama, and dance, each of these approaches is consonant with the culture from which these children come and honors that which they bring to the learning experience.

Conclusion

Young children about to enter the portals of academe generally look forward to going to school. It signifies a rite of passage, a way to be more "grown up," a giant step into the world at large. They bring to this experience energy, eagerness, hope, and enthusiasm for the rich world of learning that awaits them.

Yet, a one-size-fits-all curriculum driven by standards, "drill and grill", and testing, and often unrelated to anything relevant to the children, is a recipe for failing a substantial number of them. Rather than serving as a "boost up", education can become a step down, particularly for those children from homes that lack many of the resources identified as essential for school success - abundant literacy materials, caregivers with both the skill and time to read to them, fluency in the English language, as well as adequate resources in the areas of nutrition, housing, and medical care.

What all children need most in educational contexts is culturally sensitive teaching that respects and includes their unique and individual ways of making meaning. Do we really want our children to experience the loss of creativity described in Harry Chapin's (1978) song, *Flowers Are Red that* is based on his son's experience at school? The disheartening tale told in its lyrics about a child who uses original colors and shapes to draw flowers and who is compelled by a teacher to draw flowers that are "real", i.e. flowers that are red and leaves that are green. When the child changes schools, he no longer creates his unique floral expressions, instead repeating his previous teacher's admonition that "flowers are red and green leaves are green." The song is all the more poignant in that it describes the process of depriving young children of the freshness of expression they bring to schooling as they confront rigidity and disrespect for the creativity they bring to learning.

Arizona's 2008 Teacher of the Year, Robert Kerr, a primary grade teacher, believes in the role of teachers as change agents for their students. He maintains

> It is a teacher's responsibility to ensure curriculum meets the needs of students, advances them academically, and empowers them as thinkers. ... Cultural relevancy is not only empowering to students, it also recognizes students for who they are and pushes them to think and act with their realities (Arizona Republic, 2007).

Empowers! Should not the role of education be, from children's earliest years, to empower them? Empower them to think great thoughts, to dream great dreams, to do great things? It is within the purview of the arts, as dynamic components of education, to develop creativity and fluidity of thinking, to develop parts of the brain neglected in a one-size-fits-all curriculum. And, more importantly, provide children with a broad repertoire of intellectual and social tools for success, both in the present and in the future. Let the arts be, as Gandini (2005) declared, "a reaction against the concept of the education of young children based mainly on words and simple-minded rituals" (p. 7). Let the arts enable each child to become, as Vygotsky (1978) put it, "a head taller" (p. 102).

References

Amabile, T. M. (1986). The personality of creativity. *Creative Living, 15*(3), 12-16.

Banks, J. (1994). *Multiethnic education: Theory and practice* (3rd ed.). Needham Heights MA: Allyn & Bacon.

Baylor, B. (1976). *Hawk, I'm your brother.* New York: Scribner.

Bernstein, B. (1972). A critique of the concept of compensatory education. In C. B. Cazden, V. John, & D. Hymes (Eds.), *Functions of language in the classroom,* (pp. 135-150). New York: Teachers College Press.

Blatner, A. (1995). Drama in education as mental hygiene: A child psychiatrist's perspective. *Youth Theatre Journal* 9, 92-96.

Blackledge, A. (2000). *Literacy, power, and social justice.* Stoke-on-Trent, UK: Trentham Books.

Bruner, J. (1996). *The culture of education.* Cambridge, MA: Harvard University Press.

Bruner, J. (1999). Narratives of aging. *Journal of Aging Studies, 13*(1), 7-10.

Bruner, J. (2004). Life as narrative. *Social Research, 71*(3), 691-710.

Catterall, J. (2002). The arts and the transfer of learning. In Critical links: Learning in the arts and student academic and social development. [Online report] Compendium of the Arts Educational Research Studies. Available: http://www.aep.org

Chapin, H. (1978). Flowers are red. On *Living Room Suite* [Album]. New York: Elektra Records.

Chapman, L. H. (2005). No child left behind in art? *Art Education, 58*(1), 6-16.

Chapman, L. (2007). An update on No Child Left Behind and national trends in education. *Arts Education Policy Review, 109*(1), 25-36.

Dewey, J. (1934). *Art as experience.* New York: Perigee.

Drohojowska-Philp, H. (2004). *Full: bloom: The art and life of Georgia O'Keeffe.* New York: W. W, Norton.

Edwards, C., Gandini, L., & Forman, G. (Eds.). (1998). *The hundred languages of children: The Reggio Emilia approach—Advanced reflections* (2nd ed.). Norwood, NJ: Ablex.

Gallas, K. (1994). *The languages of learning: How children talk, write, dance, draw, and sing their understanding of the world.* New York: Teachers College Press.

Gandini, L. (2005). From the beginning of the *atelier* to materials as languages. In L. Gandini, , L. Hill, L. Caldwell, & C. Schwall (Eds.), *In the spirit of the studio: Learning from the atelier of Reggio Emilia* (pp.6-16). New York: Teachers College Press.

Gardner, H. (1994). *The arts and human development.* New York: Basic Books.

Gardner, H. (1999). *Intelligences reframed: Multiple Intelligences for the 21st century.* New York: Basic Books.

Gay, G. (2000). *Culturally responsive teaching: Theory, research, & practice.* New York: Teachers College Press.

Holt, J. (1995). *Freedom and beyond* (Rev. ed.). Portsmouth, NH: Boynton/Cook Publishers.

Jalongo, M. (2002). *The child's right to creative thought and expression: A position paper.* Washington, D.C.: The Association for Childhood Education International.

Klug, B., & Whitfield, P. (2003). *Widening the circle: Culturally relevant pedagogy for American Indian children.* New York: Rutledge Falmer.

Nagel, N., & Guest, S. (2007). Savage inequalities: STILL – An interview with Jonathan Kozol. *Democracy & Education, 17*(1), 3-6.

No Child Left Behind Act of 2001. Pub. L. No. 107-110 (HR1). http://www.ed.gpv/nclb

Ohanian, S. (1999). *One size fits few: The folly of educational standards.* Portsmouth NH: Heinemann.

Paley, V. (1986). *Molly is three: Growing up in school.* Chicago: University of Chicago.

Paley, V. (1988). *Bad guys don't have birthdays: Fantasy play at four.* Chicago: University of Chicago.

Perret, P., & Fox, J. (2004). *A well-tempered mind: Using music to help children listen and learn.* New York: Dana Press.

Pestalozzi, J. H. (1915). *How Gertrude teaches her children.* (L. C. Holland & F. C. Turner, Trans.) Syracuse, NY: C.W. Bardeen. (Original work published 1801)

Rea, D. (2001). Maximizing the motivated mind for emergent giftedness. *The Roeper Review, 23*(3), 157-164..

Roskos, K., & Christie, J. (2002). Knowing in the doing: Observing literacy learning in play. *Young Children, 57*(2), 46-54.

Russ, S. W., Robins, A. L., & Christiano, B. A. (1999). Pretend play: Longitudinal prediction of creativity and affect on fantasy in children. *Creativity Research Journal, 12*(2), 129-139.

Sidelnick, M., & Svoboda, M. (2000). The bridge between drawing and writing: Hannah's story. *The Reading Teacher, 54*(2), 174-184.

Smilansky, S. & Shefatya, L. (2004). *Facilitating play: A medium for promoting cognitive, so-cio-emotional, and academic development in young children.* Silver Springs, MD: PS&E Publications.

Smith, K. (2002). Dancing in the forest: Narrative writing through dance. *Young Children, 57*(2), 90-94.

Vygotsky, L. (1962). *Thought and language.* Cambridge MA: MIT Press.

Vygotsky, L. (1978). *Mind in society.* Cambridge MA: Harvard University Press.

Whitfield, P. (2005). No Child Left Behind: Leaving the arts behind in young children's literacy. *Journal of Children & Poverty, 11*(1), 43-54.

_____. (2008). *Opening minds through the arts (OMA).* Tucson Unified School District. *http:www.omaproject.org/index.php/about/ results.*

_____ (2007). Flagstaff educator top Arizona teacher. *The Arizona Republic,* November 9, 2007.

Patricia T. Whitfield
Professor Emerita
Lyon College, Arkansas USA

Dr. Patricia T. Whitfield has been a teacher educator for nearly 30 years in both public and private higher education, working primarily with underserved popula-tions. Her roots are in elementary education, and after working in public schools she entered higher education, serving as a professor, program director, division chair, assistant dean, and dean of Education. Her research interests are: multicul-tural education, diversifying the teaching force, and supervision of instruction. She is strongly committed to social justice, especially in education.

Part Three
Visions

Chapter 9
Empowering Pre-service Teachers to Design a Classroom Environment that Serves as a Third Teacher

Katherina Danko-McGhee and Ruslan Slutsky

Abstract This chapter focuses on ways to empower pre-service teachers to design a quality learning environment for young children. Two approaches of preparing pre-service teachers to think about the learning environment as the *third teacher* are shared with implications for teacher preparation programs.

Keywords classroom environment, aesthetics, third teacher, Reggio Emilia

Introduction

With each passing year, more and more children are spending time in group care outside the home. Children who are entering preschools and childcare centers are there because their parents work. The amount of time parents spend at work, limits the amount of time they have to interact with their children on a daily basis. Subsequently, this leads to children spending more time with adults and caregivers who are not related to them.

In 1999, over 60% of U.S. children, ages three to five, spent some part of their day in daycare centers and preschools (U.S. Department of Education, 2003). These findings are not limited to the United States, but are true internationally as well. For example, with over 800 million of 0 to 6 year old children in the world, more than two thirds have benefited from early childhood programs (Korintus, 2000).

With so many children enrolled in preschools and childcare centers, the question of quality in these settings becomes vital. Childcare quality is not only impor-

University of Toledo, USA

University of Toledo, USA

M. J. Narey (ed.), *Making Meaning.*
© Springer 2009

tant to parents, but to educators and policy makers because research has found that a high quality experience has a more positive impact on children's overall development (Barnett, 1995; Brooks-Gunn et al., 1994; Burchinal et al., 1997; Feagans & Appelbaum, 1995; Lamb, 1998; Ramey & Ramey, 1998; Roberts, Rabinowitch, Bryant, & Burchinal, 1989).

Research on child care quality has often focused on teachers as the cornerstone of the quality debate; suggesting that high quality teachers, those with an educational background in early childhood or a related field, have classrooms that rate higher with respect to overall classroom quality (Phillipsen, Burchinal, Howes, & Cryer, 1997). Teacher knowledge of early childhood education and development, without question, is an important factor in determining the overall quality of a classroom and the impact that it has on learning and development. High quality and developmentally appropriate early childhood classrooms expose children to nurturing relationships and appropriate early learning experiences. Alternately, children in low quality care settings are often exposed to hazardous and unstimulating environments, often due to a lack of teacher knowledge to be able to appropriately respond to children's emerging needs (Shonkoff & Phillips, 2000).

In this chapter, we want to take a look at quality experiences for young children based on the type of environment that teachers create. These quality environments become the cornerstone in which actual learning and social experiences take place. The more teachers understand early childhood development and practice, the more likely they are to engage children in an environment that is stimulating, challenging, and allows children to take on the role as constructors of knowledge. An environment that allows for these types of experiences itself becomes a teacher. In this chapter we will refer to this concept of the environment as third teacher (Cadwell, 1997).

Understanding the meaning of the environment as third teacher

How to create a nurturing environment that promotes learning is one of the most important considerations for teachers when planning a curriculum. Such an environment, as viewed in the Reggio Emilia approach, is where physical space nurtures concentration, creativity, and the motivation to independently learn and explore (McKellar, 1957).

According to Rinaldi (1995), children are considered to be naturally curious and resourceful:

> ...children can best create meaning and make sense of their world through living in complex, rich environments which support complex, varied, sustained, and changing relationships between people, the world of experience, ideas and the many ways of expressing ideas. (Cadwell, 1997, p. 93)

In Reggio Emilia schools, "it is understood that the environment should support the work and interest of the children without constant adult guidance and intervention" (Wurm, 2005, p. 40). Learning can be enhanced when teachers make choices about how to design learning environments that enable them to support independent explorations and creative problem solving.

There is attention to design and placement of objects to provide a visual and meaningful context. The objects within the space are not simplified, cartoon-like images that are assumed to appeal to children, but are 'beautiful' objects in their own right (Tarr, 2001).

Classrooms as third teachers are set up to invite conversation, exploration, and collaboration. Natural and manufactured materials are aesthetically displayed in transparent containers, many of which are set upon mirrors to provide multiple vantage points in order to engage children. The work of children, both in visual images and in text format, is highly regarded and is on display throughout the school for all to view. Children can revisit their work to reflect upon previous learning that has taken place. An environment set up as a third teacher fosters revisiting experiences and sets the stage for continuous learning that the teacher does not need to regulate. By designing environments this way, we provide children with experiences that allow them to explore multiple perspectives and to reconstruct knowledge based on continuous exploration.

Carefully prepared environments nurture critical thinking skills. They are designed in a provocative kind of way to encourage a child to learn, and can entice a child to look and ponder and become engaged in discovery, problem solving, and creative thinking. The teacher's charge is to provide these materials to invoke thought that will set the stage for constructive thinking. The child then uses these materials as a language to communicate a thought or idea.

The environment as the third teacher is grounded in the educational philosophy of John Dewey and the constructivist learning theory of Lev Vygotsky (Malaguzzi, 1998).

> Constructivists believe that learning is accomplished through exploring, experimenting, and manipulating objects or materials. This theory directly relates to the development of creative thinking and the necessity for active participation in the process. Using the constructivist theory as a basis for environmental design, the classroom should contain a variety of materials that can be explored and combined in many different ways. (Isbell & Raines, 2003, pp. 15-16)

The Reggio Emilia environment, as previously described, does just as Isbell and Raines (2003) suggest. However, it is important to bear in mind that how the environment is prepared is driven by the teacher's image of the child and their knowledge of early childhood education and development. In Reggio, the child is highly regarded, respected, and is viewed as: intelligent, curious, interested in engaging in social interactions, capable of constructing his/her own learning, eager to interact with everything that the environment has to offer (Gandini, 1998). If a teacher does not operate within this framework, then the environment can be designed to be stifling and condescending inasmuch as it:

...isolates particular aspects of a culture which simplifies visual forms, and protects children from the outside world. 'It's visual aesthetic reflects mass marketing and craft store culture. It does not challenge children aesthetically to respond deeply to the natural world, their cultural heritage, or to their inner worlds. (Tarr, 2001)

We typically find this type of environment in North American schools. A paradigm shift in thinking must take place in order to understand and be able to design suitable environments for young children. What better place for this to occur than in methods classes for early childhood education pre-service teachers.

Creativity, Aesthetics, and the Environment as a Third Teacher?

Young children seem to be naturally inclined to be creative (Isbell & Raines, 2003; Torrance, 1969; Williams, 1982). They have a zest for exploring new materials and are not afraid to use them in innovative and unique ways. This, of course, is provided that their environment supports these explorations. Jalongo and Stamp (1997) suggest that to nurture creative responses from young children, they must have a supportive environment that allows for investigation where they can freely pursue their own answers. Therefore, it is essential that teachers provide open-ended explorations for young children. However, in reality, this is not always the case. Children are often in learning environments that are not aesthetically pleasing and do not nurture creative thought (Tarr, 2001).

Kerka (1999) suggests that stimulating environments that nurture creativity provide the necessary resources and time for investigative play and experimentation. A nurturing environment is one in which children are free and motivated to make choices and to explore for answers without feeling threatened or intimidated. Duffy (2002) adds that:

> The way in which we organize and use the available space inside and out is crucial in creating opportunities for children to express their creativity...the range of resources and organization we provide will determine what and how the children can create and how creative they can be. (p. 105)

However, we should also remember that a stimulating and creative environment is aesthetic as well. According to Isbell and Raines (2003), "Aesthetics is an area of art concerned with feelings and responses to color, form, and design (p.117)." Schirrmacher (2006) notes that it is a basic human instinct to have aesthetic experiences and to appreciate the world. Broudy (1988) further adds that everyone engages in aesthetic experiences. An aesthetic moment "...is not limited to things in galleries and museums" (Eisner, 1992, p. 5). Therefore, if the environment is made conducive to allow for such experiences, aesthetic moments can occur in common everyday places, such as classrooms.

Duffy (2002) believes that, creativity and imagination are often linked with aesthetics. Taking this point a step further, Eisner (1972) refers to 'aesthetic organizing' which

> ...is characterized by the presence in objects of a high degree of coherence and harmony... the overriding concern is in the aesthetic organization of qualitative components. Decisions about the placements of objects are made through what may be called a qualitative creativity. (p. 220)

This 'qualitative creativity' is also implied in Duffy's statement that, "in an early childhood setting, whatever is available is organized in a tidy way" (2002, pp. 105-06). The aesthetic way materials are presented to children will determine how creatively they can use them in their given environment. The more aesthetically and creatively materials are displayed in the classroom, the more intrigued children may be to use and explore them. Duffy further notes that,

> It is frustrating for children and adults if they are delayed and possibly distracted by being unable to find a resource or piece of equipment at a crucial moment. Examination of the work areas of artists and crafts people often reveals well-organized space where everything is easy to locate and readily at hand (2002, p. 106).

McKellar (1957) reinforces this point by noting that the way a space is aesthetically organized can assist in concentration and can increase one's motivation to work in creative ways. These types of settings can also further the opportunity for children to construct knowledge and revisit previous learning experiences.

Eyestone-Finnegan (2001) also sees the importance of a creative and aesthetic environment, and suggests that it should be considered as a third teacher, where images and objects are displayed that relate to the interests of young children. Gandini (1998, 2002) echoes those thoughts and adds that environments and the way they are set up by teachers should become invitations for exploration and construction of knowledge. As a promoter of the Reggio Emilia philosophy, she too sees the environment as a third teacher.

Designing an Environment that Can Serve As a Third Teacher

In order for children to be creative, teachers must model creative behavior (Schirrmacher, 2006). One way to model creative behavior is through the design of the teaching/learning environment. If a teacher bears in mind the importance of the environment as the third teacher, this will help with the selection of materials and how they are arranged. Remember that the environment as third teacher must provoke children to want to learn and explore. Therefore, just making materials available for children is not enough. The teacher must take the time to speculate how the children may react to certain materials and then display them accordingly. For many teachers, this requires a paradigm shift in thinking. Instilling this new way of thinking should begin with pre-service teachers. This was done during one academic year with two separate courses at a university.

We wanted to look at two approaches with regard to the environment as third teacher and what type of experience would impact the pre-service teachers the most. One approach was to provide a theoretical foundation along with a hands-on experience where students had the opportunity to design an environment as a third teacher. The second approach involved students in discussions to form a theoretical foundation, similar to the first approach, but they did not have an opportunity to design an environment.

First Approach:

Before the students arrived for the semester, the classroom environment was thoughtfully prepared. Because the classroom is housed in a museum setting and also serves as a learning environment for young children, care was taken to prepare the environment for both children and pre-service teachers. There was a concerted effort to design learning experiences that related to the museum collection. Learning areas were set up all around the room. Each one focused on a different work of art. Materials were displayed to provoke children to use them in creative ways, while at the same time, making their own connections to the art reproductions displayed. For a more detailed account of this prepared environment, see Danko-McGhee (in press).

When students arrived in the fall, they were first given a pre-test to determine what they knew about the learning environment and how it can serve as a third teacher (see Tables 9.1, 9.2, & 9.3). Their responses indicated that while they thought that the learning environment was important for young children, they were unfamiliar with the concept of environment as third teacher and did not feel confident that they could design an appropriate environment for young children.

Table 9.1 Student Responses to Pre-Test Survey Regarding the Learning Environment for Young Children n=20

Criteria for a Quality Learning Environment	Student Responses in Percentages
Learning environment is important for young children	100%
	(20)*
Environment should be inviting	10%
	(2)
Environment should be bright and colorful	70%
	(14)
Children's artwork and other art work should be displayed	5%
	(1)

Table 9.1 (continued)

Environment should be creative	5%
	(1)
Environment should provide multi-sensory experiences	10%
	(2)

*( ) indicates the number of students

Table 9.2 Student Awareness of the Environment as Third Teacher n=20

Student Awareness of:	Unfamiliar	Somewhat Familiar	Familiar
The Environment as Third Teacher	85%	15%	0%
	(17)*	(3)	
Reggio Emilia Approach	65%	1%	34%
	(13)*	(1)	(6)

*( ) indicates the number of students

Table 9.3 Student Self Conception n=20

Students felt they had:	Yes	Some	Very Little	None
Artistic ability	0%	5% (1)*	95% (19)	0%
Creative skills	0%	5%(1)	95% (19)	0%
The ability to create a Reggio inspired environment	0%	0%	10% (2)	90%(18)

*( ) indicates the number of students

As the semester continued, students were asked to explain how their classroom environment challenged them to think and then to conjecture about how young children might react to this space. There were many discussions about Reggio Emilia and the environment as third teacher. Students were required to read, *In the Spirit of the Studio* (Gandini, Hill, Cadwell, & Schwall, 2005). This further helped with students understanding of the environment and the aesthetic arrangement of materials. A DVD from the North American Reggio Emilia Alliance (2005) entitled *North American Reggio-inspired Environments*, was shown to the class for further inspiration. This DVD showcases Reggio-inspired environments across the United States and provides many good examples of the environment as third teacher. Students were also shown slides of environments from the Reggio Emilia schools in Italy.

Much time was spent discussing children's graphic and aesthetic development and ways to meet their needs in developmentally appropriate ways, which included safety concerns and issues of sequential skill development, such as hand-eye coordination, fine and gross motor, visual discrimination, social, and sequencing skills. Brain research supports the principles of developmentally appropriate practices that include meaningful experiences matching the child's level of development. "The best learning for young children is active, hands-on, meaningful, integrative, and responsive" (Isbell & Raines, 2003, p. 19). Additional discussions included explorations of various art media and how to use them in creative ways with young children. Schirrmacher's (2006) book, *Art and Creative Development for Young Children*, was used as an additional textbook for the class and served as a basis for many of these studio experiences.

A concerted effort was made to educate pre-service teachers about the dangers of restrictive or stifling art experiences. As Szekely (1991) points out, "...learning the right technique, following the correct procedure, can be self defeating" (p.13). Schirrmacher (2006) follows this line of thought by adding that, "...an emphasis on conformity and convergent thinking can kill the creative spirit" (p.13). Numerous examples of creative versus uncreative art experiences were demonstrated and discussed with the students.

After being provided with the necessary theoretical underpinnings, university students were challenged to make some changes and additions to our classroom learning environment. Using the classroom designed by the professor as a launch pad, they had to come up with their own ideas on how to extend upon the design in order to improve the classroom environment. Students divided themselves into work groups of four and decided on an area of the classroom environment that they wanted to change or enhance. Students were instructed to come up with a plan that included their ideas and the means by which they would implement them. The professor offered continuous feedback. In the true spirit of creativity, students had to be original, fluent, and flexible (Torrance, 1969) as they reworked their ideas into viable solutions. As Jalongo and Stamp (1997) note, "Truly creative teachers know how to establish the conditions and provide the opportunities for their students to be creative" (p. 128). These pre-service teachers also had to bear in mind that with regard to creativity,

> ...the more experiences a child has with people, places, or materials, the more possibilities will exist for use in creative activities. Young children's worlds should be filled with interesting experiences that build on their level of development. These should include many opportunities to experiment and combine a variety of materials and objects in different ways and should allow them to make choices. (Isbell & Raines, 2003, p. 24)

With this in mind, students had to make sure that the environment they designed met the following criteria: it had to be aesthetically appealing; the experiences they were providing would provoke critical thinking in young children; would be open-ended; and would nurture creativity. Experiences also had to focus on artworks housed in the museum, because the classroom is in a museum setting and had to reflect that. Once plans were finalized, students were ready to actually become environmental designers. Two of their designed environments will be discussed.

Project One: Literacy Area

The existing literacy area was made more comfortable by adding assorted large blue pillows for little children to sit upon while reading. These pillows were made with a variety of aesthetically appealing fabrics that were carefully chosen to enhance this learning space using the blue color scheme. Small journals with blank pages were made using wallpaper scraps for the covers. Sumptuous papers were selected to enhance the aesthetic appeal. The pre-service teachers believed that placing these attractive journals in this area would serve as a provocation for children to write in them. The journals were placed in a basket along with writing tools. A small note invited children to write.

A mailbox was placed on one of the bookshelves in this area to encourage children to write letters to the people in the painting that was hanging in this space. The painting was a reproduction of *Two on the Aisle* by Edward Hopper (1927). In this painting, three people, a man and two women, are guests at the theater. One woman, beside the man, is getting ready to sit down in her chair. The other woman is seated in her chair and is reading the theatrical program, which she holds in her hands. Students were careful to only select reproductions of paintings in the museum where the subject matter included individuals who were engaged in reading (Fig. 9.1).

Fig. 9.1 Portion of Literacy Area that invited children to write letters to people in the painting

Empty picture frames were placed on the blackboard to encourage children to draw pictures and to write a story within the frame. Through our observations, children already had demonstrated that they enjoy drawing on the chalkboard. So, this activity capitalizes on that interest by helping the child to focus more on a work of art that was displayed nearby and to respond to it in various ways.

Project Two: Monet's Water Lilies

Another area displayed a reproduction of Monet's (1919) *Water Lilies*. The students who were working on this project had a very difficult time. Their vision was to cover the wall with paper that was cut out as a large pond of water lilies. They then wanted to paint the pond using the colors of Monet by 'smudging' the paint onto the paper to create an 'impressionistic' look. They really struggled with this until a technique was demonstrated to them so that they were successful in achieving the effect that they desired. The final product served as an aesthetically pleasing backdrop (Fig. 9.2).

They then created puzzles by cutting up small reproductions of Monet's *Water Lilies*. These puzzle pieces were placed on a magnet board hanging on the wall. Children were to put the puzzles together and could view the reproductions of *Water Lilies* displayed in this area as a guide to correctly assemble the puzzle. Children's books about Monet were included in this area, along with painting supplies for children to create their own lily ponds on paper.

These are two examples (literacy and water lilies) of how these pre-service teachers began to think in terms of setting up an environment as the third teacher by providing materials that would provoke thought, exploration, and creativity in young children. While the water lilies environment was the most aesthetically pleasing, it fell short of meeting the other assigned criteria in that it did not provide open ended experiences or foster critical thought like the literacy area did.

Fig. 9.2 Portion of Pre-service teachers' *Water Lilies* learning center

For example, there is less critical thought involved when children are asked to correctly replicate the painting by putting together a puzzle. However, another experience in this area provided children with materials to paint their own version of a lily pond, a more open ended experience. Nevertheless, students could have challenged themselves by designing more creative and open-ended experiences for young children.

At the conclusion of this course, pre-service teachers were given a post-test to determine how their thoughts on the environment had changed.

After their experience of designing their own learning environment, students felt that the environment should inspire and sustain innovative thinking and should be aesthetically pleasing. While they felt that the opportunity was very challenging, it was useful in preparing them for designing their future classrooms. (See table 9.4).

Table 9.4 Students Impressions About Designing an Environment – Post Test Survey n=20

Criteria for a Learning Environment	Percentage of Responses
Experiences should be open-ended	75% (15)*
Aesthetically Pleasing	70% (14)
Learning from the Experience	**Percentage of Responses**
Helped them to be more thoughtful	65% (13)*
Felt challenged when designing the environment	100% (20)

*( ) number of students responding

Second Approach

Emergence of Themes

The second approach was conducted with 26 students who enrolled in a two-week summer course on the Reggio Emilia approach. Students were asked to complete a pre-test to determine what they knew about the learning environment during the first day of class. All 26 students completed the pre-test. Their responses indicated that while they thought that the learning environment was important, they were unable to articulate the important role that a quality environment plays in the learning process. A few themes arose as students discussed their initial thoughts on environment: 1) importance of materials; 2) organization of space; 3) providing learning opportunities; and 4) centers. Of the four themes, the first, importance of materials, was the one that students believed was the most important one to implement. Some of the student responses for all four themes are listed below.

Theme 1: Importance of Materials

- The environment plays a vital part in sustaining children's creative, innovative thinking and learning; children are predominantly visual learners; children learn by exploring their environment and touching, using, and looking at everything. Around them, children need plenty of materials in the environment as well.
- Provide them with a lot of different materials to use and lots of opportunities to use them. Leave the material use open-ended and not give the children specific instructions.

Theme 2: Organization of Space

- Having an organized classroom also plays a major role in the learning experiences of children. Allowing the children to have an abundance of materials and space to work gives them a variety of options that will allow them to express themselves in different ways.
- It is important to keep the classroom as organized as possible. All materials should be labeled and there should be a spot for everything in the room. When a room is organized children can better express themselves.

Theme 3: Providing Learning Opportunities

- Provide experiences and materials the child would not encounter in his/her home or neighborhood.
- Offer opportunities for choice, risk-taking, collaboration with peers and mentors in a challenging environment.

Theme 4: Centers

- The teachers can create an open, flexible, fun and creative environment that promotes learning by setting up different learning stations such as dramatic play, sand/water table, reading area....also, have developmentally appropriate toys easily accessible for the children.

- The classroom can be inviting and warm, with many areas to look at and have students work to help them along. But if it is plain and unchanging all year, then it can be hard on the child, and definitely uninspiring.

New Theme: Environment as Third Teacher

Throughout the first week of the two-week course, students were provided with many examples of how the environment can serve as a third teacher. It was stressed that a quality environment should be able to teach a child even when the teacher is not readily available. Through interaction with the environment, the children could engage in an authentic and meaningful learning experience, whether alone or with peers. Along with our class discussions, students in this second approach, as in the first approach, were required to read, *In the Spirit of the Studio* by Gandini, Hill, Caldwell, Schwall, & Vecchi (2005), watch a DVD from the North American Reggio Emilia Alliance (2005) entitled, *North American Reggio-inspired Environments*, and were shown slides on Reggio Emilia school environments on the first day of class (after the pre-test). The second week of class included the same type of experiences found in the first approach with the only exception being that students did not have an opportunity to create an environment.

During the last day of class, a post-test was given to all 26 students to see if their perceptions of the environment had changed. All 26 students completed the post-test. After reviewing the post-test, a new theme emerged, environment as third teacher, as well as some returning ones: importance of organization of the environment and materials. Student comments about the environment at the conclusion of the two-week course demonstrate these themes.

Environment as Third Teacher

"A classroom environment is the third teacher and should be created by the children. Hands-on activities and projects will inspire critical thinking, as well as, creative and innovative thought process."

"The environment can play a huge role in a child's learning …in fact, it is the third teacher! A beautiful environment lets a child feel valued. Supplies, layouts, etc. serve as protagonists for learning, sparking interest & curiosity."

"The classroom environment would inspire creative and innovative thinking because it can be filled with so many open-ended experiences. The classroom can serve as the third teacher. It can open up so many experiences for the children to explore and learn from. When children are given time to explore and learn on their own they will be able to use their critical thinking skills."

Organization of Space:

"A classroom can inspire interest by having the environment revolve around them, children need to feel a sense of ownership and feel they belong to class, they will then be more interested in being there, thus artwork and projects put up by students around the room will motivate children to want to be at school and learn that the environment is a teacher."

"A classroom environment that allows children to explore themselves creates better time management because the teacher does not always have to get supplies."

"If the classroom is set up with interesting materials and children have time and support to explore and interact with materials, peers, and teachers, quality learning experiences can happen."

"The classroom environment plays a major role in the learning process for young children. In our schools today, many classroom environments are full of secular materials that were bought at a store. There is absolutely no creativity or independent thought. In order for our classrooms to inspire children, I believe we must allow the children to control the environment. The work of the children, and their creative ideas should decorate the classroom. If we give the children this freedom, they will sustain innovative thinking and independent thought."

Importance of Materials:

"Display work that the children have done around the room. Include materials for the children to use around the room. Rather than having coloring books and commercially made decorations, include blank materials to inspire the students' interest."

"When children have multiple languages to work with that are laid out for them to use, they have the freedom to explore. When they have the freedom to explore different materials freely, children use their critical thinking skills. When teachers give children the materials to use to solve problems, it stifles their creativity and their critical thinking. Children need to be able to choose their own materials so they can utilize their critical thinking skills, which they NEED in Early Education!! Lots of materials and open space is what they need to flourish!"

"Lots of materials, anything that you find: paint, clay, glass, recyclables, hair gel, demonstrates the idea of the 100 languages. Children have many

tools at their disposal to express how they feel or what they want to get across. Without different materials or supplies, children are limited and their learning experience will not be rich."

In the pre-test, students focused on the very basic elements in the environment, such as materials and space, without any true regard for setup, aesthetics or quality. In the post-test, students, after the two week course, became astute to the aesthetic appeal that materials can have on the environment itself and how they can promote quality learning engagement. Additionally, students began thinking of the environment and describing it as a third teacher. Even when students described the environment as an organization of space in the post-test, their perspectives of that space shifted from a more teacher directed to a child directed space. Additionally, the importance of materials was re-conceptualized in the post-test remarks as well, with students paying more attention to the quality of materials that should be present that best address children's interests. The paradigm shift that students experienced in this two-week course suggests their new understanding that the environment as a third teacher goes well beyond just the set up. It is how children are allowed to interact with the environment and the materials in it that is the key.

Conclusions

We found that both approaches, talking about the environment versus actually designing one, can be used to provide meaningful experiences for pre-service teachers interested in exploring the complexity of the learning environment and its impact on children. However, we feel that providing pre-service teachers with the opportunity to design an environment is a much more powerful approach. This adds a hands-on opportunity that assigned readings and class discussions lack. By actually allowing pre-service teachers to manipulate the environment, they are engaging in critical thought processes that allow them to make decisions and changes to a real environment rather than a hypothetical one. Anytime teacher educators can implement a hands-on model for pre-service teachers to interact with authentic experiences (such as environmental design), it offers them a better transition and scaffold when they actually have to implement this type of experience in their own classrooms.

Teachers that understand the importance of letting children explore and construct knowledge, while serving as a facilitator in the learning process, are critical to the establishment of a quality learning environment. A teacher who chooses to set up the classroom environment as a third teacher, allows children to have open-ended explorations of materials with time to test their ideas. Teachers must also be willing to be co-learners in the learning process and the construction of knowledge.

References

Barnett, W. S. (1995). Long term effects of early childhood programs on cognitive and school outcomes. *The Future of Children, 5*(3) 25-50.

Broudy, H. (1988) Aesthetics and the curriculum. In W. Pinar (Eds.), *Contemporary curriculum discourses* (pp. 332-342). Scottsdale, AZ: Gorsuch Scarisbrick.

Brooks-Gunn, J., McCarton, C. M., Casey, P. H., McCormick, M. C., Bauer, C. R., Bernbaum, J. C., Tyson, J., Swanson, M., Bennett, F. C., Scott, D. T., Tonascia, J., & Meinert, C. (1994). Early intervention in low-birth-weight premature infants: Results through age 5 from the Infant Health and Development Program. *Journal of the American Medical Association, 272*(16) 1257-1262.

Burchinal, M. R., Campbell, F. A., Bryant, D. M., Wasik, B. H., & Ramey, C. T., (1997). Early-intervention and mediating process in cognitive performance of children of low-income African American families. *Child Development, 68*(5), 935-954.

Cadwell, L. (1997). *Bringing Reggio Emilia home: An innovative approach to early childhood education.* New York: Teachers College Press.

Danko-McGhee, K. (in press). The environment as third teacher: Pre-service teacher's aesthetic transformation of an art learning environment for young children in a museum setting. *International Art in Early Childhood Journal.*

Duffy, B. (2002). *Supporting creativity and imagination in the early years.* Buckingham, England: Open University Press.

Eyestone-Finnegan, J. (2001). Looking at art with toddlers, *Art Education, 54*(3) 40-45.

Eisner, E. (1992). Arts can counter school reforms standardizing aims. *ASCD Update, 34*(5) 5.

Eisner, E. (1972). *Educating artistic vision.* New York: Macmillan Company.

Feagans, L., & Appelbaum, M. (1995). Validation of language types in learning disabled children. *Journal of Educational Psychology, 78,* 358-364.

Gandini, L. (1998). Educational and caring spaces. In C. Edwards, L. Gandini, & G. Forman (Eds.), *The hundred languages of children: The Reggio Emilia approach - advanced reflections* (pp. 161-178). Greenwich, CT: Ablex.

Gandini, L. (2002). The story and foundations of the Reggio Emilia approach. In V. Fu, A. J. Stremmel, & L. T. Hill (Eds.), *Teaching and learning: Collaborative explorations of the Reggio Emilia approach* (pp. 13-22). Upper Saddle River, NJ: Merrill Prentice Hall.

Gandini, L., Hill, L., Cadwell, L., Schwall, C., & Vecchi, V. (2005). *In the spirit of the studio.* New York: Teacher's College Press.

Isbell, R. & Raines, S. (2003). *Creativity and the arts with young children.* New York: Thompson Delmar Learning.

Jalongo, M. & Stamp, L. (1997). *The arts in children's lives: Aesthetic education in early childhood.* Boston, MA: Allyn & Bacon.

Kerka, S. (1999). Creativity in adulthood. Washington, DC: Office of Educational Research and Improvement, ERIC Document Reproduction Service No. ED429 186.

Korintus, M. (2000). Early childhood in central and eastern Europe: Issues and challenges. (Monograph) UNESCO Educational Sector, 13, 1-62.

Lamb, M. E. (1998). Nonparental child care: Context, quality, correlates. In W. Damon, I. E. Sigel & K. A. Ranninger (Eds.), *Handbook of child psychology, Vol. 4: Child Psychology in Practice* (pp. 73-133). New York: John Wiley and Sons.

Malaguzzi, L. (1998). History, ideas and basic philosophy: An interview with Lella Gandini. In C. Edwards, L. Gandini, & G. Forman (Eds.), *The hundred languages of children: The Reggio Emilia approach - advanced reflections* (2nd ed.) (pp. 49-98). Greenwich, CT: Ablex.

McKellar, P. (1957). *Imagination and thinking: A psychological analysis.* London: Cohen and West.

Phillipsen, L. C., Burchinal, M. R., Howes, C., & Cryer, D. (1997). The prediction of process quality from structural features of child- care. *Early Childhood Research Quarterly, 12*(3), 281-303.

Ramey, C. T., & Ramey, S. L. (1998). Early intervention and early experience. *American Psychologist, 58*(2), 109-120.

Rinaldi, C. (1995). Projected curriculum constructed through documentation – progettazione. In C. Edwards, L. Gandini, and G. Forman (Eds.) *The hundred languages of children*. Greenwich, CT: Ablex.

Roberts, J. E., Rabinowitch, S., Bryant, D. M., & Burchinal, M. R. (1989). Language skills of children with different preschool experiences. *Journal of Speech and Hearing Research, 32*(4), 773-786.

Schirrmacher, R. (2006). *Art and creative development for young children*. Clifton Park, NY: Delmar Learning.

Shonkoff, J. P., & Phillips, D. A. (2000). *From neurons to neighborhoods: The science of early childhood development*. Washington, DC : National Academy Press.

Szekely, G. (1991). *From play to art*. Portsmouth, NH: Heineman.

Tarr, P. (2001). Aesthetic codes in early childhood classrooms: What art educators can learn from Reggio Emilia. *Art Education, 54*(3), 33-39.

Torrance, P. (1969). *Creativity*. Belmont, CA: Fearon Press.

U.S. Department of Education, National Center for Education Statistics (2003) Digest of Education Statistics (NCES 2003-060), Table 45.

Williams, F.E. (1982). Developing children's creativity at home and school. G/C/T Gifted, Creative, and Talented, 24(1) 2-6.

Wurm, J. (2005). *Working in the Reggio way: A beginner's guide for American teachers*. St. Paul, MN: Redleaf Press.

Katherina Danko-McGhee
University of Toledo
Toledo, OH   USA

Dr. Katherina Danko-McGhee is a Full Professor and Early Childhood Art Education Coordinator at the University of Toledo and also acts as a consultant to the Toledo Museum of Art Early Childhood Programming. Published nationally and internationally, Dr. Danko-McGhee's main focus in research has included early childhood aesthetic preferences, art and literacy, as well as aesthetic learning environments. She is the author of the book, T*he Aesthetic Preferences of Young Children* (2000, Mellen Press) and co-author of the book, *The Impact of Early Art Experiences on Literacy Development* (2007, National Art Education Association).

Ruslan Slutsky
University of Toledo
Toledo, OH   USA

Dr. Ruslan Slutsky is an Associate Professor of Early Childhood Education at the University of Toledo, Judith Herb College of Education. Dr. Slutsky is published both internationally and nationally on such topics as art and literacy, the arts and standardization, and critical thinking through the arts. He is co-author of the book, *The Impact of Early Art Experiences on Literacy Development*.

Chapter 10
Rewiring and Networking Language, Literacy, and Learning through the Arts:

Developing Fluencies with Technology

Lynn Hartle and Candace Jaruszewicz

Abstract In this chapter we present an ecological approach (Bronfenbrenner, 2007) to address the changing needs, opportunities, and challenges of teaching young children literacy in the 21st century. We provide examples to illustrate how technology works to develop fluencies that make learning meaningful for young children and their teachers. Implications for teacher education are offered.

Keywords Arts, early childhood, multi-literacy, visual literacy, teacher education, technology

Shifts in Early Childhood Teacher Education: Fluid and Static Mediums for the 21st Century…and Beyond…

Child Meaning-Making

Learning, making, and using symbols are at the essence of being human. Babies and young children tune in to objects that are significant. A teddy bear can be a sign of security for some, while a blanket soothes others, and therefore, are signs that carry meaning for the child. The field of semiotics, the study of all systems of signs, symbols and how these are used to communicate provides a framework for understanding the processes children use in making meaning (Gordon, 2003). Sig-

University of Central Florida, USA

College of Charleston, USA

M. J. Narey (ed.), *Making Meaning*.

nificant symbols differ for individual children depending on their experiences or contexts. Cuddling with a teddy bear at home may evoke feelings of security, but at preschool that same bear may trigger signs of embarrassment. Young children are also influenced by the modern world of symbols through exposure to visual media and interactive media, advertisements, and videos, as well traditional forms, such as books, and storytelling (Anning & Ring, 2004).

The child brings cognitive skills and personal contextual experiences, such as the home, friends, family, school, television, radio, or digital audio players (MP3) to symbolic investigations that extend their family histories to the external world (Labbo, 1996; Labbo & Reinking, 1999). Dyson's (1993) research suggests that children use any available symbol systems or languages at their disposal, such as music, dance, or drawing to express themselves and make sense of their world. Through drawing, for example, children liberate themselves from the here and now. In a literature review of trends in research on the intersections between literacy and visual/communicative arts, Sweet (2005), makes the case that the arts "...offer students a way of pushing the boundaries of their learning..." (p. 274). In fact, for some young children, their drawings reveal in-depth and important knowledge and perception beyond the level, skill, or aesthetic quality expressed in their verbal or written language.

With appropriate scaffolding, young children are capable of representing their ideas in creative, symbolic, and concrete forms with multiple media and in *one hundred languages* (Edwards, Gandini & Forman, 1998). The notion of the *hundred languages of children*, first realized by preschool programs in Reggio Emilia, Italy, is particularly relevant when discussing the potential of 21st century media tools for enabling children to express emerging ideas about their internal (feelings, imagination) and external (objects, people, places) worlds. The New London Group (1996), expands upon the notion by explaining that the concept of multiple literacies, or "multi-literacies...focuses on modes of representation much broader than language alone" (p. 61). Writing, drawing, gesture, creating with a graphic organizer, and play are examples of traditional media that young children may use to express what they know and can do (Dyson, 1993; Vygotsky, 1978). Taking and using digital photos to research a topic, using software to create books, and engaging in web quests are examples of digital literacies that expand children's understandings of those arts and verbal and visual signs, symbols (Labbo, 1996). Digital representation requires children and teachers to understand the multiple realities of how new technologies can enhance learning experiences (Labbo & Reinking, 1999; Partnership for 21st Century Skills, 2002).

Expanded Teacher Roles

Not only do teachers need to know how children become literate in the 21st century; teachers need to develop information fluency & literacy and then teach this to young children. In other words, teachers must learn how to access and discriminate among multiple forms of information, such as more traditional books, journals, or newspapers, but also the new Web 2.0 technologies of wikis, blogs, and electronic documents posted on websites. At the forefront of information fluency is the use of sound investigative techniques to select appropriate information and strategies to support diverse learners. Our role as teachers is to critically analyze texts and scaffold children's development of visual literacy and critical analysis as well. Rather than considering only four areas of literacy – listening, speaking, reading, and writing, the International Reading Association and National Council of Teachers of English (1996) standards also foster the important development of children's viewing skills to critically analyze visual text and images and visual representations using knowledge of how images and video document and represent meaning.

While not always practiced in schools, strategies for developing those information fluency skills are now included in the revised National Literacy Standards of the International Reading Association and National Council of Teachers of English (1996), signaling a need to shift teaching practices from less drill, practice, and passive learning to increases in actively pursuing inquiry questions, taking responsibility for learning in small group activities, and communicating through multiple avenues to others in the community and beyond. Socio-cognitive orientations (Vygotsky, 1978) help teachers reposition their views on how children develop literacy symbols through visual and performing arts and modern technologies to realize the interdependent nature of children who live in highly fluid, dynamic and complex social contexts.

An Ecological Model of Teacher Education

Like young children, teachers need opportunities to integrate their new knowledge in settings with other teachers, children, and array of old and new media relevant to the children they teach. Teachers need time and support to explore strategies and reflect on their value for children (Putnam & Borko, 2000). Rather than merely "retooling" teachers with arts, creativity, or technology skills, Loveless, Burton, and Turvey (2006) suggest a more *ecological model* (Bronfenbrenner, 2007) of professional development to address and respect teachers' deep professional needs, values and ideas. Loveless, Burton, and Turvey found technologies were best learned in the context of real settings with children and teachers of varying experience levels working together to explore possibilities. This kind of authentic model is further discussed in *The Arts Education Partnership – Champions of Change: The Impact of the Arts on Learning* (Fiske, 1999) and *Third Space: When Learning Matters* (Stevenson & Deasy, 2005). These examples present how teachers and administrators in these high needs schools across the United States transformed school culture, reaching children who otherwise might not have been reached until they engaged with their preferred learning styles through the multi-literacies. For example, when children engaged in the processes of combining images with words to make movies, this process tapped visual learning styles, making learning more authentic and meaningful for these children who previously saw no connections between school and their community contexts (Bull, Park, Searson, Thompson, Mishra, Koehler, & Knezek, 2007). Not only the children, but also the teachers realized a newfound energy in their teaching craft through their shared processes, products, and productions. This synergistic nature of academic and aesthetic learning, inspired one elementary school, reported in the *Third Space* to rename their art space the "Heart Room"(Stevenson & Deasy, 2005).

As experienced teacher educators, we (co-authors) have adopted an ecological model of teaching with exciting new as well as old favorite arts and technology tools that stretch beyond simply elevating young children and adults' motivation and excitement about learning. Our focus upon multiple literacies aligns with research-based teacher education practices and with contemporary cognitive learning theory and brain-based teaching (Bransford, Brown, Cocking, 2000; Gazzaniga, 2008). Multi-literacies allow for children's proficiency across diverse disciplines, affording greater learning, generalization and neuro-transfer. Dual coding through two or more forms of representation fosters children's deep meaning through diversification in the brain cells (Paivio, 1986). Arts also allow for self-exploration and self-expression using parts of the brain not accessed through traditional communicative means. Infusing these visual literacies to teach across disciplines is not simply to connect content knowledge, but also to foster inquiry, imagination, deep mental activity, problem solving, and democratic processes (Eisner, 2002). We believe that an ecological model for developing teachers' understandings of 21st century classrooms can be best represented through the rich tradition of the characteristics of play and the natural ways young children explore their world (Isenberg & Quisenberry, 2002).

To illustrate our perspective, in this chapter we present examples of project-based activities from one Southeastern university campus early learning demonstration preschool. These examples show how multi-literacy development can be supported by thoughtful teachers who scaffold children's abilities to express themselves through visual as well as verbal languages. The program philosophy is inspired by the Reggio Emilia schools in Italy and follows the basic premise to encourage life long learning. This center's teachers and surrounding community have strong appreciation for and focus on the arts. The teachers take advantage of local events, taking the children on excursions to performance rehearsals, puppet shows, and visual art displays. In the classroom, teachers routinely encourage the children to explore sensory materials and media and express themselves freely. Teacher-directed activities as well as mass-produced art are discouraged; the preschool emphasized process over product. A technology support person is available on call with resourceful information about new technologies, especially open source and share ware, available free or at little cost. The art room (Atelier) contains found (recyclable) and purchased art materials and computers, digital cameras and other technology peripherals are found in each classroom. While these examples are drawn from the admittedly ideal setting of a university-based preschool, the principles and practices presented are only limited by the imagination and risk-taking of any good teacher.

The (He)art of Multi-literacies: Making the Magic

DePlatchett (2008) describes how the recognition of the magical role of the arts to make learning meaningful and address the needs of all children's learning styles can lead to changes in teacher education. Yet, in many instances, the educational community fails to see the magic and misses opportunities to fully enable the child to learn through the arts.

For a visual literacy rich learning environment (DePlatchett, 2008; Kist, 2000; Labbo & Reinking, 1999), materials traditionally seen as two and three dimensional art media - paint, clay, wire, fabric, found objects, as well as performance and production media, such as props for dramatic play, photography, film, and production software should be seamlessly infused in the everyday planning and teachable moments of the school day. Two and three-dimensional materials should be out of cupboards. Computers should not just be down the hall in the computer laboratory, but also in the classroom. Technology uses must extend beyond reinforcement of reading, writing, or math skills and fluency. Once teachers awaken students' expectations with the arts, technology-integrated instruction should enhance those expectations (DePlatchett, 2008).

Mondrian Example: Using Art to Explore Mapping

During a month-long exploration, four- and five-year-old children at the university early learning center studied and discussed many examples of and a video about Mondrian's impressions of New York City. Two of the ideas teachers wanted to explore were intentionality and how children represent their ideas about three-dimensional space.

Teachers then took children outside to draw what was of interest to them on the playground. On 18" x 24" paper, children applied geometric shapes and strips of black, white, red, yellow, and blue paper to represent the playground structures in Mondrian's style. Later, use of the document camera (a high-resolution web cam mounted on a flexible arm that captures and enlarges 3D objects and images from flat surfaces) gave all the children full view wherever they wanted to project, i.e. wall or floor (like overhead and opaque projectors). Teachers observed extraordinary concentration, focus on details, and evidence that children could represent their ideas to plan and visualize abstractly (with some assistance).

This experience piqued the interest of the teacher of the three-year olds who wondered if these younger children could conceptualize beyond creation of a pretend map, such as one they constructed as part of a hunt for hidden pirate treasure boxes. Inspired by the book, *Reggio Tutta: A Guide to the City* (Davoli & Ferri, 2000), created by preschool children, the teacher asked the three-year olds if they would like to try to make a real map of their classroom. A lengthy and animated discussion about the relative location of key places of interest in the room, then, with only an orientation of the large paper to one wall in the class, each child chose a part of the map and proceeded to draw directly on the paper. The finished representation was not only proportionately accurate, but included an unexpected attention to details (Figure 10.1) and documented the children's emerging understanding of the concepts of symbolic representation of place, position, and scale necessary to mapping. A second map of the playground soon followed. To share these with families, the maps were digitally photographed and scanned to the computer. It was clear that even very young children are capable of converting three-dimensional space to a two-dimensional representation when that space is entirely familiar to them.

To encourage the type of teaching modeled by the early childhood teachers in this example, teacher educators will need to have at least some background themselves in the arts or arts-infused education or be willing to collaborate with others who do. The combined expertise of the authors of this chapter includes, for example, (a) early childhood and art education teaching certification, (b) co-teaching experiences with professors from the arts or arts education departments at their respective universities, and (c) first-hand teaching experience in and visiting many early childhood programs both in the United States and abroad, such as Reggio Emilia, Italy. Therefore, in order to prepare pre-service teachers, we highlight the need for teacher educators to build their own knowledge and skills.

Fig. 10.1 Our classroom, by the three year olds.

Expanding Meaning Making with Information and Communication Technologies

Numerous forms of technology come on the market every day. Teachers are challenged to examine these or the potential that they offer for exploring, extending or enriching arts, literacy, and learning.

Technologies: As Tools

Teachers can use an interactive electronic whiteboard with individuals or groups of children to access online resources or use light, sound, and pictures to enhance learning. Computers with internet access can be used to research content for children's projects. Those interactive projects and works-in progress can be electronically captured, saved, and printed at various stages; invaluable for both formative and summative assessment. Document cameras, the second-generation opaque projectors, are now available to enable even the youngest children, with the aid of a projection system, to investigate, magnify, and observe two or three-dimensional objects down to minutest details and from multiple perspectives. For teachers who formerly used cut-and-paste methods to construct visual documentation of student learning (Helm, Beneke & Steinheimer, 2007), the wait time needed to have film developed is no longer necessary. The digital camera is indispensable and much more forgiving in terms of the image choices it affords. The expense of printing is no longer an issue, as web-based photo-management applications such as Flickr™ (http://www.flickr.com/) make capture, organization, and retrieval of photos and video clips increasingly efficient and flexible for multiple purposes.

Technologies: Local and Global Outreach

Using a tool such as the web-based Voicethread™(http://voicethread.com) can extend photo opportunities even more, enabling individuals or groups of people to upload real-time conversation about digital photos or scanned images of artifacts. Software and Web 2.0 engineers clearly understand the potential classroom applications of these kinds of tools, so some are offered in teacher-friendly versions, specifically set up for classroom use. Interactive web applications, such as blogs, wikis, and website design tools offer privacy control solutions as well, so that ethical considerations of sharing identifiable photographs can be maintained. Families can stay connected to children's work as a class and with their own individual child. Many websites can even display digital audio and/or video files as PowerPoint™ slides for presentation or assessment documentation purposes. Through the classroom website or blog, children are also able to communicate with other classrooms anywhere in the world, creating the very real and promising possibility that children can begin at a very young age to develop concrete understandings of what it means to live in a global community.

A Typical Day at the University Early Learning Center

Most days at the university early learning center begin with a large block of time set aside for center activities and project work. Children and teachers mostly work in small groups, but some children work independently. The entire group is convened upon request, when community discussions, sharing, or decisions are needed. The human interactions of the classroom community remain central to the teaching and learning. The technology doesn't take the place of the subject matter, creative thinking, play, reading, writing, or problem solving, but rather it is used to enhance the potential and excitement for learning.

- **In the block area**, children manipulate translucent pattern blocks on the light table. Then they decide to "keep a visual" of their block patterns, especially the overlapping colors, so they get out the watercolors to reproduce the designs. The teacher suggests they also record their ideas on a digital tape recorder so they can add their spoken words to a photograph loaded on to a *Photo Story 3* (Windows™ open source, free plug-in) creation. As they continue to experiment with mixing watercolors to match the colors and shapes of the translucent blocks on the light table, they play back their conversation and decide whether or not they need to record more or if what they have accurately represents their thinking.
- **In the atelier (art room)**, children look at and discuss reproductions of paintings of famous artists. The teacher interviews (audiotapes) each of them. Later, she will post their "critiques" to a Voicethread™ project that includes electronic versions of these paintings. On their home computer later, children can view this project with their families.
- **While discussing an earlier long-term project about dinosaurs**, one child says that he wanted to see "that Dinosaur movie" they made, again. He said he forgot what the scenery looked like. The teacher leads him to the computer where they enjoy, the digital eight-minute movie – "The Dinosaurs Help" that they wrote, produced, directed, and later published to the center's web site.
- **After returning from a visit to the studio of a local artist**, the entire group of children discuss and negotiate how to describe a series of digital photos taken

during the outing as the teacher transcribes their words to her laptop and later inserts them into a PowerPoint presentation that will be available to families on the center's website. The text for the transcription in the visual documentation of their visit reads:

A visit to Redux:

1. On Monday the Blue Hermit Crabs and the Orange Butterflies [names the children chose at the beginning of the year for their classes] visited Tina at her studio. Here is what happened.

2. Last Friday, Tina had asked us what art was and we made a big list. At the studio she told us, "art is ideas." We learned that it doesn't have to be pretty but it has to show an idea.

3. This is two BIG stickers. They are part of the art that is finished. We have this book. There are objects with it. Tina says that this is art, too.

4. According to Lily, this is REAL art. (It is pretty)

5. The artists had stuff they were working on in their studios. We looked at it.

6. This is Tina's studio. Art she has finished is on the walls. Sometimes she looks at books and finds ideas.

7. This is Tina's new art. Her two boys [our students] are in the picture.

8. We saw two other artists who were at work.

9. This is one of our favorite things we saw at the art studio. Our other favorite thing was the red lights in the dark room.

10. The last thing Tina did was to show us how to make prints.

Subsequently, printmaking materials were offered and the children spent several days exploring and experimenting with different printmaking techniques. This example demonstrates how teachers integrate traditional tools and new technologies in the daily work of the early childhood classroom.

Implications for Teacher Education

The policy implications and support for information fluency are rapidly surfacing in institutions of higher education. Institutions are realizing the need to update faculty on the new technologies and the 21st century multi-literacies needed by graduates entering all aspects of the workforce (Partnership for 21st Century Skills, 2002). In both of our universities (but increasingly in many colleges and universities), technology is heavily supported. Some of the supports available to us are (a) instructional technology liaisons, (b) grant funding opportunities for exploration of new hard and software applications, (c) regular updating and replacement of equipment, (d) "smart" classrooms which include the teaching technologies to project and seamlessly move between surfing the internet, show CDs and DVDS, and present with PowerPoint to model applications and (e) hands-on professional development opportunities via faculty technology institutes and one-on-one coaching, as needed. If this is not the case, it is incumbent upon the teacher educator to pursue professional development and practical experiences, independently or partner with more experienced colleagues from other institutions who may be willing to coach or mentor.

Learning to Weave and Orchestrate Multi-literacies

Technology today represents a model of thinking about learning from an integrated and multi-dimensional perspective consistent with what we know about the creative process. Mitchel Resnick (2006) of the Massachusetts Institute of Technology (MIT) Lifelong Kindergarten Laboratory embraces the medium computers, as an artist would embrace a paintbrush; as a musician might finger her piano; or as a sculptor might stroke a block of stone to find the sculpture inside. He believes we should think of computers as more like paintbrushes and less like TV's. Computers have enormous potential as a creative design and expression tools if used appropriately with young children.

The 24-Foot Python Example

This example describes an experience inspired by the four- and five-year-old children's interest in large animals. After teachers and children found a streaming video from a waterhole in Botswana posted online by the National Geographic Society, children watched it off and on for several weeks, collecting facts from many sources about the elephants, tigers, antelopes, giraffes, and hippos they saw. Children made many observations, drawings, murals, and sculptures that represented their fascination with the watering hole animals. In the classroom during story time, the teacher read children a four-line poem "The snake problem" by Shel Silverstein (1971). A line about a twenty-four foot python instantly captured their attention and they became intensely interested in how long that python would actually be.

The children decided to make a stuffed paper snake, but were adamant it needed to be not one inch shorter or longer than 24 feet and that it should look as real as they could make it. Because their concepts of standard measurement are still immature, there was plenty of arguing about what measure to use to make the snake equal 24 feet. Finally, in an "ah-ha" moment, the children discovered that the linoleum blocks on the floor measured exactly one foot and they could count out 24 blocks to have the proper length. But since the classroom is only 16 blocks long, the paper, paints, books of pictures, scissors, tape, and staplers went out into the hallway to construct the snake.

When one of the children asked, "But how can we paint it so it looks exactly right?" someone remembered that a former graduate assistant had a three foot pet python named "Jorge" who had come to visit the previous year. Students emailed an invitation to Jorge for another visit. They waited to paint the paper snake until they had observed Jorge from every angle, made many drawings, taken dozens of digital photos, and formulated and recorded several more research questions.

They were surprised to learn that a python's belly looked different than the back and that although the snake pictures downloaded from the Internet and collected from print resources were definitely classifiable as pythons, there were slight pattern variations from one animal to the next (which they then compared to physical characteristic variations among humans). At some point, they decided the paper snake's head looked too big in comparison to real pythons. The original head came off, a new one was made that was proportionate and visually satisfying, and the painting began in earnest.

Four more days later, it was finished, and the paper python was hung around the ceiling of the classroom, with a sign indicating "Beware, 24 foot python!" This experience was immensely satisfying and bolstered the children's confidence about building to scale.

A few weeks later, when binoculars revealed a red-tailed hawk had build a nest on the church steeple across the street, they made another stuffed-paper scale model. This time they used the document camera to project their favorite downloaded (from the internet) photo on the wall. They traced the projected bird to make paper patterns for the wings, body, head, and feet. Again, perfectionism reigned and they had to make the tail twice before it met their standards. The red tailed hawk hangs from the ceiling next to the python.

In their continued reading (online and print materials), children discovered that both animals are predators. The study later shifted somewhat to include other predators that might also be found in the local region to add to their display. While this example could be described in terms of how the experience connected to any number of concepts and/or standards, it would not have happened at all without a teacher who respects these children's interests and questions and understands how much time children often need to figure things out and construct personal meaning and understanding through self-selected available mediums. The classroom teacher is familiar with each child's unique abilities and skills, and has observed that these skills are enhanced by technologies that offer the child freedom to make creative choices.

Although this teacher's masterful skills were developed through professional development of her own visual literacy, college teacher education faculty can explicitly prepare future teachers to understand and develop language and literacy skills through integration of arts and technology. Involving pre-service teachers in visual documentation of their own learning is a means by which the metacognitive dimensions of this concept become apparent in a very real and concrete sense.

In one university course, students were assigned to tell a story through building blocks and to document their own learning. When three-dimensional blocks and words were *not* enough to tell the story or create the imagery about this space traveler, pre-service teachers painted a corresponding picture of the block figure's travel through pathways in space to future stimulate the imagination of listening colleagues (see Fig. 10.2). Teachers then critically selected three sequential significant digital photos among the many digital photographs to document the entire experience.

After some modeling by the teacher-educator, pre-service teachers can individually, or preferably in groups, prepare displays (panels) using photos, scanned images of course artifacts, and textual reflections about the learning that takes place each week, constructing visual representation of the entire course by the end of the semester. The pre-service teachers are able to experience in a very real way, how the panels provide contextual referencing and a means by which they can reflect on their own learning. They witness the impact of aesthetic individuality, represented across the various attempts by their colleagues and make aesthetic decisions through the art and technology used in the documentation process.

College class activities and/or assignments should fully engage teachers with peripherals such as: digital cameras, audio-recorders, document cameras, interactive electronic whiteboards, and digital microscopes as "invisible" or infused as these would be in classrooms for children. Teacher educators then need to be explicit about the value and ways each of the technologies support content learning or specific knowledge, skills, and learning styles of young children (DePlatchett, 2008).

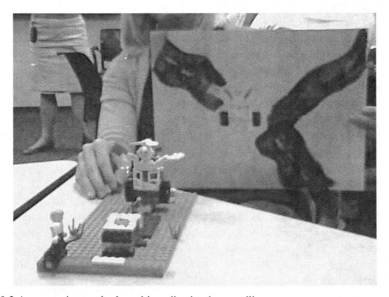

Fig. 10.2 A pre-service teacher's multi-media visual storytelling.

For example, drama can support the kinesthetic learner, digital photography helps visual learners hold memories, and certain math programs stimulate more in-depth understanding of the principles of geometry (Clements & Sarama, 2003). We suggest incorporating, at minimum, the following requirements and resources to build teacher confidence and skills:

- online courseware and assignments with typical components such as the discussion board, chat room, uploading and downloading documents
- electronic communications that require them to use email, distribution lists, and listservs
- assignments and in-class activities with online (and off-line) applications such as blogging, social networking, wikis, document-sharing, and photo and/or audio-file management
- website navigation and construction
- appropriate software, hardware, and peripheral decisions
- discussions about ethical considerations, i.e. safe space internet use, overuse of technologies, excessive screen time, and importance of physical activity

Teachers can then use their heightened awareness to realize the symbiotic relationships between media and literacies (Labbo & Reinking, 1999; Leu, 2000; Sweet, 2005). Teachers can later bank on these skills to motivate and teach to children's preferred learning styles, especially children who might not otherwise have been reached by traditional teaching methods.

Early Childhood Applications of Arts and Technology

Comfort with technologies is a necessary, although not necessarily sufficient condition for teachers to use technology in their own classrooms to advance multiple literacies. It is imperative that teacher educators seek out teachers and classrooms in their communities where the arts are valued as a dimension of multiple literacies, and where technologies are being used in the daily lives of children as an integral part of their learning process. Teachers need to see what happens when young children are engaged in creative intellectual pursuits in classrooms where technology is also viewed as a natural means for extension of the learning process. They need to see practicing teachers who are not afraid of technology, but embrace its use because they see how their work and the verbal, written, and visual literacy development of their children can be enhanced in meaningful ways.

Observing How Technology Supports Meaning-making

Pre-service teachers visiting the university early learning center profiled in this chapter immediately notice an environment that emphasizes (a) neutral colors, (b) natural elements, (c) careful and deliberate arrangement of aesthetically pleasing and intriguing objects, and (d) many examples of framed children's artwork, poetry, and writing as part of the "permanent collection." Visitors can observe technology being used to make meaning in a variety of ways.

Teacher activity includes technology use such as:

* posting digital pictures and drawings in the block center of current constructions so that children can (a) preserve their work, (b) see their skills progress over time, (c) revisit and converse with each other about their work
* inviting two children to help inventory art supplies, making a list, and then working with children to place an online order
* transcribing the progress of an illustrated story that is being written and saved on the interactive electronic white board or the computer over the course of a week
* posting current events on the center's homepage and classroom blogs

Student engagement with technology occurs on many levels:

* one child examining a shell with a hand-held magnifying glass while a group is using a document camera to look at other shells from many angles, as they all use colored pencils and pastels to record their observations in journals
* children composing an email question about fossils to send to their newly discovered 'expert' friend in the College Science Department
* children expressing great satisfaction when a visiting professor is sharing artwork, photos, and letters carried back from a village in Africa for which children had sent over bake sale proceeds for the village orphanage. When the visitor leaves, children search (again) on GoogleEarth (http://earth.google.com/) to find the exact location of the village and then compose a letter to their new friends
* children are molding plaster fossils they will later bury in the sand table to be found by other children, broken apart with a hammer, sorted, classified, and graphed by type
* children in the photography studio are cutting up sheets of digital photos they have taken that morning and labeling these for their classroom daily news

Program-wide commitment to providing evidence of meaning-making:

* a display of group-authored stories responding to a portfolio of illustrations by Chris Van Allsburg (1996).

- a looping PowerPoint on a television monitor documenting a month-long gingerbread house building/decorating project
- visual documentation of long-term projects posted to the program website (http://www.cofc.edu/~child/)
- hanging printouts of a visual journal tracking the progress of the sunflower house in the garden recording growth of the plants
- numerous books illustrated and published by children in the classrooms
- (in 2010) program and classroom accreditation folios on the program wiki

Developing Fluencies with Technology

The American Association of Colleges of Teacher Education (AACTE) Focus Council on Early Childhood Education (2004) and the National Association for the Education of Young Children (NAEYC) point to the need for teachers to be prepared to work with an ever diverse population of children with preferred learning styles (Bredekamp & Copple, 1997). This underscores the need to develop pre-service teachers' fluencies in a number of areas, including the arts and tech nology. Secondly, teacher educators need to be explicit with pre-service students about the place of technology and the arts infusion in teaching – to determine when and how each of these medium can enrich creative expression and meaning-making for children, and also decide when a medium may be an impediment or counter-productive.

In other words, the same beliefs and practices that guide teachers in making *any* developmentally appropriate instructional decisions should be applied when considering technology uses and other mediums to suit the child or the learning situation. Teachers charged with scaffolding the growth and development of the full range of literacy expression for our youngest learners must think about how to keep technology from becoming an end in itself, but rather a tool to support these multiple fluencies.

In principle, teachers should have an appreciation and acceptance of the arts as a contextual framework for promoting, supporting, extending, and illuminating intellectual growth as a dimension of multiple literacies. Teachers should be engaged in experiences with exciting new technologies and modern media. Building the infrastructure to do so in teacher education is another matter altogether, requiring:

1. Teacher educators who are disposed to and have deeply held beliefs about the value of the arts as communication, aesthetic enrichment, and creative expression.
2. Teacher educators who are technologically fluent and who keep abreast of new media.

3. Planned experiences in teacher education courses that require students to think critically about the arts as viable forms of the many multiple literacies.
4. Planned experiences in teacher education courses that involve students in hands-on exploration and application of technologies for building capacity in multiple literacies
5. Opportunities for students to observe and interact with teachers in early childhood technology-infused classroom settings where the arts are valued as an integral part of the curriculum.

Teachers making appropriate choices

Around the same time the python study was on-going, one child, Bradley was laboriously hand-illustrating and writing a fictitious story word-for-word about Transformers (i.e., a trademarked toy) using colored pencils and watercolors, only asking the teacher for assistance with laminating the pages and cover with a spiral binding machine to publish the finished book. Another child, Andrew, who is not yet writing complete sentences, but extremely interested in being viewed as a herpetologist, because he now considers himself an expert on snakes, used the digital camera to take more photographs of Jorge.

After construction of the 24-foot paper snake was completed, Andrew used those photographs to create a fact book called, *All About Snakes*. The teacher also helped him locate and print pictures of different kinds of snakes besides pythons that he had learned about during internet searches. She also transcribed his dictation on her laptop. After printing, Andrew preferred to cut and paste the text and photos himself to make the book, despite the fact that there were other, entirely computer-based software options, such as *Photostory 3* that could have been used. The teacher followed each child's lead, and made appropriate decisions about judicious use of technology to scaffold and support their individual creative and literary intentions. The teacher left Bradley to his own devices entirely, and offered, but not overwhelmed the other, Andrew with "just right" technology options. The teacher created a school world that parallels their community and home world, immersed in visual and auditory opportunities to explore, express, learn, and selectively decide which to use to communicate.

What is the status of emerging developments to fully engage young children's and early childhood teachers' multiple literacies in the next few years? We concur with the prediction: "Lightspeed Ahead with Mild Turbulence" (Kalinowski, 2001, p. 281).

References:

American Association of Colleges of Teacher Education. (2004). *The early childhood challenge: Preparing high-quality teachers for a changing society.* Reston, VA: AACTE Focus council on early childhood education.

Anning, A. & Ring, K. (2004). *Making sense of children's drawings.* Berkshire, England: Open University Press/ McGraw-Hill Education.

Bransford, J.D., Brown, A.L., Cocking, R.R. (2000). *How People Learn: Brain, Mind, Experience, and School: Expanded Edition.* Commission on Behavioral and Social Sciences and Education (CBASSE). Washington, DC: National Academy Press. Retrieved January 31, 2008 http://www.nap.edu/catalog.php?record_id=9853

Bredekamp, S., & Copple, C. (1997). *Developmentally appropriate practice in early childhood programs.* Washington, DC: National Association for the Education of Young Children.

Bronfenbrenner, U. (2007). *The ecology of human development: Experiments by nature and design.* Cambridge, MA: Harvard University Press.

Bull, G., Park, J., Searson, M., Thompson, A., Mishra, P., Koehler, M. J., & Knezek, G. (2007). Editorial: Developing technology policies for effective classroom practice. *Contemporary Issues in Technology and Teacher Education* [Online serial], *7*(3). Retrieved from the Internet November 28, 2007. http://www.citejournal.org/vol7/iss3/editorial/article1.cfm

Clements, D.H., & Sarama, J. (2003). Young children and technology: What does the research say? *Young Children 58*(6): 34-40.

Davoli, M., and Ferri, G. (Eds.) (2000). *Reggio tutta: A guide to the city by the children.* Reggio Emilia: Reggio Children.

DePlatchett, N. (2008). Placing the magic in the classroom: TPCK in arts education. In AACTE Committee on Innovation and Technology (Ed.), *Handbook of technological pedagogical content knowledge (TPCK) for educators* (p. 167-192). New York, NY: Routledge/ Taylor & Francis.

Dyson, H. A. (1993). 'From Prop to Mediator: The Changing Role of Written Language in Children's Symbolic Repertoires. In B. Spodek & O. N. Saracho (Eds.) *Yearbook in Early Childhood Education: Language and Literacy in Early Childhood Education Vol. 4.* (pp. 21-41). New York: Teachers College Press.

Edwards, C. Gandini, L. Forman, G. (Eds.) (1998). *The hundred languages of children: The Reggio Emilia approach – advanced reflections* (2nd ed.). Norwood, NJ: Ablex.

Eisner, E. W. (2002). *Art and the creation of mind.* New Haven, CT: Yale University Press.

Fiske, E. B. (Ed.) (1999). *Champions of Change: The Impact of the Arts on Learning.* Washington, DC: Arts Education Partnership. Retrieved from the Internet February 10, 2008. http://www.aep-arts.org/publications/index.htm

Gazzaniga, M. (2008). *Learning, arts, and the brain: The Dana consortium report on the arts and cognition.* New York, NY: Dana Press.

Gordon, D.T. (2003). *Better teaching and learning in the digital classroom.* Boston, MA: Harvard Education Press.

Helm, J., Beneke, S., & Steinheimer, S. (2007). *Windows on learning.* New York: Teachers College Press.

International Reading Association & the National Council of Teachers of English. (1996). *Standards for the English language arts.* Newark, DE & Irbana, IL: Authors.

Isenberg, J. P., & Quisenberry, N. (2002). *Play: essential for all children.* A Position Paper of the Association for Childhood Education International. Retrieved February 13, 2008 http://www.acei.org/playpaper.htm

Kalinowski, M. F. (2001). The Current Status of Technology in Education: Lightspeed Ahead with Mild Turbulence. *Information Technology in Childhood Education Annual,* 281-291.

Kist, W. (2000). Beginning to create the new literacy classroom: What does the new literacy look like? *Journal of Adolescent and Adult Literacy, 43*(8), 710-718.

Labbo, L. (1996). *A semiotic analysis of young children's symbol making in a classroom computer centre. Reading Research Quarterly, 31*(1), 356-385.

Labbo, L. D., & Reinking, D. (1999). Theory and Research into Practice: Negotiating the Multiple Realities of Technology in Literacy Research and Instruction. *Reading Research Quarterly, 34*(4), 478-492.

Leu, D. J., Jr. (2000). Literacy and technology: Deictic consequences for literacy education in an information age. In M.L. Kamil, P. Mosenthal, P.D. Pearson, & R. Barr (Eds.), *Handbook of reading research* (pp. 743-770). Mahwah, NJ: Erlbaum.

Loveless, A., Burton, J., & Turvey, K. (2006). Developing conceptual frameworks for creativity, ICT, and teacher education. *Thinking Skills and Creativity, 1*(1), 3-13.

New London Group. (1996). A pedagogy of multiliteracies: Designing social futures. *Harvard Educational Review, 66*(1), 60-92.

Paivio, A. (1986). *Mental representations: A dual coding approach.* New York, NY: Oxford University Press.

Partnershipship for 21st Century Skills. (2002). *Learning for the 21st Century.* Tucson, AR: Author.

Putnam, R. T., & Borko, H. (2000). What do new views of knowledge and thinking have to say about research on teacher learning? *Educational Researcher, 29*(1), 4–15.

Resnick, M. (2006). Computer as Paintbrush: Technology, Play, and the Creative Society In Singer, D., Golikoff, R., and Hirsh-Pasek, K. (eds.), *Play = Learning: How play motivates and enhances children's cognitive and social-emotional growth.* Oxford, UK: Oxford University Press.

Silverstein, S. (1971). *A light in the attic.* New York: Harper Collins.

Stevenson, L. M. & Deasy, R. J. (Ed.) (2005). *Third space: When learning matters.* Washington, DC: Arts Education Partnership.

Sweet, A. P. (2005). A national policy perspective on research intersections between literacy and the visual / communicative arts. In Flood, J., Heath, S. B., Lapp, D. (Eds.) *Handbook of research on teaching literacy through the communicative and visual arts.* Mahwah, NJ: Lawrence Erlbaum.

Van Allsburg, C. (1996). *The mysteries of Harris Burdick (portfolio edition).* Boston: Houghton Mifflin.

Vygotsky, L. S. (1978). *Mind in Society.* Cambridge, MA: Harvard University Press (Original work published in 1934).

Lynn Hartle
University of Central Florida
Orlando, FL   USA

Dr. Lynn Hartle is an Early Childhood Teacher Educator at the University of Central Florida with a research interest in preparing teachers to differentiate instruction for diverse learners. She serves on the board of the National Association of Early Childhood Teacher Educators and as facilitator of the National Association of Young Children Technology and Young Children Interest Forum.

Candace Jaruszewicz
College of Charleston
Charleston, SC   USA

Dr. Candace Jaruszewicz is an Associate Professor at the College of Charleston and the director of the Miles Early Childhood Development

Center, a nationally accredited campus lab/demonstration program. She serves on the board of the National Association of Early Childhood Teacher Educators and pursues research related to the role of reflection in teacher professional development.

Chapter 11
Lighting the Fires Within:

Pre-service Teachers Learning in and through Drama

Kelli Jo Kerry-Moran and Matthew J. Meyer

Abstract Drama has been a key mode of learning and meaning making through-out recorded history; however, drama's role in teacher education is peripheral at best. Both teacher educators and pre-service teachers, because they often lack drama experience themselves, become fearful of extending themselves through such activities as creative dramatics or process drama in their classrooms. Yet creative drama is an ideal medium for developing literacy, particularly within a multi literacies paradigm. With simple, structured and progressive creative drama techniques, teacher educators can encourage pre-service teachers to become aware of the aesthetic and multi literacy benefits of drama use in their classrooms. A sample unit designed for the teacher education classroom is included.

Keywords drama, theater, theatre, creative drama, process drama, pre-service teachers, teacher education, literacy, multi literacies

> Humans are not vessels to be filled, but fires to be kindled. (unknown, as cited in Cecil & Lauritzen 1994, p.xiii).

Indiana University of Pennsylvania, USA

St. Francis Xavier University, Canada

M. J. Narey (ed.), *Making Meaning*.

Introduction

A three-year-old recently asked his mother to play ponies with him. "I'll be the baby pony," he exclaimed, "and you be the momma pony. Now, let's get some food." The pair went on to enact growing crops on a farm, harvesting, and eating the food. The boy decided they needed some fish and searched the house for an appropriate fishing pole and bait. Armed with pole (shoe string) and bait (small, green block), mother and son fished on the stairway, bringing in a great catch before running away to hide from a giant, who was surely going to overcome them at any moment.

Young children enact make believe scenarios like this one thousands of times each day across the globe. Throughout recorded history, human beings have always used drama. Whether through informal techniques like this child's socio-dramatic play or formal theater like the ancient Greeks, drama provides a way to perceive, study, and understand our lives and the world in which we live. In the previously mentioned play scenario, the young child explored roles of leadership, nurturing, and family relationships. He tried out his knowledge of how food is grown and secured and he did all of this while practicing verbal skills, making use of symbols (the fishing pole and bait), and composing his own story. This child was engaging in a literacy-rich activity, making meaning (Kress, 1997) through his dramatic expression. We understand literacy to be the ability to create and interpret symbolic, abstract ideas and texts, using multimodal approaches. This is a literacy that moves beyond communication through reading, writing, speaking and listening to include visual images and the senses of taste, touch, and feeling through which we understand the world. It is through multiple modes of exploration and expression that children develop literacy (Kress, 1997), both in the traditional sense of reading and writing, and in the expansive sense of communicating with others and making sense of life. Young children's dramatic expression encourages literacy while developing creativity and imagination.

Imagination is not only a hallmark of childhood, it is a foundation of learning and teaching. Maxine Greene (1995) champions imagination as an essential component of pre-service teacher preparation programs.

> ... It is difficult for me to teach educational history or philosophy to teachers-to-be
> without engaging them in the domain of imagination and metaphor. How else are they to
> make meaning out of the discrepant things they learn? How else are they to see
> themselves as practitioners, working to choose, working to teach in an often
> indecipherable world? (p. 99)

But all too often pre-service teachers find their senses of imagination and creativity stifled by their formal educational experiences. Classroom applications of drama are one remedy to this situation.

This chapter is in two parts. Part 1 provides essential background for using drama as a pedagogical approach and focuses theoretical foundations and perspectives for the use of drama in teacher education. Part 2 describes a drama unit appropriate for a pre-service teacher education classroom. Linkages between the theories and perspectives outlined in Part 1 is included. In addition, the unit described in Part 2 may be adapted for the early childhood classroom. Finally, we outline the literacies developed through the drama unit.

Part 1

What is Drama?

Pre-service teachers and other adults engage in drama all the time, without calling it such. We participate in and observe drama presentations every day of our lives (Goffman, 1959). The formal ones are those we experience through the media: television, cinema, live theater and the like. The informal ones are those in our daily life at home, school or other locations. When we rehearse in our mind how we will ask our boss for a promotion or imitate a colleague telling a funny story, we are engaging in drama. The young child pretending to be a mommy feeding her baby or a bus driver taking the zoo animals on a wild ride to the park is using drama. A parent making silly faces at his infant is employing drama. Yet how does this drama differ from an actor in a stage production?

There are numerous definitions of drama and theater and most are helpful in understanding the art form within particular contexts. David Booth (2003) links theater and drama closely:

> The field of Theater encompasses such variety: children playing in a sand box, students in the school musical, young people who have entered a university drama program, students exploring a script in the classroom...Drama is an ubiquitous force in our present world, an everyday and everywhere occurrence, as evidenced by the dramatic performances we view and listen to....Drama has become our principal means of expressing and interpreting the world as we explore and communicate ideas and information, social behaviors, values, feelings, and attitudes... (p. 18)

Many artists and non-artists use the terms drama and theater interchangeably but the distinction between the two is important for understanding drama's role and its potential as a pedagogical approach for learning and teaching. Wagner (1999/1976), in discussing the drama in education approach of Dorothy Heathcote, one of the early pioneers in the field, describes it as follows:

> The goal is to learn through drama—for example, to...see what other walks of life feel like. Drama in education enables participants, either during the drama itself or after the drama in a discussion, to look at reality through fantasy, to see below the surface of actions to their meaning. (p. 1)

Drama is also described as a social activity that helps participants explore issues from diverse perspectives. (Norris, McCammon, & Miller, 2000). Eric Bentley (1964) takes this further:

> Events are not dramatic in themselves. Drama requires the eye of the beholder to see drama in something, that is both to perceive elements of conflict and to respond emotionally to these elements of conflict. This emotional response consists in being thrilled, in being struck with wonder at the conflict. Even conflict is not dramatic in itself. Should we all perish in a nuclear war, there will continue to be conflict in the realm of physics and chemistry. That is not a drama, but a process. If drama is a thing one sees, there has to be one to see. Drama is human. (p. 4)

Drama does not exist outside a social context but it is an innate part of our lives. The approach we take in this chapter emerges from informal drama that has an educational or pedagogical purpose. These types of drama are known by many names including: educational drama (Wagner, 1999/1976), creative drama (McCaslin, 2005) or creative dramatics (Bolton, 2007), process drama (Bolton, 1996), story drama (Saldaña, 1995), child drama (Bolton, 2007) and sometimes even improvisational drama (Spolin, 1986). Some educators and artists have used these terms interchangeably yet there are distinctions between them. Despite these differences, which are beyond the scope of this chapter, all can be used effectively in classroom settings. We will consider them collectively as "creative drama."

Despite the pervasiveness of drama in the lives of young children, creative drama is an underutilized teaching tool or pedagogical approach in Western teacher education. It is not unusual to find early childhood programs with little drama coursework. When one of the authors began teaching at a United States university several years ago, she was assigned a course that integrated arts methods for the early childhood classroom. The course description highlighted visual arts, music and movement but drama was conspicuously absent from the description. This circumstance is not unusual. Many pre-service teachers' limited exposure to and experiences with creative drama make it difficult for them to fully comprehend the benefits of a drama-infused curriculum approach. Pre-service teachers may read a chapter or two on drama in a college text, but rarely see it used in their pre-service classes or field experiences. We have found with our pre-service teachers that when they are exposed to creative drama, they are often unaware that they are participating in a drama activity. Instructional techniques such as role play and readers theater are recognized by many pre-service teachers, but these same students may not view these as drama.

Connections Between Literacy, Learning and Creative Drama

There are many approaches to literacy and learning. For the purposes of this chapter we see creative drama activities as a tactile and theoretical tool for classroom use and as an additional pedagogy for the classroom practitioner. When we have asked our pre-service teachers to identify ways that they could potentially use drama in the early childhood classroom, many are unable to come up with strategies. This is a consequence both of their lack of knowledge concerning drama but also their lack of experience in being taught through or using drama techniques. Yet drama holds many characteristics that make it well suited for the pre-service classroom.

Understanding that many pre-service teachers have little to no drama or theater training, we have looked to several scholars and drama practitioners on which to base our classroom activities and lessons. We use and interpret liberally Gallego's and Hollingsworth's (2000) multiple literacies paradigm: school literacies, community literacies, and personal literacies. This paradigm inspires our interpretation of how creative drama can enhance learning and teaching in early childhood and in pre-service teacher education classrooms. Each literacy category is described below with an example and explanation of how creative drama facilitates that particular literacy development.

School Literacies

Gallego and Hollingsworth (2000) define school literacies as "the learning of the interpretive and communicative processes needed to adapt socially to school and other dominant language contexts, and the use of practice of those processes in order to gain a conceptual understanding of school subjects" (p. 5). We interpret school literacies to essentially refer to the ability to learn within school, or formal contexts, particularly within the language and norms of the dominant culture. Creative drama can facilitate school literacies with a focus on language and narrative structure. It has also been used in formal school settings to help students develop problem-solving skills. Heathcote's drama in education is based upon helping children select and solve problems (Wagner, 1999/1976). Sometimes referred to as the "Man in a Mess" (Bolton, 2007) approach, Heathcote helped children select problems that had relevance to the group and work together as an ensemble in solving them. Even when playing theater games, unscripted drama activities focusing on particular tasks or skills; the problem provides necessary tension to move the action forward (Spolin, 1986). Teaching is a daily exercise in problem-solving and good teacher educators attune to the need to help pre-service teachers recognize and solve problems that will confront them in their future classrooms. Drama activities can focus on problems and situations inherent to new teachers and provide a forum for grappling with the practical, ethical and moral aspects of these dilemmas.

Community Literacies

Gallego and Hollingsworth (2000) define community literacies as "the appreciation, understanding, and /or use of interpretive and communicative traditions of
culture and community" (p. 9). We interpret community literacies to focus on acquiring the skills to function within particular communities and societies by understanding cultural norms and traditions and being able to communicate effectively with its members. All cultures including those that are dominant, minority
and/or oppressed have community literacies. Under the best circumstances, young
children develop literacy skills across several communities and a deep understanding of diverse communities that reaches far beyond written texts. These types of
literacy require the ability to see the world from multiple vantage points, understanding that circumstances appear differently depending on one's perspective.

Creative drama provides children and pre-service teachers with the opportunity
for vicarious experiences and the development of empathy. All types of drama encourage children and adults to put themselves in the place of someone else. Doing
so provides opportunities for exploring feelings, places, and perspectives beyond
oneself. We have found that pre-service teachers understand this best when they
have experienced drama in the classroom and had the "aha" experience of com-
prehending a previously foreign perspective. When one author used a readers theater script with a group of pre-service teachers, several students who had been
asked to play the role of parents commented that they had never before thought of
schooling from the parent's perspective. Readers theater made this "aha" experience possible. Eisner (1988) writes, "representation must give way to the primacy
of experience. In the end, it is the qualities we experience that provide the content
through which meaning is secured" (p. 16). When first-hand experience is not possible, drama can provide a good substitution. Through the approximation of experience, theory, practice and knowledge come together within drama.

Creative drama is also a social activity that requires collaboration and coopera-
tion. Both players and observers need to agree upon common rules (i.e. doctor's
do not hurt patients) and have a shared vision (i.e. the cash register is the shoe box
on the corner desk). In a very similar way, school personnel must collaborate with
one another and cooperate in creating school environments conducive to children's optimal development. The use of role-play or other creative drama techniques can help pre-service teachers approximate the experience of working with
colleagues to solve education problems and reach goals.

Personal Literacies

Gallego and Holligsworth (2000) define personal literacies as the critical awareness of ways of knowing and believing about self that comes from thoughtful examination of historical or experiential and gender-specific backgrounds in school and community language settings...Personal literacies reflect both the ways students believe they should join in socially accepted discourse communities and the private ways they know they can and would like to be able to participate across communities. (p. 15)

We interpret personal literacies to refer to intrapersonal skills in knowing and understanding oneself, from both an historical and introspective position. This relates to reflectivity and the ability to self-evaluate one's learning and performance. Deep learning does not take place simply by doing: it requires reflection with action. The learner must act and think about what was accomplished, what went well, what could be improved, how this learning influences personal outlooks and beliefs. Reflection is a necessary component of creative drama. Failure to include reflection in dramatic learning diminishes the experience and eliminates the presence of what Latta (2001) describes as 'aesthetic play.' During a recent teacher education class, the students were assigned to create a brief skit (commercial, infomercial, etc.) based on various instructional strategies. Many of the skits were humorous and the group had a lot of fun with the assignment. However, it was not until the students reflected on the task, and what they had learned through the process, that the educational value of it was recognized.

Finally, underlying this multiple literacies paradigm, we also believe that visual and performing arts activities further enhance a student's abilities to extend their intellectual, creative, and emotive sensibilities and talents. Creative drama has attributes that contribute to the development of each literacy type. When we have used dramatic activities with our pre-service teachers, we have found that their knowledge and imagination abilities have expanded quite remarkably. Their subsequent work has demonstrated cognitive and communicative connections between printed, aural, visual or performance-based stimuli and their creating capabilities and capacities to further understand their world have increased many fold.

The notion of infusing the arts into pedagogic practice is not new; it has been advanced for many years. Advocates include John Dewey (1934), Maxine Greene (1995), Elliot Eisner (2005), Tom Barone (2001), and David Booth (2003). It is not within the scope of this chapter to delve deeply into these pedagogues' ideas. However, we see the infusion of creative drama into the early childhood or pre-service classroom to be most successful when put into a constructivist pedagogy as typified by Lev Vygotsky (1978), which looks at a student's learning curve within an environment that considers equally a student's experience, sequential content and context building parameters.

It is in this perspective, we use a Vygotsky inspired interpretation of knowledge development to provoke and inspire our use of creative drama in promoting literacy expansion lesson plans within the multiple literacies paradigm. This follows to some degree Wertsch's (1990) "socio-cultural" concept where he looks at Vygotsky's approach to how the "human mental functioning reflects and constitutes its historical, institutional, and cultural setting" (p. 115). Liberally applied here, in a pre-service preparation program creative drama learning activity, we hope that our participants' functioning attempts to take into account the connection between literary (in our upcoming Part 2 example) or other artistic works with the creative potential of fusing learning and the awareness of a students' learning environments and literacies while reflecting on the substance and emotions represented by the literary work's characters and content. Furthermore, we hope that by infusing creative drama into reading and writing activities, pre-service teachers will increase their awareness of the way the arts in general, and creative drama in particular, are sign systems that, as Short and Kauffman (2000) advocate, are not just ways to present ideas but also ways to generate ideas. Creative drama and other artistic modes are not just ways to express oneself but also ways to learn.

In a pre-service learning environment, this can be expanded further through Moll and Greenberg's (1990) ideas of students creating "knowledge zones" which are based on their accumulated life experiences, ameliorant knowledge, and their direct ongoing classroom observations and participation. The actual tactile, intellectual and emotive participatory involvement with a creative dramatics learning experience expands the pre-service teacher's creative and pedagogic skills by provoking the pre-service teacher to reflect, "how would I create and execute such an interactive creative drama activity in my classroom?" These activities further the multiple literacies paradigm mentioned earlier by having pre-service teachers make connections between abstract thoughts and the world around them through the vehicle of creative drama. This notion is supported within a Dewey conception. Eisner (2005) expands this idea:

> Any idea that ignores the necessary role of intelligence in the production of works of art is based upon identification of thinking with use of one special kind of material, verbal signs and words. To think effectively in terms of relations of qualities is as severe a demand upon thought as to think in terms of symbols, verbal and mathematical. (p. 107)

Creative drama provides pre-service teachers with opportunities to explore the nuance of qualities through verbal expression, body language and the other tools of expression and communication people use in their interactions with one another.

This pursuit that Eisner refers to is multi-dimensional. There has been a fair amount of research that connects literacy within the multi-modalities sphere of scholarship, (Siegel, 2006; Mavers, 2007; Berghoft, 1998) semiotics and multimodality together (Hull & Nelson, 2005). These scholars profess that students have always been involved in a variety of simultaneous learning spheres. Visual and aural images create signs and signposts of a designed reality at times. Electronic media, commercial television programming, printed mediums, and web-based conventions have all created an ever-growing language of images. These images can serve as interpretive signs to understand further the world around us. From our teaching experiences with young children through pre-service teachers, we strongly believe that these interpretive signs require a connection to tactile learning.

Pre-service teachers should be able to manipulate some tactile aspects of the visual and performing arts in order to influence their students' understanding of the more abstract psycho-emotional 'signs' that are continually conjured up by electronic, visual, aural and printed communication. The following infusion of creative drama concepts within the promotion of multiple literacies should assist pre-service teachers in that pursuit, and perhaps inspire teacher educators to expand their use of creative drama in pre-service classrooms.

Part II: Sample Literacy Unit [1]

The second half of this chapter provides an example of an extended drama exercise appropriate for the pre-service teacher education classroom. The pre-service teacher can easily adapt this exercise, in part or in its entirety, depending on the age, grade and developmental level of the students involved. Suggested adaptations for primary and preschool-aged children are included; however, readers are encouraged to make their own adaptations based on their particular needs.

The purpose of the unit plan is to bring together tactile and sensory experiences in an exploratory way. Variations of this exercise have been employed at all grade levels from Kindergarten to pre-service teacher preparation programs and with various access points to other areas of the curriculum. These guidelines are the ones that we have used in our pre-service classrooms, based on a typical grade three class (children approximately 8–9 years old). The activities described below are simple enough to be implemented by teachers without drama experience and may be freely adapted to fit specific learning goals. Throughout the unit the goal is not to make dramatic presentations but rather to learn through creative drama.

1. Warm-up or Introductory Activity

Creative drama uses the self as the instrument. Participants' minds, bodies and voices are creative drama's tools so it is important to be certain that students are comfortable in participating. Creative drama involves taking risks: risks of sharing thoughts, ideas and feelings with others and risks of performing with and for one's peers. Children and adults need opportunities to develop comfort in engaging in creative drama activities. Therefore, it is important to begin small, through tasks that build individual comfort, camaraderie, and trust with peers and teachers. Several excellent sources for warm-up activities exist (see Bany-Winters 1997; Gibbs 2001; Spolin, 1986), most are effective with any age group and require no special materials, props, or skills to complete. Many activities common to the early childhood classroom, such as finger plays and creative movement, can serve as effec-

---

[1] For purposes of clarity we have employed a numerical sequencing system. Readers should feel free to alter these steps.

tive warm-up experiences for creative drama. The success-key is to begin with a simple activity or approach that puts students at ease. The following unit plan does not include prescribed warm-up activities; however, each day's lesson should begin with a brief warm-up appropriate for the particular students.

2. Puppetry

The following series of puppetry exercises has several objectives. First, to have students further their creative presentation skills; to build confidence in speaking in front and with others; to create analytical links between written, spoken and three-dimensional media; to serve as a setup protocol to the more involved writing project at the end of the unit; and for the participants to have an active, tactile, and intellectual learning experience in literacy. Second, simple puppetry provides a good foundation for subsequent creative drama activities because many people feel more comfortable manipulating a puppet than in using only their own body as a performer. The puppet provides a protective front. Finally, the exercise gives pre-service teachers personal experience in engaging in several creative drama activities for learning and teaching. Throughout this exercise, it is important to help pre-service teachers reflect upon their learning and explore possible ways that creative drama may be applied in the early childhood classroom. We suggest that every creative drama session conclude with opportunities for individual and group reflection on what was experienced and learned and how the particular creative drama method can be used in the early childhood classroom. Reflection strategies might include journaling, discussion, cooperative learning activities or any other effective reflection method.

2.1 Paper Bag Puppet Concept

The day before this unit begins, request that students find the one place in their homes where they feel most comfortable. As they sit in that most comfortable place, they should look around the room very closely and find the one object in that room to which they feel most emotionally close. For example, it could be an artifact acquired on a trip such as a seashell or rock; or a piece of clothing from a costume they once wore, perhaps a gift from a loved one; an accoutrement to daily life such as a hairbrush or barrette; a small tool or toy. The rule is that it cannot be animate such as a person, pet or facsimile thereof (i.e. photograph).

After choosing an object, they are to personify it by giving it a name, personality, age, biography, and other human characteristics. They are to come to class the next day with some item that would help describe the object but not the object itself, and its made up history. For example, a student who chose a racing trophy might bring a toy car or wheel. The teacher does the same.

Primary Adaptation: Ask the children to identify a favorite toy and imagine that the toy is suddenly transformed into a person. What type of personality does it have? What is its name and how will it look? Have the children draw a picture of their new person/toy and bring it to class.

Preschool Adaptation: Ask the children to bring a favorite, small stuffed toy that they will introduce to their friends at preschool.

2.2 Paper Bag Puppet Materials

Before class begins, the teacher secures enough of the following materials for the creation of simple paper bag puppets: at least three paper lunch bags per student, masking tape and scissors to cut and secure finger openings for the thumb and pinkie fingers if so desired, crayons, markers or colored pencils.

Primary Adaptation: Paper lunch sacks may be too large for some primary-aged children to manipulate easily. In this instance, smaller paper sacks may be available through craft or hardware stores or stick or sock puppets may be used.

Preschool Adaptation: Paper lunch sacks are too large for some preschool-aged children to manipulate. Stick puppets, such as those made by securing a piece of cardstock to a wooden tongue depressor, are more easily manageable for younger preschool-aged children.

2.3 Object Introduction: Exercise in Imagination and Personification

At the beginning of class, have the students form a circle with their chairs. Each person in turn (after the teacher) will present his or her personified object. This should be no more than one minute per participant. They will introduce their objects now as *personified* objects. They themselves are now the objects along with the items to serve as descriptors. The teacher can contrive a story line such as 'the first day of school for this object' to initiate the presentation. If the class has a large enrollment, we suggest the teacher divide the class into groups of no more than five participants each, where each group member presents to the other group members.

Primary Adaptation: Have each child introduce their toy, using their picture as a prop and sharing key information such as the toy's name, likes, dislikes, etc. This activity is best in small groups with teacher support; however, if it is impossible to provide this support through teachers or aids, a large group activity is preferable. Teachers may need to structure this activity further to suite group dynamics and particular learning needs.

Preschool Adaptation: In a small, relaxed group such as circle time, have each child introduce their stuffed toy to their classmates. The children should be encouraged to tell the toy's name and any special likes or dislikes. Young children should not be forced to participate but many will have already personified their stuffed toy with a name, feelings, etc. as a natural part of their play. The teacher can encourage creative thinking and personification by following up with questions such as "what is __'s favorite thing to do at the park?"

2.4 Improvisation: Exercise in Creativity, Personification and Character Development

After all the presentations are complete; the teacher divides the participants into 5 person groups and has them, in character, do a brief improvisation exercise in which the setting is lunch time and each group member talks about her lunch. The described lunch contents must be particular to the character's persona. For example, the student representing the racing trophy might bring wax or polish. The purpose of this exercise is several fold: first, to have students listen to each other; second, to further the students' creative conversation abilities; third to develop characterization and fourth, to work towards a group identity. Additionally, this activity builds on previous exercises so that the students move sequentially from the simple to the more complex.

Primary: Depending on the children's experience-level with creative drama, it will be necessary to structure the activity so that expectations are clear. Young children work best when they are aware of important guidelines for time (about three but no more than five minutes), space (children should remain seated as if at a lunch table), and behavior (respect others' personal space, use inside voices, etc.) limitations.

Preschool: Have the children use their toys to sing a simple nursery rhyme or favorite song or to act out part of a book or story. Regardless of which activity is used, the children should be encouraged to use the toy as part of the performance.

2.5 Puppet Bag Creation: Exercise in Creativity and Visual Representation

Have participants draw face sketches of what they believe their persona would resemble if it were an animate object. Then distribute one paper bag to each participant. Students will create a paper bag puppet of their persona. Each participant can choose to either use the bottom half (at the fold) as its head [to place fingers as a sort of mouth or cut finger holes on the sides for arms (thumb and pinkie)]. We strongly suggest putting masking tape around any holes and the bag opening edges to curtail paper destruction. Using coloring crayons, chalks, markers or pencils participants will create their puppets.

Primary: It will be necessary to demonstrate the way to structure the paper bag puppet so that the mouth can move and "arm" holes can be made. Adult supervision is required for the cutting of any holes.

Preschool: Young children should be given latitude in determining what kind of puppet to make; however it is best to avoid television or movie characters as these are typically so well defined in terms of personality and actions that much of the creative benefit of this exercise will be lost. Children may want to make their toy or a different character based on a book or favorite play theme.

If using stick puppets and cardstock, be sure to encourage creative expression by not using pre-cut forms or patterns. Many young children are unable to use crayons to make dark marks that can be seen from a distance. Puppets are best viewed with vivid, high contrast colors so non-toxic, water-based paints or markers are better materials than crayons. With adult assistance, young children may be able to trim the cardstock once their creations are complete.

2.6 Paper Bag Puppet Scenarios: Exercise in Creativity, Improvisation and Narrative Development

Over the next few days, assign participants into groups of four or five and have them, in their personas and using their puppets, act out daily life scenarios from the perspective of their puppet. Possible scenarios might include cleaning out the puppet's attic, basement or closet (what types of things would be in the attic? how would the task be approached?), caring for a pet, or writing a birthday wish list. Regardless of the scenario, it must be enacted from the perspective of the puppet, not the student. Each scenario should be a maximum of 3 minutes with a clear beginning, which the instructor creates, and a student created middle and ending.

Primary: Children should have some knowledge of narrative structure and be encouraged to plan the action. Children may also need help in moving the action along through dialogue. It might be desirable to have the children revisit the same scenario more than once so that they gain practice in self-evaluating their work and revising for improvement. It is vital that the teacher circulate amongst the groups during this activity to provide support. Following each creative drama session, it is important to lead the children in reflecting on the activity and identifying things that went well and things that can be improved for the next session.

Preschool: Be prepared for very short scenes or scenarios from this age group. Additionally, very young children might enact scenarios through sociodramatic play rather than with the use of puppets. This is appropriate and may be better suited to some groups. If so, the teacher should encourage this dramatic play by providing props that extend and support the dramatic play. Teachers may also need to help the play move along by entering the play as a participant or through the use of questioning (i.e. "What is under ___'s bed?) or side coaching.

2.7 The Sock Puppet: Exercise in Creativity and Narrative Representation

After about four such scenarios, the group is ready to move on to the sock puppets. Each participant should bring to class a good size sock. The instructor will assemble, buttons, crafts materials such as wool, ribbon(s), lace, craft glue, small glue guns and glue sticks, threads, felt marker pens, and any other materials that could be used as accoutrements to the sock. Students may also be encouraged to bring craft and found items. Just as in the paper bag puppet creation, guide the participants into creating their own individual sock puppet either based on their original puppet or a new creation. All participants, regardless of age, need reminding of basic safety procedures in using a hot glue gun.

Primary: If a glue gun is used, only the teacher or assisting adult should handle it.

Preschool: Non-toxic craft glue should be used rather than glue guns and care should be taken to ensure that no part of the puppet presents a chocking hazard. Consequently, buttons and commercial eyes are not recommended for this age group but small pieces of felt may be substituted. The puppets must be sturdy so teachers will need to supervise the gluing and provide adequate drying time before the puppets are used.

3. Story Book Introduction: Theme

This exercise begins after a brief (depending on age and background) discussion of theme that focuses on emotions. The example used here is based on Maurice Sendak's (1963), *Where the Wild Things Are* but additional books, stories, and texts that are thematically related should be added. Begin by reading the texts aloud either to the entire class or in small groups. The reading may be done by the instructor or students, as long as the reader is well prepared and reads with expression.

When adapting this unit for the early childhood classroom, a different aspect of literature or literacy may be used based on the learning needs of the children and the curricular demands of the school. This unit is most effective with a high quality text that the children find personally engaging. The text should also have a strong theme and vivid imagery. More independent readers will benefit most from a text that they can read independently or with little assistance.

Preschool: Young children will want to hear the story several times. Help them explore each story through enactment. The techniques suggested for primary-aged children are appropriate for many preschool-aged children as well.

Primary: Read the story aloud to the students taking sufficient time to show them the illustrations as you go along. The story may be read more than once before moving on to the next step. After the reading, discuss the story by posing several questions. The questions should help the students explore aspects of the theme and might include the following: what is going on in this story? What kinds of things do you hear? What do you see? How does Max feel when he..., Why does Max...?

Young children need opportunities to demonstrate their understanding through multiple modes of communication. In addition to discussing the story, provide opportunities for children to explore these prompts through: visual arts (i.e. draw a picture about why you think Max decides to sail home), dramatic expression (i.e. make a face that shows me how Max feels when he is sent to his room), creative movement (i.e. walk across the rug the way you think Max walked up to the Wild Things when he reached the island), and music (i.e. use your rhythm instruments to make the kind of music that reminds you of the Wild Things' rumpus).

3.1 Descriptive Language

After the story is read, go to the board and have the students relate to the class one (preferably) or two word descriptors that stood out to them in the story or describe characters in the story.

As the words come forward, attempt to group them on the board – perhaps in three or four columns: actions, abstracts/ emotions, and time (Table 1). We suggest that students help determine the groupings and that titles are added towards the middle or end of this exercise. After each column has about 7-10 words. Ask the participants to identify idea patterns from both within each group and between groups. Ask the participants to select the most significant idea patterns.

Table 11.1. Where the Wild Things Are

Actions	Abstract Ideas	Feelings	Time
roars	imagination	defiance	sailing
made mischief	rudeness	courageous	night-time
forest growing	bossy	love	weeks
ocean tumbled	regal	afraid	day
leaving	loneliness	hungry	year

Primary: Young children will need help in thinking about and identifying descriptive words. The teacher will need to provide examples while giving the children opportunities to create their own descriptive words (i.e. of themselves, their friends, family members, familiar characters, etc.). A big book is ideal for this activity so that the children can follow along and identify descriptive words as the story is re-read. These words should be organized into a simple chart to facilitate the children's discovery of patterns and commonalities in descriptive words. If the children are not yet able to read, descriptive words can still be discussed and symbolized through pictures. Additionally, the following adaptations recommended for preschool are also appropriate for primary-aged children.

Preschool: Themes should be kept very basic for this group and explored multiple times and in multiple ways. Rather than focusing on descriptive language, additional books focusing on the same theme can be read and explored through enactment, age-appropriate discussion, art, and movement. Picture books such as *When Sophie's Angry—Really, Really Angry* (Bang, 1999) and *Alexander and the*

Terrible, Horrible, No good, Very Bad Day (Viorst, 1987) can help young children better understand emotions and the expression of anger and relate to those themes as they are presented in various contexts and characters. The broad theme should be emphasized with each activity and children invited to apply the theme to themselves (i.e. "I feel angry when…" or "When I am angry I…"). Unfamiliar vocabulary may be explored in a similar way.

3.2 Thematic Statement

As a class, discuss the theme of the story or stories read as part of this unit. Develop a thematic statement that represents all the texts and is no more than one sentence.

Primary: Introduce the concept of theme in a developmentally appropriate way and keep themes simple and direct. Primary-aged children will benefit from several examples of theme and multiple opportunities to express themes from familiar stories.

Preschool: A discussion of theme is not appropriate for preschoolers but young children can display their understanding of what a story is about through discussion, artwork, music, movement and dramatic play. Keep themes simple and discuss similarities in the stories.

4. Theme And Sock Puppets Together

4.1 Scenario Assignment

Participants are put into suggested groups of five maximum. Using their sock puppet characters they must create a scenario that depicts the class developed thematic statement, not the *Where the Wild Things Are* story. The following instructions should be taken as guidelines and adapted to the learners' needs and particular curriculum goals:

>   The scenario can be no longer than 3 minutes
>   There must be a beginning, middle and ending
>   There can only be 2 action sequences
>   All puppets must be involved, but not necessarily equally

Rehearsal guidelines such as behavior expectations and time and space limits should be provided. It is also important to emphasize that students should practice their performance before presenting it to the group. If possible, provide separate practice space for each group. As the students prepare their scenarios, the teacher circulates amongst groups to assist and help the group remain on task. He or she makes only those suggestions necessary to keep the scenario storylines in place and to ensure that all students are involved (not necessarily equally).

Primary: Young children need clear structure and defined limits such as scenario time length, clearly defined physical space for rehearsal and performance and basic staging directions (i.e. puppets should face out towards the audience, be sure to speak loudly enough to be heard, etc.). They will also need more teacher support. Depending on the level of experience the children have with similar activities, it might be advisable to divide the scenario development, rehearsal and performance over a few days.

Preschool: With adult support, preschool-aged children can develop simple theme-based scenarios and enact them with the puppets. For example, if the theme is anger and appropriate ways to express anger, the children can discuss situations in which they feel angry such as when another child takes a toy from them. The teacher can serve as narrator with the children performing the simple scenario with their puppets. The teacher and children would then discuss appropriate ways to behave in each situation and act these out with the puppets. Preschool-aged children can also explore these themes through sociodramatic play or simple role-play.

4.2 Performance/Discussion

After a brief rehearsal period, the scenarios are presented to the class. A puppet stage is unnecessary and the audience will focus on the puppets and not the puppeteers if the puppeteers look at their own puppets rather than at the audience. However, an impromptu puppet stage can be created by stretching a flat sheet across the front of the room and having two student volunteers hold it at a comfortable height for the puppeteers. We give our pre-service teachers a choice between performing with or without the impromptu puppet stage. This exercise can be repeated several times using different thematic statements.

It is important to include group discussion following the scenarios to help students reflect upon the activity and make connections between the drama and any curricular goals.

Primary: Appropriate audience behavior should be discussed prior to the performance. Remind the children that each child will have a turn to participate and have the group generate a brief list of audience guidelines (i.e. attentive listening, kind words or no put downs, clapping at the end, etc.). Focus on how it looks and sounds to be a good audience and have the children practice this behavior prior to the performances. As each small group performs, reinforce good behavior through recognition and praise. This discussion should be framed and conducted in a way that is appropriate to the child's developmental level.

Preschool: No formal performance is given (see 4.1) but some children might want to perform their puppet scenario for a parent or guardian. If so, assist the child or children and be sure to explain the process to the parent or guardian.

5. Original Short Story or Poem

Finally, the students are asked to create an original work of some kind such as an original short story or poem formulated on the thematic statement. The teacher can assign specific content and stylistic components as fits the course curriculum goals, interests and abilities of the students. If desired, students may be assigned to create an original work based on a non-written form of literacy such as an oral story, play, dance or painting.

Primary: Young children may complete this exercise individually or as a group. The adaptations suggested for preschool children may also be used for the primary level; however, many primary-aged children will not require as much adult assistance.

Preschool Adaptation: The task must be developmentally appropriate and themes for this age group should be straightforward and simple (i.e. share with others, be kind to animals, etc.). The teacher should help the children explore this theme through multiple modalities (additional story books, drawings, songs, etc.) and to make personal connections to the theme (i.e." I can share my trucks with my brother" or "I can pet my dog softly"). These personal connections can be explored through dramatic play. As the children identify ways they can apply the themes in their own lives and act it out through dramatic play, it is beneficial to explore the theme over an extended period of time. Older preschool and kindergarten children may create a group story that can be transcribed by a teacher or other adult. Preschool-aged children may choose to draw a story that is narrated and subsequently transcribed by an adult.

Connecting the Unit and the Multiple Literacies Paradigm

Infusing the tactile (puppets and dramatic play) with the storybook (thematic understanding), our treatment and application of the multiple literacies paradigm is both multi-modal in appearance and practice and multi-dimensional (simultaneous understandings of personal, sociological, and physical spaces) in the cognitive and aesthetic aspects of the participants' learning experience. From the school literacies perspective participants further their understanding of established and expected grade level language skills. Students also identify textual patterns and themes both within the story and as predictions in their small group scenarios. Throughout the unit, individual and collective imagination abilities expand as students create the stories, signs and symbols that connect the established Sendak (1963) story themes with their own creations and simultaneously develop a deeper understanding of these stories, signs and symbols through creative drama activities.

From the community literacies perspective, participants' creations establish environmental and cultural contexts that are indicative of their individual and group creations. Their created storylines and character personalities have self imposed limitations and boundaries which can be historically, culturally, and geographically designed to bring about a verisimilitude that connects their imagined reality to the real world. Components of the unit move from individual to large group to small group activities that help the students make connections between themselves and others and gives them practice in working with different group types. When we have implemented variations of this unit in classrooms of all types, some common themes inevitably emerge as students share their personified objects. These shared themes, as well as acknowledged differences, help build classroom community across gender, racial and socioeconomic diversity.

Finally, the personal literacies, especially as created through their characters and then character associations with other characters (from the story and or from their puppet personas and subsequent interactions with other puppet personas) furthers the students' language and language understanding of their immediate community settings. This takes on a variety of perspectives. For example, do their puppet creations of a personified physical object have a gender, or a social role in a specific community? If so, how does its language, and its social context, interact with the other communities within the evolved story line world? The initial assignment to choose a location of comfort and a physical object with which one holds a strong emotional connection, invites students to consider their personal histories and how physical objects and surroundings connect with our lives.

In addition to these multiple literacies, the actual tactile experience of building the puppet and creating its personality and environments expands the participants' creative artistic imagination and immerses them in the physical, psychological, emotional, and environmental construction of a character. The participants' awareness of time, space, imagination, social behaviors and multiple literacies expand and can be built upon for ongoing learning experiences in this multi-modal framework.

Conclusion

We introduced this chapter with a quotation: "Humans are not vessels to be filled, but fires to be kindled" (unknown, as cited in Cecil & Lauritzen, 1994, p. xiii). Creative drama in the classroom is about kindling fires, helping students of all ages to fully engage their minds and bodies in learning, making personal connections with ideas and shaping them so that they become their own. Humans are creatures of habit and comfort. It is unreasonable to expect that pre-service teachers, who do not regularly experience and participate in creative drama, will utilize it in their own early childhood classrooms. Our conception of literacy is multimodal and multifaceted; creative drama represents one approach that can attend to all the modes of communication in which human beings engage. As teacher educators who want to infuse a love of learning and a passion for literacy in our students, we must use in our own classrooms every pedagogical approach that we hope our students will use in their work with young children. With perseverance and multiple literacy strategies including creative drama, we can inspire our students to kindle their own fires and pass the flame to future generations.

References

Bang, M. (1999). *When Sophie gets angry—really, really angry….* New York: Scholastic Inc.

Bany-Winters, L. (1997). *On stage: Theater games and activities for kids.* Chicago: Chicago Review Press.

Barone, T. (2001). *Touching eternity: The enduring outcomes of teaching.* New York: Teachers College Press.

Bentley, E. (1964). *The life of drama.* New York: Applause Theater Books.

Berghoff, B. (1998). Inquiry about learning and learners. *The Reading Teacher, 51*(6), 520-523.

Bolton, G. (1996). Afterward: Drama as research. In P. Taylor (Ed.) *Researching drama and arts education: Paradigms & possibilities* (pp. 187-194). Washington, DC: Falmer Press.

Bolton, G. (2007). A history of drama education: A search for substance. In L. Bresler (Ed.), *International handbook of research in arts education* (pp. 45-61). Dordrecht, The Netherlands: Springer.

Booth, D. (2003). Towards an understanding of theater in education. In K. Gallegher & D. Booth (Eds.), *How theater educates convergences & counterpoints* (pp. 14-22). Toronto, ON: University of Toronto Press.

Cecil, N. L., & Lauritzen, P. (1994). *Literacy and the arts for the integrated classroom: Alternative ways of knowing.* White Plains, NY: Longman.

Dewey, J. (1934). *Art as experience.* New York: Capricorn Books.

Eisner, E. (1988). The primacy of experience and the politics of method. *Educational Researcher, 17*(5), 15-20.

Eisner, E. (2005). The role of intelligence in the creation of art in D. A. Breault & R. Breault (Eds.) *Experiencing Dewey: Insights for today's classroom* (pp. 106-108). Indianapolis, IN: Kappa Delta Pi.

Gallego, M., & Hollingsworth, S. (2000). Introduction: The idea of multiple literacies. In M. Gallego & S. Hollingsworth (Eds.), *What counts as literacy: Challenging the school standard* (pp. 1-23). New York: Teachers College Press.

Gibbs, J. (2001). *Tribes: A new way of learning and being together.* Windsor, CA: Center Source Systems.

Goffman, E. (1959). *The presentation of self in everyday life.* New York: Doubleday.

Greene, M. (1995). *Releasing the imagination: Essays on education, the arts, and social change.* San Francisco: Jossey-Bass.

Hull, G. & Nelson, M. (2005). Locating the semiotic power of multimodality. *Written Communication, 22*(2), 224-261.

Kress, G. (1997). *Before writing: Rethinking the paths to literacy.* New York: Routledge.

Latta, M. (2001). *The possibilities of play in the classroom.* New York: Peter Lang.

McCaslin, N. (2005). Seeking the aesthetic in creative drama and theatre for young audiences. *Journal of Aesthetic Education, 39*(4), 12-19.

Mavers, D. (2007). Semiotic resourcefulness: A young child's email exchange as design. *Journal of Early Childhood Literacy, 7*(2), 155-176.

Moll, L., & Greenberg, J. (1990). Creating zones of possibilities: Combining social contexts for instruction. In L. Moll (Ed.), *Vygotsky and education: Instructional implications and applications of sociohistorical psychology* (pp. 319-348). Melbourne, Australia: Cambridge University Press.

Norris, J., McGammon, L., & Miller, C. (2000). *Learning to teach drama: A narrative approach.* Portsmouth, NH: Heinemann.

Saldaña, J. (1995). *Drama of color: Improvisation with multiethnic folklore.* Portsmouth, NH: Heinemann.

Sendak, M. (1963). *Where the wild things are.* New York: Harper Collins.

Short, K. G., & Kauffman, G. (2000). Exploring sign systems within an inquiry system. In M.A. Gallego & S. Hollingsworth (Eds.), *What counts as literacy: Challenging the school standard* (pp. 42-61). New York: Teachers College Press.

Siegel, M. (2006). Rereading the signs: Multimodal transformations in the field of literacy education. *Language Arts, 84*(1), 65-77.

Spolin, V. (1986). *Theater games of the classroom: A teacher's handbook.* Evanston, IL: Northwestern University Press.

Viorst, J. (1987). *Alexander and the terrible, horrible, no good, very bad day* (2nd ed.). New York: Alladdin Paperbacks.

Vygotsky, L. (1978). *Mind in society: The development of higher psychological processes.* Cambridge, MA: Harvard University Press.

Wagner, B. J. (1999/1976). *Dorothy Heathcote: Drama as a learning medium* (Rev. Ed.). Portsmouth, NH: Heineman.

Wertsch, J. (1990). The voice of rationality in a sociocultural approach to mind. In L. Moll (Ed.), *Vygotsky and education: Instructional implications and applications of sociohistorical psychology* (pp. 111-126). Melbourne, Australia: Cambridge University Press.

Kelli Jo Kerry-Moran
Indiana University of Pennsylvania
Indiana, PA   USA

Dr. Kelli Jo Kerry-Moran received her B.A. and M.A. in theatre arts with a focus in children's theatre from Brigham Young University and her Ph.D. in Education from Iowa State University. She is a former preschool teacher and has taught drama, creative movement, music and visual arts for various cultural arts organizations. She is an Associate Professor in the Professional Studies in Education department of Indiana University of Pennsylvania and the Coordinator of an urban-focus collaborative elementary education program between Indiana University of Pennsylvania and the Community College of Allegheny County.

Matthew J. Meyer
St. Francis Xavier University
Antigonish, NS   Canada

Dr. Matthew J. Meyer is an Associate Professor in the School of Education at St. Francis Xavier University, Antigonish, Nova Scotia, Canada. He teaches B.Ed and

M.Ed. courses in educational administration and drama-theatre educational practices. His research interests are in two distinct areas: leadership and organization aspects of school principal succession; and arts based research projects that focus on drama-theatre practices in the classroom and teacher-administrator professional development. He completed his doctoral work at McGill University.

Chapter 12
Learning to See the Boa Constrictor Digesting the Elephant:

Pre-service Teachers Construct Perspectives of Language, Literacy, and Learning through Art

Marilyn J. Narey

Abstract In this chapter, the process of making meaning through arts learning is explored in the context of an elementary education methods course. Common theories-in-use are discussed alongside of current theory, research, and practice to facilitate new perspectives of language, literacy, learning, and art. Examples of learning experiences promoting pre-service teachers' abilities to teach art as a visual language to inform, express, narrate, and persuade are provided.

Keywords meaning making, early childhood, pre-service teachers, critical thinking, language, literacy, inform, express, narrate, persuade

> Once when I was six years old I saw a magnificent picture in a book, called *True Stories from Nature*, about the primeval forest. It was a picture of a boa constrictor in the act of swallowing an animal...In the book it said: "Boa constrictors swallow their prey whole, without chewing it. After that they are not able to move, and they sleep through the six months that they need for digestion." I pondered deeply, then, over the adventures of the jungle. And after some work with a colored pencil I succeeded in making my first drawing...I showed my masterpiece to the grown-ups, and asked them whether the drawing frightened them. But they answered: "Frighten? Why should any one be frightened by a hat?" My drawing was not a picture of a hat. It was a picture of a boa constrictor digesting an elephant. But since the grown-ups were not able to understand it, I made another drawing: I drew the inside of a boa constrictor, so that the grown-ups could see it clearly... The grown-ups' response, this time, was to advise me to lay aside my drawings of boa constrictors, whether from the inside or the outside, and devote myself instead to geography, history, arithmetic, and grammar. (de Saint Exupéry, 1943/1971, pp. 3-4)

East Stroudsburg University of Pennsylvania, USA

M. J. Narey (ed.), *Making Meaning.*
© Springer 2009

"Is it a hill?" "Maybe...a snail?" "...melting ice cream?" "A hat?" Like the grown-ups who Antoine de Saint Exupéry (1943/1971) describes at the start of his classic tale, *The Little Prince*, my students (early childhood and elementary education majors) fail to decipher the image that I have scanned from the book and projected on the screen. I shake my head, feigning a hint of professorial concern at their inability to understand the child's drawing, "Oh, my! It appears that we have some work ahead of us!"

On this first day of our university methods course, I am well aware that most of my students are somewhat disconcerted by this initial activity. Coupled with their dislike of not knowing the "right answer," pre-service teachers tend to be surprised that the subject of a child's drawing is an important topic for discussion. Most view the arts as a free-time activity, a release from the *real* thinking involved in the *important* subjects that they will teach. Expecting to come away from the course with some ideas to keep little hands busy or to give older children a break from the rigors of the school day, their conceptions of children's art are primarily limited to holiday decorations or colorful expressions of emotion, rather than products of inquiry that involve critical thinking and problem solving.

Presenting my students with the problem of identifying the subject of the child's first drawing from the illustration in de Saint Exupéry's (1943/1971) book, followed by a discussion of the opening text, has proven to be a provocative way to introduce the concept of art as a critical and creative thinking process that contributes to making meaning. The activity challenges my students' previous notions of children's art as we deconstruct the events: the child's encounter with the "magnificent picture in a book... of a boa constrictor swallowing an animal" (p. 3); followed by deep pondering of the text that leads him to wonder how a boa constrictor might digest a *really* huge creature; next, his drawing to help him understand how this amazing feat might look; his desire to share the awesomeness of the phenomenon he has depicted with the grown-ups, asking if "the drawing frightened them" (p. 4); and, finally, the grown-ups' responses to the child's image and the impact that this had upon the child. My students are drawn in to the meaning making underlying the image. Through our own search for meaning, the invisible has become visible.

It is a good beginning; yet, each semester, I wonder, "How might I help this particular group of students to better understand, appreciate, and learn to teach art as a meaning making process? How can reflection upon our own meaning making processes in this arts methods course extend and enhance our perspectives of teaching and learning in general? How might I bring my students to become teachers who are able to see boa constrictors digesting elephants instead of hats?"

Seeing Hats: A Metaphor for the Problem

The ability to look deeply, and to search beyond our initial assumptions, is as critical to the broader context of the classroom as it is to the art experience. Unfortunately, there are too many in our early childhood education community who do not take time to look for the boa constrictors; who make hasty judgments; who label young children's abilities and behaviors with little thought or reflection. Conditioned by personal experience and culture, we see what we expect to see (Bolman & Deal, 1991). Typically, many of us do not subject our observations to an inquiry that may help us understand in a more complex manner what might lie beneath the surface of our immediate perception. Children who do not appear meet our expectations are labeled as "struggling learners" or "behavior problems" and we rush to correct the deficit, rather than take the time to look beyond the perceived deficiency to discover the children's abilities and strengths; abilities that often surpass our expectations, but remain unrecognized because they do not conform to our narrow perspectives for success.

> With limited information, we then interpret through our own perceptual lenses, and we make assumptions about what we observed, often without further discussion with others and with no attempt to confirm our interpretations. From these observations, we draw conclusions that affirm our assumptions. The actions we finally take, the decisions we make, reflect these conclusions. In brief, we see the world as we want to see it and act accordingly...As a result, the assumptions that we draw may not be accurate, and the decisions that we make may be flawed. (Osterman & Kottkamp, 2004, p. 30)

The adults in de Saint Exupéry's (1943/1971) story accept their initial perceptions without scrutiny, and thus fail to recognize the child's drawing as the visual traces of his critical thinking and problem solving, even when the child presents his second drawing "so that the grown-ups could see it clearly" (p. 4). This, in essence, becomes the metaphor for the problem that we face in early childhood teacher education: a large majority of our early childhood education community maintains unexamined assumptions about art, language, literacy, and learning, thus causing past patterns of practice to continue despite knowledge of theory, research, and practice that may contradict these beliefs. If we, as teacher educators, seek to interrupt these patterns, we must look beneath the surface of our own assumptions: focusing "not only on observable actions and outcomes but also on the unobservable—our thoughts and intentions, our feelings and the feelings of others" (Osterman & Kottkamp, 2004, p. 18).

The experiences described in this chapter are drawn from my observations and reflections as a teacher educator working with pre-service teachers enrolled in my art methods course and related field experiences. In most arts methods courses, education students typically learn about art materials, techniques, and processes, engage in hands-on assignments, and review current art education literature (Kalin & Kind, 2006). In these courses the pre-service teachers' learning may be targeted to, and assessed through, any number of observable actions and outcomes related to knowledge and technical skill. While these are important components of teaching and learning, and art making, for that matter, they are not likely to provide the understandings that will interrupt past patterns of practice regarding the arts in our classrooms. Therefore, in addition to addressing knowledge and technique, I attempt to seek out the larger issues that influence my students' learning, to attend to the cultures of our university and public school classrooms, to get a sense of the whole. Eisner (1994) makes this stance clear as he relates teaching to the aesthetic principle of art wherein everything must work together:

> …everything matters…We need to pay attention to matters of mix…the intentions that give direction to the enterprise, the structure that supports it, the curriculum that provides its content, the teaching with which that content is mediated, and the evaluation system that enables us to monitor and improve its operation. (p. 11)

In this chapter, I provide examples of learning experiences that may be adapted to other teacher education settings (e.g., literacy and language arts courses, in-service professional development). However, rather than focus on the clearly observable (e.g., readings, rubrics), I have chosen to uncover the less visible meaning making underlying our work in the course. Extending the metaphor of *The Little Prince*, I offer the equivalent to the child's second drawing (i.e., showing the elephant inside the boa constrictor) to assist others in understanding that which is "invisible to the eye" (de Saint Exupéry, 1943/1971, p. 87). I begin by examining the common theories-in-use that work to influence pre-service teachers' understandings of art, language, literacy, and learning along with alternate perspectives from current theory, research, and practice. This is followed by my descriptions of learning experiences that demonstrate the link between visual and verbal languages/literacies and that reveal the critical/creative thinking that contributes to understanding. My discussion is enriched by two former students' personal stories of how they became teachers who see boa constrictor digesting elephants instead of hats.

Examining Theories-in-use: A Fertile Ground for Learning

Like the arts, teaching and learning is a reciprocal and interactive creative process of making sense of human experience:

> Authentic education is not carried on by "A" for "B" or by "A" about "B," but rather by "A" with "B," mediated by the world—a world which impresses and challenges both parties, giving rise to views or opinions about it. These views, impregnated with anxieties, doubts, hopes, or hopelessness, imply significant themes on the basis of which the program content of education can be built. (Freire, 2002, p. 93)

As a teacher educator, I need to understand, with my students, the views that challenge our individual perspectives of teaching and learning. An examination of classroom teachers' common theories-in-use provides a fertile ground for discussion and deeper understanding.

Common Theory-in-use: Art Is about Feeling, Not Thinking

Teachers frequently operate under the assumption that art is an emotional release that requires little thought, and, as such, many see it as an activity that serves to provide students a break from the rigors of other subjects. Yet, almost anyone who has produced authentic work in the arts will agree with John Dewey's (1934/1980) position on art and intelligence:

> Any idea that ignores the necessary role of intelligence in production of works of art is based upon identification of thinking with use of one special kind of material, verbal signs and words. To think effectively in terms of relations of qualities is as severe a demand upon thought as to think in terms of symbols, verbal and mathematical. Indeed, since words are easily manipulated in mechanical ways, the production of a work of genuine art probably demands more intelligence than does most of the so-called thinking that goes on among those who pride themselves on being "intellectuals." (p. 46)

Part of the problem stems from the false separation that is made between affect and cognition. As Elliot Eisner (1994) points out, affect and cognition are processes that cannot exist, one from the other, but rather, "interpenetrate just as mass and weight do. They are part of the same reality in human experience" (p. 21). Arguing against the widely accepted notion of cognitive development offered by narrow, fact-oriented conceptualizations of knowledge and limited modes of teaching, he illustrates this interpenetration of cognition and affect: "Intellectual life is characterized by the absence of certainty, by the inclination to see things from more than one angle, by the thrill of the search more than the closure of the find" (p. 71). Underscoring that these are qualities inherent to work in the arts, Eisner contends that schools actually lead students away from the intellectual life by ignoring the arts. Rudolf Arnheim (1969/1997) explains further, "Thinking requires more than the formation and assignment of concepts. It calls for the unraveling of relations, for the disclosure of elusive structure. Image-making serves to make sense of the world" (p. 257). Karen Gallas (1994) extends the views of these theorists with her observations as a teacher and researcher in her own classroom:

> ...the arts become a way of thinking about thinking...this way is very natural and accessible to children. The process and dynamics of the art experience best capture the way children make their world sensible from very early years on. What is unfortunate in American education, however, is that as soon as children enter school they are gradually taught that their natural way of understanding the world is not an important and valid way...(p. 116).

As these voices from theory, research and practice attest, art involves thinking *and* feeling.

Common Theory-in-use: Children should be Left Alone to Create

Holding to the image of an unkempt, paint-spattered artist wildly flinging brilliant splotches of color at a canvas, or that of a young child who is up to her elbows in finger paint, many early childhood teachers believe that art is freely expressing oneself with art materials. Unfortunately, this belief is reinforced by teacher-educators and textbooks that admonish teachers to not interfere in the child's artistic endeavors, but rather, advise teachers to merely provide an abundance of materials and leave the child alone to create (Bresler, 1993, 1994; Kindler, 1996). As a result, many teachers mistakenly take a hands-off position to children's art and this often extends to sheltering children from any external influence that they believe might inhibit artistic development. Thus, teachers refrain from presenting their own art, or the work of professional artists, for fear of frustrating the child who is often perceived by the teacher to be unable to sustain adult levels of concentration (Beetlestone, 1998), skill, or complexity of thought. Others, acting on the belief that art must be engaged in a solitary fashion, often prevent children from assisting each other (Kindler, 1996).

Theory, research, and practice offer contradictory perspectives. For instance, rather than advocating a hands-off approach to children's art learning, many scholars and researchers insist that teacher interaction, guidance, and instruction are essential (Frisch, 2006; Thompson, 1997). Further, as the wealth of examples from children attending the schools of Reggio Emilia (Edwards, Gandini, & Forman, 1998), or from the children in Karen Gallas' (1994) classroom demonstrates, when teachers interact with children and respond to their interests and ideas with thoughtful planning and support, children are capable of sustained and exceptionally complex artistic work. In these art-based learning spaces, children work in collaboration with teachers and peers to generate, critique, and build upon ideas. Unlike the mindless-messing-with-materials stereotype of free expression embraced by many classroom teachers, these examples show how very young children may achieve sophisticated levels of meaning making and underscore the need for teachers to take an active role in children's art learning.

Common Theory-in-use: Whatever Children Do in Art Is OK— There Is No Right Way

In a culture that is predicated on knowing the correct answers, art seems to be the one area that many teachers believe has no right answer. While this may be valid to the extent that there is no *one right way*, there are frequently many answers in art that are decidedly better than others. This becomes clear when art is viewed as problem-solving: there are many possible responses to a problem and some responses will be more effective than others based upon the desired purpose and the variables involved. Unfortunately, many teachers adopt an unconditional acceptance stance towards children's art and avoid any critique of children's work. Even when the child who is struggling to make a drawing "look right" initiates the request, a common response from the teacher is "just do your best, you can't really make a mistake in art." In part, this belief is due to the teacher's fear of inhibiting the child's free expression as just discussed, as well as the concern for the impact critique will have on the child's feelings of self-worth. Gilbert (1996) explains that in teachers' minds, acceptance of the artwork is equated with acceptance of the child. Yet, as she points out, to refrain from critique is an abdication of teachers' responsibilities to help children learn. Children's work in art, as in any other sub-ject area, requires diagnostic and formative assessment in order to appropriately determine the teaching strategies that the child needs for further development. Cri-tique is not about criticizing or prescribing, but about facilitating dialogue regard-ing the artist's intent and the viewers' interpretations (Barrett, 1997; Beattie, 1997). To analytically respond to the child's work with worthwhile, formative feedback, is not a devaluation of the work, or the child, but rather is the teacher's responsibility as much as analyzing a child's reasoning to determine his/her diffi-culty in solving a math problem, or understanding a scientific concept.

Common Theory-in-use: Verbal Language Development Is More Important than Visual Language Development

Despite some early childhood educators' recognition of emergent literacy (i.e., reading and writing behaviors that precede formal literacy training), most have not re-envisioned their notions of literacy (Siegel, 2006). Language and literacy de-velopment remains focused upon written language, with emergent literacy seen as an early stage on the continuum, with non-verbal components like children's drawings or dramatic play only a means to a preferred verbal end. This view does not align with the present need to develop facility with a full range of multimodal texts in our current social, cultural, and economic worlds, or acknowledge the im-portance of valuing and supporting the various ways individuals make meaning.

Texts today are highly visual. Meaning is carried as much through graphics and images as it is through words. Teachers' perspectives of language and literacy de-velopment must take into account multimodal texts in both print (e.g., newspapers, magazines) and non-print form (e.g., film, video, and Internet websites). "As edu-cators we need to determine the specific features of reading that occur and that are needed for the synchronous functioning of the modes of print, image, movement, colour, gesture, 3D objects, music and sound on a digital screen" (Walsh, 2006, p. 36).

Children make meaning in a variety of ways. Yet, as Robert Sternberg (1997) points out, our educational system is a closed system that privileges certain abili-ties over others, causing teachers to label children who possess the privileged abilities as intelligent, and those who do not as deficient. Sternberg argues that this practice results in a great loss of potential for both the child and our society, as the deficient-labeled students believe that they have nothing to offer and often give up. In a similar vein, Janet Olson (1992) argues that many students who are as-signed to special education as "learning disabled" may be visual learners who "do not respond to the traditional verbal approach to learning" (p. 114). Levine (2002) encourages the abandonment of this deficit view of children's abilities, to instead "tolerate, educate, and celebrate all kinds of minds" (p. 307). Teachers must be open to the perspective that children with strong visual abilities are not necessarily slow, but may merely think differently. Albert Einstein's (1963, cited in Adams, 1986) reliance on non-verbal thinking is widely known as he explains, "words do not seem to play any role in my mechanism of thought. The psychical entities which seem to serve as elements in thought are certain signs and...images which can be 'voluntarily' reproduced and combined" (p. 36). When schools adopt curricula that include attention to children's multimodalities, "those youth who experience substantial success are the very ones who've been labeled 'struggling reader' or 'learning disabled'" (Siegel, 2006, p. 73). The children did not change, the teachers' perspectives of language and literacy changed. Rather than label children with strong visual language skills and weak verbal language skills as deficient, and those with strong verbal skills and weak visual language skills as advanced, we need to recognize the value of visual and verbal abilities equally.

Common Theory-in-use: Teaching Art Is the Art Teacher's Job

Most art specialists have had years of schooling in the arts. Typically, to be certified as an art teacher, candidates must earn a bachelors degree that includes numerous studio courses, along with courses in art history, pedagogy, and technology, plus a semester of student teaching. Although, this information is enlightening to some of my students who are often not aware that art teachers require higher education, for in-service teachers, it establishes an area of expertise that many feel is clearly beyond their grasp. Further, for many art teachers, their university studies were preceded by years of secondary school art classes and/or private lessons. It should not be surprising, then, that a large portion of early childhood and elementary teachers, who usually have taken only one art methods course in their teacher education program, feel inadequate when they are confronted with the expectation to include art in their curriculum (Thompson, 1997).

Beyond the issue of specialized schooling, this theory-in-use is most likely reinforced by several beliefs discussed previously. Revisiting the belief that art does not involve thinking, many teachers, consciously or unconsciously, privilege their work over that of the art teacher. While they may be quick to offer compliments regarding their art colleagues' efforts, the general classroom teachers readily accept typical hierarchical school practices of canceling the art class, rather than the math class, when an assembly, testing, or weather-related event shortens the school day, or the reassignment of the art teacher to a non-teaching responsibility (e.g. duties, coverage) more frequently than the non-arts faculty.

A related belief that art is a special talent also contributes to the theory-in-use that only the art specialist should teach art. In her study of elementary classroom teachers involved in an arts partnership, McKean (2001) found

> When the arts are viewed too much from the perspective of requiring special talents found only in certain few individuals, teachers acknowledge feelings of inadequacy and inaccessibility. For the teachers in this study, recurrent statements such as "I can't draw" or "I can't sing" reflected this sense of inadequacy and lack of talent that impeded their

own experimentation within the art forms and their confidence in teaching the arts to their students. As one teacher said, " I can't teach what I can't do. If I had the talent to do it, I would." (p. 28)

Some might question if this rationale would be offered if the areas in which the teacher lacked talent were in math or spelling.

Common-Theories-in-Use: Other Influences

This discussion of classroom teachers' common theories-in-use must also acknowledge the role of art teachers and educational policies in contributing to the perpetuation of several of these beliefs. Due to their educational backgrounds and personal biases, many art teachers embrace these same narrow understandings of children's art that underlie the general classroom teachers' beliefs. Further, educational policy has had a particularly heavy-handed influence as the pressure of preparing for high-stakes tests steal time and attention from the arts.

Pre-Service Teacher Education: Constructing New Perspectives

Pre-service teachers need more than subject matter knowledge and pedagogical skills in order to teach well, and they require more than new concepts or fresh strategies in order to construct alternative perspectives of the classroom. Eisner (1994) points out that those of us who enter the field of education "have had years to internalize a set of expectations regarding what teachers do and what schools are like" (p. 6), therefore, "the most difficult task for educators may very well be relinquishing the yellow school bus mentality that conceives of both the purposes and the forms of schooling in terms conditioned by familiar and comfortable traditions" (p. 69). Understanding the common theories-in-use that influence pre-service teachers is critical to interrupting these patterns of practice. Unless teacher educators engage their students' initial understandings, new concepts may not be comprehended, or students will merely espouse them for the length of the course, but then revert to their earlier beliefs when the course is over (Hammerness, Darling-Hammond, & Bransford, 2005). When theory and research are juxtaposed against the reality of views and opinions encountered in the authentic contexts of classroom practice, pre-service teachers are empowered to question and construct their own perspectives, to make their own meanings.

It is equally important to open up the teacher education classroom for inquiry. In an ethnographic study of the process of learning to teach, Segall (2002) examined how the discourses and practices within a methods course helped construct prospective teachers' understandings and attitudes toward teaching. Rather than merely presenting teaching as "something to be practiced with some other bodies someplace else in the future" (p. 156), he proposes that teacher educators destabilize the images of teaching that students bring to the program by bringing the analysis of teaching directly to the university classroom where students can experience the teaching/learning experience first hand. Segall maintains that if teacher educators want prospective teachers to become change agents, they must provide them the opportunity to begin by questioning their own learning experiences as students at the university. If we expect pre-service teachers to question their own practice to expand their perspectives of language, literacy, learning, and the arts, then we, as teacher educators must model this in the teacher education classroom.

The learning experiences that I describe in the following sections are framed in the larger context of inquiry into our beliefs, and our past and current experiences of practice, as we, teacher educator and pre-service teachers, construct broader perspectives of teaching, learning, and art. These experiences provide only a sample of our work within the course and should be viewed as threads woven into the fabric of this larger context. What is important in their selection for this chapter is not so much the content that is displayed, but rather the meaning making processes that these enable me to illustrate.

Learning Experiences in the Arts Methods Course

After establishing the perspective of the course with the experience based upon the excerpt from *The Little Prince* (discussed at the beginning of the chapter), we spend the remainder of the semester explicitly exploring how art as a visual language is used by adults and children to *inform, express, narrate,* and *persuade* and the implications this perspective has for teaching.

Introducing Art as Visual Language

In my art methods course, the students are introduced to the work of a wide range of theorists, researchers, and practitioners who view art as a language, from John Dewey's (1934/1980) classic, *Art as Experience,* to current scholars' explorations of multiliteracies. According to Dewey, "Because objects of art are expressive, they are a language. Rather they are many languages. For each art has its own medium and that medium is especially fitted for one kind of communication" (Dewey, 1934/1980, p. 106). He goes on to claim, "...art is the most effective mode of communication that exists" (p. 286). Building upon Dewey's work, over the past several decades Elliot Eisner has also advocated for the need to conceive of art as a language. In an early work, *Reading, the Arts, and the Creation of Meaning,* Eisner (1978) writes,

> We know most of what we know not in one way, but in a variety of ways. Each of our
> sensory modalities puts us in contact with the environment, and each modality enables us

to create a knowledge system that we use to know and express our conceptions of reality. (p. 15)

Numerous other theorists (e.g., Arnheim, 1969/1997; Kress, 2003; Vygotsky, 1978) along with researchers and practitioners (e.g., Anning, 1999; Dyson 2003, 2004; Gallas, 1994; Heath & Wolf, 2005; Olson, 1992; Piro, 2002) continue to explore and advance this concept of art as language. Their works, and those of others, are offered to the students in the form of readings, case studies, and quotes interspersed throughout the course. Students also read the NCTE (National Council of Teachers of English, 2005) Guideline on multimodal litercacies that explicitly states that the arts should not be considered luxuries, but instead must be viewed as integral components of the interplay among meaning making systems that teachers and students need to learn and to critically use.

Establishing and Modeling a Meaning Making Perspective

If pre-service teachers are to understand art, teaching, and learning as making meaning processes, it is important for the teacher educator to establish and model this perspective throughout the course. As Freire (2002) contends,

Education is suffering from narration sickness. The teacher talks about reality as if it were motionless, static, compartmentalized, and predictable... Instead of communicating, the teacher issues communiqués and makes deposits which the students patiently receive, memorize, and repeat. This is the "banking' concept of education, in which the scope of action allowed to the students extends only as far as receiving, filing, and storing the deposits... Knowledge emerges only through invention and re-invention, through the restless, impatient continuing, hopeful inquiry human beings pursue in the world, with the world, and with each other... The more students work at storing the deposits entrusted to them, the less they develop the critical consciousness which would result from their intervention in the world as transformers of that world. (pp. 71-73)

Therefore, concepts are not presented to my class as indisputable truths, but initially, are offered to the students as questions for their thoughtful examination. *Is art a language? Why might people consider art a language? What is language?* This questioning leads us to analyze the nature and purpose of language, and to identify the multiplicity of forms and the varying structures used. During the inquiry process, students recognize languages such as sign language, Morse code, and Braille, and discuss the concept of body language; they note the sensory aspects of various languages: aural, visual, tactile; they decide that language is a communication system that has rules for combining symbols or signs that may be heard, seen, and/or felt; and they recall from their English classes the varied purposes of language: *to inform, to express, to narrate,* or *to persuade.* Finally, most come to the conclusion that art *is* language.

As hooks (1989) suggests, teacher education needs to teach teachers to "talk back" to experiences, or what Schon (1983) calls a reflective conversation with the situation. By taking this problem-posing approach early in the course, I hope to develop these pre-service teachers' abilities (and willingness) to take a thought-ful and questioning stance to teaching and learning, rather than passively take for granted whatever they are told, or what they initially perceive, as unexamined truth. Further, because they are actively engaged in constructing the foundation for their own knowledge through inquiry into the concepts, it is more likely that the students will internalize what they have discovered and better comprehend the concepts under study (Kukla, 2000).

Art as Visual Language to Inform

"Learning to slow down perception so that one can really see is as important in bi-ology or literature as it is in the visual arts" (Eisner, 2006, p. 11). When the pur-pose of language is to inform, attention is given to carefully observing and authen-tically portraying the subject through precise descriptions of the sensory details. The ability to collect data through careful observation and accurate description is an important skill across the early childhood/elementary curriculum. The visual arts are a particularly effective means of developing this skill, and despite com-mon-theories-in-use that underestimate young children's artistic abilities, class-room teachers can develop their students' *visual language to inform*.

Mini-action Action Research Assignment

In order for my arts methods students to begin to understand how they might best facilitate this development, a mini-action research project assignment is modeled in the university classroom and then implemented by the students with small groups of children at their professional development school field experience. The assignment was adapted from one designed and implemented by Gilbert (1998) in several studies of her education students' field experiences. It involves three strategies that the pre-service teachers test with three different groups of children:

1. Strategy A: Just tell children to draw a selected subject (animal, flowers).
2. Strategy B: Provide the selected subject, tell children to look carefully to draw.
3. Strategy C: Provide the selected subject, interact with children to focus obser-vation and encourage rich description before telling them to draw, and then, re-inforcing this during the drawing.

This assignment provides the pre-service teachers with some initial understand-ings of how they might best develop children's *visual language to inform* and, for some, as described in a pre-service teacher's story later in the chapter, it provides the first glimpse of the pedagogical aspects of teaching art.

Having dealt with the "how" through the mini-action research project, the next step is to understand the "why:" why would a general classroom teacher be con-cerned with developing children's *visual language to inform*? This understanding is developed through art explorations that engage the pre-service teacher in authentic learning experiences applicable to the elementary curriculum.

Art Exploration: Coral Reef Fish

In this learning experience, the pre-service teachers gain first hand experience of why developing art as a *language to inform* is important to their work in the early childhood/elementary classroom. Like the other experiences described in this chapter, it is modeled in the university classroom as a problem to solve, then, after some introductory exercises and explanation, my students complete the majority of the work as an out-of-class assignment. Later, they incorporate understandings from the learning experience in the design of lessons that they then teach in their professional development school classrooms.

As described earlier, the concept of art as a *language to inform* draws heavily on the artists' research capabilities. Marshall (2007) elaborates further on how art functions as research:

> Clarity and meaning are engendered when ideas, concepts, or information is transformed into visual images, objects or visual experiences. This transformation...allows information to be seen differently in a fresh, more meaningful, personal, and experiential way ...[and] produces new insights and learning. (p. 23)

During the Coral Reef Fish Art Exploration, students engage in visual and verbal research and visually share their findings. The comprehensive project consists of clearly delineated phases to be completed within specific time frames. This enables students' out-of-class work to be supported by brief clarifications and/or further in-class instruction, as well as individually through email and conferencing outside of class. To model the attention that the pre-service teachers might give to staging a learning experience, the university classroom is prepared to simulate an underwater environment with projections of coral reef fish on the walls and various props related to diving on hand. The problem is then presented to the students who are cast in the role of novice scientific illustrators and museum display designers: "select a coral reef fish for study and accurately communicate these observations in a color illustration and a three-dimensional model that will be exhibited in our university classroom to inform visitors of the physical appearance of the selected fish." Examples of scientific illustrations are presented and discussed, along with possible resources for the students' research of coral reef fish and issues for consideration when selecting images (e.g., clarity of image, available views, authenticity of source).

Phase One of the exploration requires both verbal (Fig. 12.1) and visual (Fig. 12.2) data collection. The visual data is critiqued by peers to assess the accuracy of the artist's depiction of observations of line, shape, color, and texture in the accompanying photograph. This important step serves to interrupt the pre-service teachers' previous understandings of practice by providing experience in establishing and employing purpose-based assessment criteria. Rather than perpetuate the belief that there are no right answers in art, they learn that children's works of art may, and should be assessed on criteria related to purpose, which in the case of this particular illustration is to accurately depict the observable physical characteristics of the subject. Discussion also includes the purposes of assessment, which is not to assign a grade but to lead the artist to contemplate the need for corrections or revisions.

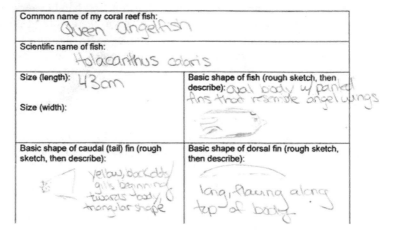

Common name of my coral reef fish: Queen Angelfish	
Scientific name of fish: Holacanthus coloris	
Size (length): 43cm Size (width):	Basic shape of fish (rough sketch, then describe): Oval body w/ pointed fins that resemble angel wings
Basic shape of caudal (tail) fin (rough sketch, then describe): Yellow, darkddy gills beginning towards body triangular shape	Basic shape of dorsal fin (rough sketch, then describe): long, flowing along top of body

Fig. 12.1 Phase one verbal data collection: Pre-service teacher's data collection form.

Fish: Queen Angelfish
http://cs.brown.edu/~twd/fish/Bonaire/doeppne-070.jpg

Fig. 12.2 Phase one visual data collection: A pre-service teacher's observational drawing.

The concept of critique as "informed criticism concerning their work from others...to enable them to secure a more sensitive and comprehensive grasp on what they have created" (Eisner, 2002, p. 49) is also important to my students' development as reflective professionals (Schon, 1983). Quality in art or in education is not achieved by perfecting a formula, but rather by examining what it is that we are doing and then imagining how we might do it better (Eisner, 2002).

Once the pre-service teachers have collected accurate data, they are ready to move on to Phase Two of the assignment. In this phase, they will experiment to discover what materials and techniques will best replicate the skin surface of the coral reef fish that they have selected. Through this process, students develop critical and creative thinking skills as they observe, analyze, imagine, experiment, and evaluate their experimental work.

They begin by verbally analyzing their visual observation (Fig. 12.3). This models for pre-service teacher a strategy for reinforcing use of descriptive language across the curriculum. Next, they generate and evaluate possible ideas for replicating the surface of the coral reef fish (Fig. 12.4), followed by testing the ideas and selecting the final materials and techniques to complete their model.

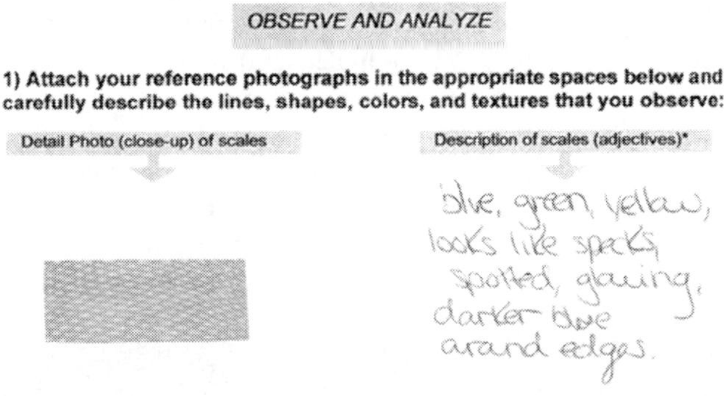

OBSERVE AND ANALYZE

1) Attach your reference photographs in the appropriate spaces below and carefully describe the lines, shapes, colors, and textures that you observe:

Detail Photo (close-up) of scales   Description of scales (adjectives)*

blue, green, yellow,
looks like specks,
spotted, glowing,
darker blue
around edges.

Fig. 12.3 Phase two analyses of data: Example of a pre-service teacher's verbal description.

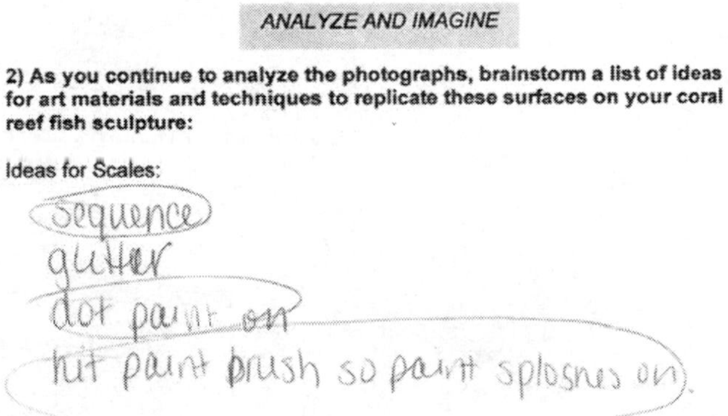

ANALYZE AND IMAGINE

2) As you continue to analyze the photographs, brainstorm a list of ideas for art materials and techniques to replicate these surfaces on your coral reef fish sculpture:

Ideas for Scales:

sequence
glitter
dot paint on
hit paint brush so paint splashes on).

Fig. 12.4 Phase two analyses of data: A student's ideas for further experimentation.

In the third and final phase, the pre-service teachers are required to construct a three-dimensional model from the six-foot lengths of brown roll paper that are provided at the beginning of the project. The students are not provided with any step-by-step instructions for the construction of the model; instead, the problem is presented to the class for discussion of possible solutions. The students take these ideas and combine them with their earlier experiments to create the final work, then, they collaborate to showcase their work in the "museum" exhibit in our university classroom (Fig. 12.5).

Reflections

It is important to note that initially my students were less than enthusiastic with what became known as "The Fish Project." Many were intimidated by the open-ended nature of the work: used to recipe-like art projects, how-to-draw books, or step-by-step crafts kits, being required to observe, and to accurately render a subject in the two and three-dimensional formats seemed overwhelming. A number of my students, concerned about grades, worried that they did not possess the "talent" to successfully complete the project. Some complained that they were not going to be teaching art, so they did not understand why they needed to spend time on this kind of project. Anticipating these concerns, I had set up the course to allow them to question assignments, to express their needs, and to facilitate interaction among all of us, teacher and students working together, in order to make meaning of the learning experience. This allowed me to address the common theories-in-use in the authentic context of the teacher education classroom and their accompanying field experience in the professional development school.

Fig. 12.5. Students' *Exhibit of Coral Reef Fish* in the university classroom.

This "permission to question" the learning experience resulted in a more positive attitude as they moved forward. As demonstrated in their written reflections, by the end of the project many of the students had developed new perspectives regarding the arts, teaching, and learning. The following excerpts from several students' reflective statements demonstrate these new understandings:

"I realized that I had many more skills than I thought. I realized that it was not that I can't draw, I just had to practice looking more carefully!"

"At first I felt angry and overwhelmed because this was a lot of work and I did not really see the purpose of such a big project, but then the way we did it in phases, it made it more doable. Even if it wasn't step-by-step instructions, I could handle it, it made sense and it was better than instructions, because I had to really think on my own and I was really proud of the idea that I came up with to do the scales. I could see myself doing this in the classroom and I would make sure that I would do it in phases so my students won't be overwhelmed."

"I have learned a lot just in doing the preliminary activities. For instance, if I had not had to brainstorm and test out the ideas, I would have just done whatever first came to my mind. Since I tested my ideas and really brainstormed, I felt that I ended up with a much better solution."

"I have seen how art can actually teach other subjects. Art was what made me do all this research to accurately depict my fish, but I actually learned a lot of science content."

"I learned teamwork, because some of us got together to share supplies and ideas and I learned that working with others can help you achieve what first appears to be an unattainable product."

Not all students' reflections were positive. As one student wrote, "I thought that this project was very tedious. It would take up too much time and be too hard for children." To make the possible connections more explicit for these students, I followed up with a class debriefing where students shared how they adapted, or might adapt the project for various levels of learners.

The most interesting evidence of the learning prompted by "The Fish Project," came in the form of unsolicited reflection after the course was over. One student who had worked on her fish sculpture in her basement with some of her classmates stopped by the following semester to tell me, "Remember how I told you my kids drove us crazy while we were working on those fish? Well, my son was in the bookstore and he's yelling, 'Mom! Look, Carly's French Angelfish is on the cover of that book', and sure enough, it was a French Angelfish." Another example of learning that extended beyond the course came in a recent email:

> Dr. Narey--I thought you would like to know that over my honeymoon I was able to spot 10 of the fish that people created last semester. We went scuba diving in the Caribbean and I kept pointing out fish to my husband. I explained, once we surfaced, that the ones I pointed out were ones that were created in class and he got a kick out of it, I thought you would too. Hope you summer is going well! (Kerri, personal communication, June 10, 2008)

Art as Visual Language to Express

Many of the pre-service teachers enter the course with the belief that expression is the primary purpose of art. Yet, operating under the common-theory-in-use that expression means emotionally pounding clay, or spattering paint, they typically do not understand that expression requires further skills in visual literacy (i.e., the ability to "read" and "write" images). To a great extent, our work with expression relies on an understanding of semiotics (i.e., the study of signs), in that instead of using design elements (i.e., line, shape, color, texture) to describe observed visible physical properties of the subject matter, as we did in art as *visual language to inform*, we now draw upon these same elements to communicate emotional or conceptual qualities of the subject to be depicted. For instance, we begin this learning experience by exploring questions such as, "what color is anger?" and "what differences might there be between drawing a line to show agitation and a line to show rage?" This is followed by viewing and analyzing works of art that demonstrate visual language to express, such as Gaspare Diziani's drawing, *Flight into Egypt*, that communicates the urgency of a family fleeing for their safety with active, diagonal, scribbled lines, and Pablo Picasso's, *Old Guitarist*, that conveys the melancholy of an aged musician with colors of blues and grays and the drooping lines of the figure.

Art Exploration: Poetry Book

For the art exploration, students are given the problem of creating a book using poems they have written in their reading methods course. In this assignment, my students move beyond the notion that the only purpose of art is to illustrate text with representational imagery. Instead of a literal interpretation of the subject matter, each student is required to critically analyze and define the overall expressive quality that he/she intends to communicate. Next, students determine the lines, shapes, colors, and textures that communicate the identified quality. After some additional work with lettering and graphics, students create pages on which to layout the poems. In the example shown (Fig. 12.6), the student used diagonal lines of reds and oranges to express the explosive action that she identified as the essence of her poems. This is seen in both the surface composition and the ideogram technique (i.e., lines and shapes created with letters or words).

Reflections

Although my students seem surprised when our investigation into communicative aspects of design elements contradicts their beliefs about what is meant by expression, they readily grasp this new concept. Many are also able to make connections to their work in the field.

Fig. 12.6. Cover and page sample with ideogram from a pre-service teacher's poetry book.

Understandings of art *to express* were incorporated into discussions of book illustration with the children in their field experience classrooms as well as into other subject areas. One student used the art concept in a lesson in which the children designed mini-posters of science vocabulary. In her lesson plan reflection she wrote, "The children really showed their understanding of the science words by the way they used colors and lines to express the meaning. My mentor teacher loved this lesson so much she hung their work in the hall!" Further insights into the teaching and learning process came about several days later as the student related that another teacher in the building had attempted to replicate the activity in her classroom, but had not achieved the same results. Knowingly, my student informed me, "I think that teacher must have skipped the art parts [of the lesson] and just told the students to draw the vocabulary words... If you want students to understand how to express effectively, you have to *teach* them the art!"

Art as Visual Language to Narrate

Despite their familiarity with the adage, "every picture tells a story," most of my students have not considered how artists go about telling stories. We begin to explore art as a *language to narrate* by inquiring:

- What kinds of stories do artists tell? What kinds of stories do children tell?
- How do artists tell stories? How do child artists tell stories?
- How might we compare and contrast visual and verbal narrative texts?
- Are there texts that are both visual and verbal?
- What kinds of literacies are required to "read" and "write" each of these texts?

Next, we engage in activities that relate to my students' work in the field and that build upon the earlier course learning experiences, such as

- analyzing artwork from a variety of cultures to identify methods of sequencing, character and setting, and other elements, such as point of view, used by artists to tell stories (e.g., Lakota Winter Counts, Ancient Greek pottery, Bayeux Tapestry, paintings by Latina artist Carmen Lomas Garza, installations by Nam June Paik).
- dramatizing characters from fairy tales and legends in a variety of action poses, then observing and drawing the characters' facial expressions and figures (builds upon the visual language to inform experience).
- analyzing graphic novels, comic books, and comic strips for visual and verbal literacy elements and devices (builds upon visual language to inform and express experiences).

Art Exploration: Comic Book as an Instructional Material

In this assignment, my students are required to create a comic book that they can reproduce as an instructional material to help teach a social studies or science concept (e.g., Japanese tea ceremony or the water cycle). They draw upon the knowledge and skills learned at the beginning of the course as they research and collect visual data and develop the expressive qualities of their comic book images and text to effectively tell the story that explains the selected concept.

Reflection

The learning experiences for art as a *language to narrate* gave my students a better understanding of how to more effectively address the art component of traditional early childhood reading /language arts activities. Rather than follow the common practices of merely telling children to illustrate a story, or to draw a picture that the teacher then translates into a verbal sentence, many of my students commented that they now spent more time preparing the children for the visual aspects of these activities. Further, although my students demonstrated a growing understanding of art as a visual language for children's learning, most did not view it as a language for teaching. Therefore, the art exploration of creating a comic book to teach offered them a new perspective, as well as authentic purpose.

Art as Visual Language to Persuade

The overwhelming proliferation of multimodal texts encountered through television, Internet, billboards, and print-based media has generated increasing attention to the importance of media/visual literary. These texts exert a powerful influence upon children and adults not only in the promotion of products, but also in the advancement of beliefs and values (Barrett, 2003; Chung, 2005; Kilbourne, 2000). Those who are not visually literate are in the greatest danger of being manipulated by those who are (Chandler, 2002). Therefore, this final learning experience is a particularly important area for exploration. We begin with investigation of what it means to persuade, and the purposes and means of persuasion, followed by deconstructions of historic posters and contemporary print advertisements in terms of

- aesthetics: color, contrast, font, camera angle, etc.
- targeted audience: age, gender, etc.
- identification of persuasive technique: flattery, bribery, bandwagon, etc.
- denotation and connotation: explicit messages and implicit messages

Discussions of the implications of media influence in the contemporary commercial advertisements are connected to concerns that have potential relevance to my university students' personal experiences, such as body image or social status.

Art Exploration: Posters to Draw Attention to the Problem of Hunger

Noting that persuasion may be used for ideological (e.g., to encourage recycling) as well as commercial purposes, students are required to create a poster that draws attention to the problem of hunger that will be displayed at a campus fundraising event for a local food charity. Students must draw upon the knowledge and skills developed throughout the course, and critique the effectiveness of their work based upon new understandings of art as a *visual language to persuade*.

Reflection

Relating the implications of media influence to issues of body image and social status appeared to resonate with many of my students. Their discussions revealed a new awareness of an image's potential power to influence beliefs and actions. Several students became quite passionate about the teacher's responsibility to teach media literacy, and went on to design such lessons for the children in their field experience classrooms. One student confidentially shared that her friend suffered from an eating disorder and related that the second grade girls in her field experience classroom were already talking about weight and dieting.

Further, the students also realized art as language to persuade involves research into audience and content, and brings about subsequent learning in a variety of areas. For instance, researching facts for the awareness of hunger poster brought some students to understand the issue in relationship to students in their classroom. As one student reflected, "I guess I had always just thought of it (hunger) as something that happens in undeveloped countries...It really opened my eyes when we researched for our posters and I found out that 13 million children in the United States go to bed hungry! These could be my students...I've got to do something about this."

Pre-Service Teachers Make Meaning

When the course is over, I invite students to share their reflections of the course and their continued experiences of integrating art during their final student teaching semester. These reflections (along with the informal feedback of students who stop by to share stories) provide me with the opportunity to understand how some students perceive the arts beyond the time that they are enrolled in the course. The following stories were written by two of these former students.

Ms. Ammermann's Story

"We don't have time for art in the classroom!" That is all I heard during my pre-service teaching experience. Most of the cooperating teachers were not willing to give up "core curriculum" time for "art." I needed to find a way to teach my art lessons within that context.

Now I was not the average student. This was my second career. I took art many years ago. My early perception of art was "arts and crafts." I had no formal training in what I now consider "art." Most of my younger peers had similar experiences with little or no background in art. It was difficult for many of my peers and I to successfully plan a lesson for art that was both meaningful and educational with the little experience we had. My art class during my pre-service teacher training was quite a challenge. After all, what did I know about art?

One of the most valuable assignments for me during this our methods course was the mini-action research project. We placed a vase with flowers on a table and used three different strategies to teach three different groups of students (A, B, and C) to draw them. This was a great learning experience for me, not just in art, but across the general curriculum as well. This activity made me realize that as teachers, we need to challenge students' thinking in order for them to learn. In Groups A and B, nothing was learned. There was no dialogue, no instruction, and basically the children did not learn anything new. They drew from their past experience but gained no new knowledge. However, in Group C, the students learned to look at more detail with a little instruction. We as teachers have a great responsibility to challenge all learners and guide them in the learning process.

I also learned how to utilize the arts to address the varying abilities and learning modalities of the students. When students learned about different types of storms, we discussed the characteristics of a hurricane with damaging winds, rain, thunder and lightning and I introduced the Beaufort Wind Scale. This is a tool that meteorologists use to classify the wind and the damage it can cause. This is where I integrated art. The objective of the lesson was to have students observe and discuss the lines, shapes, and colors selected artists have used to depict different types of wind in works of art. Another objective of the lesson was for students to use the expressive qualities of line, shape, and color to depict a specific wind speed (based upon science understandings) in a tempera painting. I introduced the students to several artists (e.g., Van Gogh, Yoshitaki, Hokusai) that portray wind in their paintings by displaying art panels that included these pictures. Prior to their creating their own wind painting, the students and I discussed the art panels in detail:

- Can you "see" the wind in the paintings?
- How did the artist achieve the feeling of wind in each painting (i.e., color, texture, etc.)?
- How did the artist show the speed of the wind in each painting (i.e., landscape changes, etc.)
- What shapes did the artists use to create the wind?
- What colors were used to illustrate the wind?

Then the students picked a number on the Beaufort scale (1-12) and had to create a painting based on the wind scale rating. I was amazed by the results. They truly understood the varied effects of different degrees of wind on the environment. This lesson had a profound affect on how I viewed art for all my lessons that followed. Art integration facilitated the students' learning. Art had a new meaning for me. It was not just painting and creating holiday crafts. Art was a tool that I used to expand students' understanding.

Pre-Service Teachers Make Meaning: Ms. Perry's Story

While reading a slow moving and detailed story by Beverly Cleary (1990) called Ramona and Her Father, I could sense that my third grade students were getting bored. So, after completing the first three chapters, I used important events and dialogue in the story to create a script. The script consisted of six scenes and I included a speaking part for each student. Because the students had not previously participated in this sort of activity, I wanted to be sure they did not feel pressured or uneasy. The assignment of roles was a group decision. My goal was for everyone to participate without feeling forced to do so or anxious about the task. Once the roles were assigned the students highlighted their lines, met with the rest of the cast in their scene, and immediately began rehearsing. I spent time with each group, working on positioning, gestures, entrances and exit, and props. The students considered studying their lines part of their homework!

On the day of the play, the students brought in props and costumes. The class was their own audience, and they we discussed how to behave as an audience. In between scenes, while the cast and props were changing, I spoke with the students to review what they just saw; what they remember happening next and any predictions they might have. This strengthened their comprehension. The play was delivered beautifully and the students had a great time doing it. After the next three chapters, I decided to write another script. The students were even more eager to *participate! When the book was finished, the class had collectively performed three plays.*

The benefits that came from doing the plays are immeasurable. The students' comprehension levels skyrocketed. Suddenly, the book made a lot more sense. The students could recall more facts and even relate the story to their lives. The students were able to practice many aspects of public speaking, such as tone, volume and pace. By the third and final play, each student was speaking slowly and clearly and consistently faced and made eye contact with each other and the audience. They learned to pay close attention to punctuation and to add inflection to certain words or phrases.

This play was an opportunity to involve the students who did not often volunteer. One student, in particular, stands out in my mind. A quiet, seemingly distant student opened up and showed an outgoing and downright hilarious side during the play. I believe it strengthened her ability to interact socially. The opportunity to interact with each other was particularly beneficial for two of the students with learning disabilities. These students were often pulled out during shared reading time, and the play provided valuable social interactions, not to mention the benefits of better comprehension and public speaking. I'll never forget the excitement on their faces when they were performing.

The plays really brought the class together. The students sincerely enjoyed and learned from the activities. After each play, the class held a discussion about likes, dislikes, funny moments, and prior and future scenes. But more importantly, the students were using memories of their friends on stage to recall important events. They were relating to the characters in ways they could not possibly relate by simply reading the story.

Shared reading is sometimes complicated because the students are required to read a certain book; they do not get to make the choice. The reading levels within a classroom vary widely, therefore making it difficult to find a book that each student can both read and understand. Incorporating theatre into the classroom brought an average shared reading book to life and energized and motivated the students. I believe each student found something within themselves during the process; They were proud of their work and displayed high levels of confidence. During one discussion, I asked the students, "Why do you think we did these plays?" One student raised her hand and summed it up perfectly: "It helped us read better, have fun, and know the story!"

Teacher Education: Preparing Pre-service Teachers to See Hats or Boa Constrictors Digesting Elephants?

As teacher educators, we, along with the pre-service teachers, must search beyond the visible and attempt to understand what we bring to our courses and what we take away. Will my students go on to teach art as a meaning making process?

Have they learned to look beneath the surface of their assumptions about teaching and learning as well as art? What have I learned from our work together?

Through these course experiences, most of my students end the semester with new perspectives of language, literacy, learning, and art. Through their field experiences, they also may have had an impact upon the views of the classroom teachers and the children with whom they worked. Through my reflections upon our interactions in both settings, I have advanced my understandings of others' beliefs and concerns. Our attempt to make meaning has challenged some common theories-in-use and, perhaps, has caused a small interruption in the patterns of practice that have become engrained in many early childhood classrooms.

Will my students see the boa constrictors digesting elephants? At least they will understand that they should look.

References

Adams, J. L. (1986). *Conceptual blockbusting: A guide to better ideas.* Reading, MA: Addison-Wesley.

Anning, A. (1999). Learning to draw and drawing to learn. *International Journal of Art and Design Education, 18*(2), 163-172.

Arnheim, R. (1969/1997). *Visual thinking.* Berkely, CA: University of California Press.

Barrett, T. (1997). *Talking about student art.* Worcester, MA: Davis Publications.

Barrett, T. (2003). Interpreting visual culture. *Art Education, 56*(2), p 6-12.

Beattie, D. K. (1997). *Assessment in art education.* Worcester, MA: Davis Publications.

Beetlestone, F. (1998). *Creative children, imaginative teaching.* Buckingham, UK: Open University Press.

Bolman, L. G., & Deal, T. E. (1991). *Reframing organizations: Artistry, choice, and leadership.* San Francisco: Jossey-Bass.

Bresler, L. (1993). Three orientations to arts in the primary grades: Implications for curriculum reform. *Arts Education Policy Review, 94*(6), 29-34.

Bresler, L. (1994). Imitative, complementary, and expansive: Three roles of visual arts curricula. *Studies in Art Education, 35*(2), 90-104.

Chandler, D. (2002). *Semiotics: The basics.* London: Routledge.

Chung, S. K. (2005). Media/visual literacy art education: Cigarette ad deconstruction. *Art Education, 58*(3), 19-24.

Cleary, B. (1990). *Ramona and her father.* New York: HarperCollins.

de Saint Exupéry, A. (1943/1971). *The little prince.* New York: Harcourt, Brace & World, Inc.

Dewey, J. (1934/1980). *Art as experience.* New York: Perigee.

Dyson, A. H. (2003). *The brothers and sisters learn to write: Popular literacies in childhood and school cultures.* New York: Teachers College Press.

Dyson, A. H. (2004). Diversity as a "handful": Toward retheorizing the basics. *Research in the Teaching of English, 39*(2), 210-214.

Edwards, C. P., Gandini, L. & Forman, G. E. (Eds.) (1998). *The Hundred Languages of Children: The Reggio Emilia Approach - Advanced Reflections* (2nd ed.). Greenwich, CT: Ablex.

Eisner, E. W. (1978). Reading and the creation of meaning. In E. W Eisner (Ed.), *Reading, the arts, and the creation of meaning* (pp. 13-31). Reston, VA: National Art Education Association.

Eisner, E. W. (1994). *Cognition and curriculum reconsidered* (2nd ed.). New York: Teachers College Press.

Eisner, E. W. (2002). *The arts and the creation of mind*. New Haven, CT: Yale University Press.

Eisner, E. W. (2006). Two visions of education. (The Arts Education Collaborative Monograph No. 2). Pittsburgh, PA: Arts Education Collaborative.

Freire, P. (2002). *Pedagogy of the oppressed*. New York: Continuum.

Frisch, N. S. (2006). Drawing in preschools: A didactic experience. *International Journal of Art and Design Education, 25*(1), 74-85.

Gallas, K. (1994). *The languages of learning: How children talk, write, dance, and sing their understanding of the world*. New York: Teachers College Press.

Gilbert, J. (1996). Developing an assessment stance in primary art education in England. *Assessment in Education, 3*(1), 55–74.

Gilbert, J. (1998). Through language the child moves from looking to seeing: Action research into language as a tool to teach drawing. *International Journal of Early Years Education, 6*(3), 277-90.

Hammerness, K., Darling-Hammond, L., & Bransford, J., (with Berliner, D., Cochran-Smith, M., McDonald, M., & Zeichner, K.). (2005). How teachers learn and develop. In L. Darling-Hammond & J. Bransford (Eds.), Preparing teachers for a changing world: What teachers should know and be able to do (pp. 358-389). San Francisco: Jossey-Bass.

Heath, S. B., & Wolf, S. A. (2005). Focus in creative learning: Drawing on art for language development. *Literacy, 39*(1), 38-45.

hooks, b. (1989). *Talking back: Thinking Feminist, thinking Black*. Boston: South End Press.

Kalin, N., & Kind, S. (2006). Invitations to understanding: Explorations in the teaching of arts to children. *Art Education, 59*(3), 36-41.

Kilbourne, J. (2000). *Can't buy my love: How advertising changes the way we think and feel*. New York: Simon & Schuster.

Kindler, A. M. (1996). Myths, habits, research, and policy: The four pillars of early childhood art education. *Arts Education Policy Review, 97*(4). 24-30.

Kress, G. (2003). *Literacy in the new media age*. London: Routledge.

Kukla, A. (2000). *Social constructivism and the philosophy of science*. New York: Routledge.

Levine, M. (2002). *A mind at a time*. New York: Simon & Schuster.

Marshall, J. (2007). Image as insight: Visual images in practiced-based research. *Studies in Art Education, 49*(1), 23-41.

McKean, B. (2001). Concerns and considerations for teacher development in the arts. *Arts Education Policy Review, 102*(4), 27-32.

National Council of Teachers of English. (2005). Multimodal literacies. Retrieved March 2, 2008 from http://www.ncte.org/about/over/positions/category/literacy/123213.htm

Olson, J. (1992). *Envisioning writing: Toward an integration of drawing and writing*. Portsmouth, NH: Heinemann.

Osterman, K. F., & Kottkamp, R. B. (2004). *Reflective practice for educators: Professional development to improve student learning* (2nd ed). Thousand Oaks, CA: Corwin Press.

Piro, J. M. (2002). The picture of reading: Deriving meaning in literacy through image. *The Reading Teacher, 56*(2), 126-134.

Schon, D. (1983). *The reflective practitioner: How professionals think in action*. New York: Basic Books.

Segall, A. (2002). *Disturbing practice: Reading teacher education as text*. New York: Peter Lang.

Siegel, M. (2006). Rereading the signs: Multimodal transformations in the field of literacy education. *Language Arts, 84*(1), 65-76.

Sternberg, R. (1997). What does it mean to be smart? *Educational Leadership, 54*(6), 20-24.

Vygotsky, L. S. (1978). *Mind in society: The development of higher psychological processes*. Cambridge, MA: Harvard University Press.

Thompson, C. M. (1997). Teaching art in elementary schools: Shared responsibilities and distinctive roles. *Arts Education Policy Review, 99*(2), 15-21.

Walsh, M. (2006). The 'textual shift': Examining the reading process with print, visual and multimodal texts. *Australian Journal of Language and Literacy, 29*(1), 24-37.

Marilyn J. Narey
East Stroudsburg University of Pennsylvania
East Stroudsburg, PA   USA

Dr. Marilyn J. Narey is a faculty member in the Early Childhood and Elementary Education Department at East Stroudsburg University of Pennsylvania. She has taught preschool children through adult learners in public and private settings throughout the state. Her research, presentation, and publication interests center upon issues of educational quality, diversity, and social justice and include the areas of multimodal literacy, semiotics, technology integration, critical/creative thinking, interdisciplinary curriculum, teacher quality, and reflective practice.

Dr. Narey acknowledges Ms. Laura Ammermann and Ms. Laura Perry for the contribution of their individual narratives to the chapter, and thanks all of her students for their thoughtful artworks, reflections, and discussions that have helped us all to make meaning.

Index

Lightning Source UK Ltd.
Milton Keynes UK
23 September 2010

160214UK00006B/96/P

9 780387 875378